# SUPERNATURAL BEINGS

*Hero and the Traitor*

THIERRY KOUAM

ISBN 978-1-950818-42-6 (paperback)

Copyright © 2020 by Thierry Kouam

All rights reserved. No part of this publication may be reproduced, distributed, or transmitted in any form or by any means, including photocopying, recording, or other electronic or mechanical methods without the prior written permission of the publisher. For permission requests, solicit the publisher via the address below.

Rushmore Press LLC
1 800 460 9188
www.rushmorepress.com

Printed in the United States of America

# CONTENTS

Introduction ................................................................. 5
Chapter 1:   The mission of the magician supernatural beings ........ 9
Chapter 2:   The mysterious witch enemy ................................ 40
Chapter 3:   Hero the traitor ........................................... 55
Chapter 4:   The mysterious supernatural being in class ............... 66
Chapter 5:   The War Between the Supernatural Beings ............. 109
Chapter 6:   The death of the ghost of Matt ............................ 156
Chapter 7:   The tradition festival of supernatural beings ........... 179
Chapter 8:   Hero sentenced to death for treason ...................... 186
Chapter 9:   The ghost of Hero prisoner ............................... 196
Chapter 10:  The mysterious ghost enemy and the torture
             of Hero .................................................. 244
Chapter 11:  The initiation of Angel as a supernatural being ....... 296
Chapter 12:  The hanging of Hero ..................................... 333

# INTRODUCTION

This story is happening in a huge world called Winnipeg, in North America between Canada and the United States. Winnipeg is divided between two states called two worlds that are the world of natural human beings, and the world of supernatural human beings., Since, Winnipeg is made up of two different race types who are the race of natural human beings and the race of supernatural human beings. So, the inhabitants of Winnipeg are the natural human beings and the supernatural human beings called again, supernatural beings.

The world of supernatural beings is very far away from the world of natural human beings, and natural human beings do not know about the existence of the race of supernatural beings in Winnipeg.

The supernatural beings were the mysterious creatures who had the shape of natural human beings, but who were not the natural human beings. The supernatural beings were instead kind of the animal species despite the fact that by looking at them, we thought that they were the natural human beings. The supernatural beings were the creatures who had the phantoms called again ghosts, and their ghosts were the animals. The supernatural beings were born with ten senses, gifted with a lot of abilities and Latin as their language.

There were the supernatural beings of the world of tiger and the supernatural beings of the world of eagle. The supernatural beings of the tiger world had the tiger as their ghosts, and the supernatural beings of the eagle world had the eagle as their ghosts. So, the supernatural beings who had the appearance of natural human beings and who were looking exactly like the natural human beings were the tigers and eagles. The supernatural beings were able to turn into their phantoms, so a supernatural being from the tiger world was able to turn into a tiger, and a supernatural being from the eagle world was able to turn into an eagle.

And the ghosts of the supernatural beings were always inside their bodies, because their phantoms were their souls. But when the supernatural beings were in danger, they removed their ghosts from their bodies because they were afraid that their phantoms could get hurt or get killed, and by removing their ghosts from their bodies; they were protecting themselves. It was because when their phantoms were not inside their bodies, they had the empty bodies, and that's the reason why it was almost impossible to kill the supernatural beings. The only way to kill them, was to kill their ghosts first.

And when the ghosts of the supernatural beings were out of their bodies, and if their ghosts were wounded somewhere; the supernatural beings had the wounds of their ghosts on their bodies, and if their ghosts were tortured somewhere; they would feel the same torture of their ghosts on them. So, if their ghosts were killed somewhere, they would die, too. And when the supernatural beings die, their ghosts were buried according to the rules of their tradition, and their dead bodies were burned, and it was the reason why when the supernatural beings were feeling that they were dying; they removed their ghosts from their bodies to prevent that their ghosts be burned inside their dead bodies.

Although the fact that the supernatural beings were a rare species of animals that had the shape of the natural human beings, they were the creatures with a lot of abilities, and they were able to do a lot of things that both ordinary animals and natural human beings could not do. And the supernatural beings could act like both ordinary animals and natural human beings. They were stronger than ordinary animals and the natural human beings. They had a superpower and that superpower allowed them to adapt in any world without a problem. The supernatural beings were very smart. Their thinking ability was superior to those of natural human beings and ordinary animals. Some supernatural beings were born with the magic and powers that they had inherited from their ancestors.

The world of supernatural beings was led by a magician king who had all the powers, but those powers were based in respect for

## SUPERNATURAL BEINGS

traditions and culture because the king was the leader and keeper of the traditions. And that magician king was the powerful supernatural being and had the mysterious powers to communicate with the ancestors to control the world of supernatural beings.

The supernatural beings were educated on the base on their traditions and they believed in their ancestors as their gods. They prayed in the name of their ancestors, and the skulls and skeletons of the ghosts of their ancestors were exposed to a place called the sacred place. All the feasts in the world of the supernatural beings were based on their culture and traditions. There were special dates that symbolized the historical events that had happened in the world of supernatural beings. The supernatural beings grew up by reading the holy book that was based on their history and traditions.

And by reading that holy book, they found out that each supernatural being had an important mission, and that mission was to eradicate the entire race of natural human beings. Each supernatural being was full of anger and the desire of revenge by reading the holy book. Chapter nine of the holy book was talking about a tragedy that had happened in the world of the supernatural beings more than a century ago. All the supernatural beings had their eyes wet of tears and their faces full of sadness when they read chapter nine of the holy book; and that chapter was talking about a tragic story that had happened between natural human beings and supernatural human beings more than a century ago.

The supernatural beings grew up with the anger and the hatred of the race of natural human beings. Their only purpose and dream were to take their revenge on the race of natural human beings for what they had done over a century ago to the race of supernatural beings. After a lot of generations, the dream and the goal of supernatural beings were still the same to destroy and to put an end to the race of natural human beings.

After more than a century ago, many generations of supernatural beings had failed to eradicate the race of natural human beings. But now, there was a new generation that was different from the previous generations because this new generation of the supernatural beings was led by two magicians who were twins. And since the existence of the race of supernatural beings; it was the first time to see the supernatural beings who were twins and who had the special magic and powers that were different from the magic and powers of other supernatural beings.

And the supernatural beings were seeing that those two twin magicians were sent by their gods to eradicate the race of the natural human beings. They all believed that those twin magicians were born for a special mission who was to destroy the race of the natural human beings. Although, there is anger and determination that this generation of the supernatural beings had against the race of natural human beings, would they be stronger enough to succeed to eradicate the race of natural human beings? Would this new generation of supernatural human beings led by the two magician twins were going to make that dream come true that their parents and grandparents failed to do; by destroying the race of natural human beings? Would those magician supernatural beings succeed in avenging their ancestors by putting an end to the race of natural human beings?

# CHAPTER I

# THE MISSION OF THE MAGICIAN SUPERNATURAL BEINGS

The world of tiger was led by a king named Philip who was living in a palace, and who had all the powers that were based in respect for traditions. All the decisions that Philip could take were based on the tradition of the tiger world. In the tiger world called again family of tiger, the law was based on the rules of the tradition, and the inhabitants of the tiger world were living according to those rules of tradition, and they were educated to respect and obey those rules of tradition. The supernatural beings of the tiger world were born with blue eyes. They had a beauty mark below the right side of their chins, with a mark that looked like a tattoo on their left shoulder that had the tiger's head and they have the hair that reached their necks.

Although the fact that the supernatural beings of the tiger world had long pointed canine teeth that were the teeth of their ghosts, they did not drink blood. But they could kill natural human beings by using those teeth of tigers and they were usually using those teeth to fight and to defend themselves. When the supernatural beings of the tiger world wanted to turn into their ghosts that were the tigers, their blue eyes were becoming dark blue and they took the shape of their phantoms. When they were in danger, a mysterious light got out from their eyes and it was their phantoms that they had removed from their bodies. Once they had removed their phantoms from their bodies, they could no longer turn into tigers until they made their phantoms come back into their bodies.

There were only the vampires, the magicians, the zombies and the wizards who could see that mysterious light that got out from the eyes of the supernatural beings, so the natural human beings who did not have the magic could not see that mysterious light that got out from the eyes of the supernatural beings, except if those natural human beings had the magic.

The supernatural beings of the tiger world born with the powers called the powers of vampirism again called the powers of animals that were located in their ghosts and some born with six powers of vampirism while others born with nine powers of vampirism. And there was only King Philip who was born with eleven powers of vampirism and the number of eleven was the highest. According to their traditions there was only the king who was born with eleven powers of vampirism. Those powers of vampirism were the strengths of the supernatural beings, so those who were born with nine powers of vampirism were stronger than those who were born with six powers of vampirism.

But an unexpected event happened in the world of tigers seventeen years ago. That event had turned the traditions and culture of the tiger world upside down; terrifying everyone. No one in the world of tiger understood what was going on, even King Philip could not explain that mysterious unexpected event. Most inhabitants were very afraid and for them. It was a curse that had happened because according to the tradition of the tiger world, all the events that happened against the rules of traditions were considered like a curse and those events were not welcome in the tiger world. The event that had happened seventeen years ago had happened against the rules of traditions of the tiger world and two women named Sarah and Jessica had given birth to the twins on a Monday at 12:00 p.m.

And since the existence of the tiger world, no woman had given birth on a Monday because Monday was a sacred day for the tiger world. Monday was a remembering day to the ancestor's memory and no activity was done on that day because it was made for prayers and rituals. Those twins were the first twins of the history of the tiger world, so it was the first time for everyone to see the twins. The worst was that those twins was not born with six or nine powers of vampirism but they were born instead with fourteen powers of vampirism. So those twins had more powers of vampirism than King Philip and it meant that those twins were stronger than Philip. It was the first time in the world of tiger that a supernatural being was born with more powers of vampirism than a king because in the culture of the tiger world, only in the family of kings that we could see a child born with eleven powers of vampirism and this child who was born with eleven powers of vampirism was the future king.

It is because eleven powers of vampirism were one of the signs to know the future king of the tiger world. But now with those twins who had fourteen powers of vampirism, everyone was completely lost and they were even scared that even Philip did not know what to do. And more than ninety-eight percent of supernatural beings believed that those twins were a curse sent by the devils and they were not welcome in the tiger world while less than two percent of supernatural beings believed that those twins were a blessing sent by their ancestors to protect them.

The birth of those twins had put the fire in the tiger world and no one had gone to see those twins not only because they had been banned by Philip to get a visit but because most of them had said that those twins were cursed. The ritual ceremonies for the births of children that the tradition of the tiger world required to do when a child was born in the tiger world had been forbidden for those twins. And Philip had not only banned the ritual ceremonies of the birth of those twins, he had also banned those twins to wear the name Tiger, because the name Tiger was the family name of all inhabitants of the tiger world. Philip had banned everything that was in report with the tradition to those twins. So those twins were not recognized as children of the tiger world.

Most supernatural beings were asking Philip to kill those twins and to not let them grow up by saying that if those children grew up, they would destroy the tiger world. And although the fact that those twins had all the marks of supernatural beings of the tiger world, most supernatural beings were saying that those twins were not the children of the tiger world and that they were the fake supernatural beings. They were coming from the race of natural human beings that those twins and that they were natural human beings with fake marks of the supernatural beings on them. It was in the world of natural human beings that there were twins and that if those twins existed in the world of tiger, it was meant to destroy it. While there were few supernatural beings who were asking Philip to let those kids grow up. And Philip wanted to kill those twins because he shared the idea of those who were saying that those twins were the cursed children who were born to destroy the tiger world. Philip did not have the entire power to decide to kill those twins without consulting the ancestor, because his powers were based on the rules of tradition and the tradition meant the ancestors.

So, before killing those twins, Philip should consult the ancestors first by using his powers and magic to talk with the ancestors who were the gods. Then, Philip organized a meeting in the sacred house of the tiger world with all its inhabitants. The sacred house was the house where all important decisions were made. Philip had announced to everyone that he was going to consult the ancestors about the decisions to make about the mysterious twins who were born in their world. And everyone had been happy about the decision of Philip, he had added that the dads of those twins would stay in jail till, and the moms would be watched by the police till the decision of the ancestors were made.

Everyone had been happy by the decision of Philip to consult the ancestors about those twins but there were few of them who were unhappy about sending the dads of those twins to jail till the decision of the ancestors., The decision to send the dads of those twins to jail was coming from Philip. It is according to the rules of the tradition of the tiger world that a supernatural being was sent to jail at the moment when the king wanted to communicate with the ancestors. The supernatural being lost all his rights as an inhabitant of the tiger world, and was not sent in a comfortable prison, that was the reason why usually the king did not send supernatural beings in the jail when he wanted to communicate with the ancestors. Robert and George who were the dads of those twins had been sent to jail. Robert had been taken out from the hospital to be sent to jail, because before Sarah who was one of the moms of those twins and Robert's wife gave birth, Robert was already sick.

And the doctors who were taking care of Robert had told the police that he was very sick and could not stay in prison. Mostly, there would be nobody in prison to take care of him because the rules of the tradition forbade to take care of the prisoners who were sent to jail when the king wanted to communicate with the ancestors. And the police answered the doctors that the decision to send Robert to prison was not coming from them, but instead from the king.

The whole inhabitants of the tiger world were enthusiastic about the decision of the ancestors because according to the rules of the tradition, it will take three days for the king to communicate with the ancestors. After two days, the only talked about from the inhabitants of the tiger world was on those twins and most of them were sure that the ancestors will order the king to kill those twins. It was the eve of the third day and most inhabitants were in the sacred house waiting for the king to get out of his secret room to announce to them the decision of the ancestors. The secret room was a mysterious room where the king communicated with the ancestors. It was 5:00 a.m., the supernatural beings who had spent the night at home woke up and went to the sacred house where they joined those who had spent the night there. They were all looking at the clock on the wall, counting the time, and turning their heads through the corridor where Philip should walk to join them in the sacred house.

After an hour, their hearts had started beating faster than normal, as they were all waiting for Philip to walk inside the room and to announce to them the decision of the ancestors. After half an hour, most of them in the sacred house started to worry and they were wondering what was going on, because Philip should have walked in the room at 6 am to announce to them the decision of the ancestors. Hours were passing, and Philip had still not walked inside the sacred house, and no one understood what was going on, and it was the first time that the king spent more than 72 hours in the secret room. It was already evening, some supernatural beings had left the sacred house without Philip getting out of the secret room, and the rest of them had decided to spend the night in the sacred house to wait for Philip.

The days were passing, Philip was still inside the secret room, and the supernatural beings had started to get worried because they were wondering what was going on. Most of them were saying that it was those twins who were preventing Philip from getting out of the secret room, and the inhabitants had started to go to the sacred place to pray, asking the ancestors to protect their king and to protect the tiger world. Robert's health was getting worse in the jail, and he was abandoned alone because there was nobody to take care of him. After nine days, the worst had happened in the tiger world, Philip was still in the secret room, Robert was dead in jail, George had succeeded to escape from the jail and two of the twins had mysteriously disappeared. It was a tragedy in the tiger world, supernatural beings were very afraid even for their own life, and they all said that those twins were born to end the race of supernatural beings, that those twins were responsible of Philip being still inside the secret room. Also, they were afraid that maybe Philip was dead inside the secret room.

The worst part was that nobody could enter the secret room to verify if Philip was still alive, because only the king had the right to get in the secret room. And they were saying that even if Philip was still alive, he would be dying of thirst and starvation, because he had not eaten food nor drink water during his stay in the secret room. The question that was going on in everyone's mind was how those twins had disappeared? But unfortunately, nobody could answer that question, even the moms of those twins.

On the eleventh day, Philip got out of the secret room, he was very tired, and had lost weight. He had organized a meeting in the sacred house, with all inhabitants of the tiger world. Everyone had been surprised when Philip had announced to them that those twins were welcome in the tiger world, and that they were sent by their ancestors to protect the tiger world and his inhabitants. Philip had told them that the ancestors had named them Hero and Prince, and that they were special kids, and the magician supernatural beings. Everyone had been very happy to know that those twins were not the

## SUPERNATURAL BEINGS

cursed kids, and they all organized the ritual ceremonies for the tradition required for the birth of kids, and Philip had given the family name of Tiger to those twins.

When those twins were growing up, everyone found out that they had the magic, and that Hero had the power to communicate with the future, while Prince had the power to communicate with the past. Both Hero and Prince had magic eyes, and also could communicate with the present. Thanks to their magic. Hero had two phantoms, a ghost that was tiger-like. All the inhabitants of the tiger world called his identity phantom, and another phantom who was his double, called his invisible ghost, while Prince had only a phantom that was a tiger-like. All inhabitants of the tiger world, but Prince was able to do a lot of things through his magic that Hero could not do. The magic of Hero and Prince were different from the magic of supernatural beings and those supernatural beings who had the magic had inherited their magic from their ancestors who were the magicians, while Hero and Prince had not inherited their magic from their ancestors.

~~And~~ When the supernatural beings asked Hero and Prince where were their twins? Hero answered that her twin went to a world called Mont Coupe', because she was not happy in the tiger world. And they demanded Hero where the world of 'Mont coupe' was? Hero answered that it was a mysterious world of the magicians. Philip asked Hero if he could ask his twin to come back in the tiger world? Hero answered that it was impossible, because he was not in touch with his twin. They asked Prince where his twin was? Prince answered that he had no idea about where his twin was. Hero and Prince who were the most hated children of the tiger world, had become most loved after the ancestors had accepted them as children of the tiger world. Hero and Prince grew up with many who loved them, all inhabitants of the tiger world loved them, and they were like the advisors of Philip. Hero was a little taller and skinnier than Prince.

Hero and Prince grew up with kids of their age, they were going to school together, and they spent their time doing the same activities. Most of their free time, they were in the forest playing, they were turning into phantoms to run and climb on the trees. But kids were also required to follow a disciplinary rule that was imposed by their education and culture, as they were required to practice different sports, the cricket and volleyball were the traditional sports of the tiger world. Most of time, kids of the tiger world were focused on training like the tradition required, so Prince, Hero and the other kids spent their time to do some activities that were related to their culture like learning to fight, learning to protect themselves, learning how to use their phantoms to fight, and learning how to use their ghosts in case of danger. Also, learning their tradition and history of their world.

But Hero and Prince did not appreciate each other. They were not good friends, because both Hero and Prince were not only the most loved kids of the tiger world, but they were the smarter, too, who had the same number of powers of vampirism, and the only kids who had the special magic. They also had a lot of abilities. And the fact that Hero and Prince were the smarter kids who had the special magic, and a lot of things in common, had caused a problem between them. They fought to know who the best between them. Hero and Prince hated each other which had caused the division in the tiger world, because one part of youth was behind Hero, and another part of the youth was behind Prince.

Hero was going everywhere with his friends, and Prince was going everywhere with his friends, too. Everywhere where Hero and his friends go, they meet Prince and his friends, so they always fight. Philip and the inhabitants of the tiger world had tried to put an end to the war that was going on between the two of them but did not succeed. The war between Hero and Prince was affecting the relationship between the families too. all, some parents were angry with other parents, because their kids got hurt during the fight against other kids.

It was an evening; Hero and his friends were wandering in the forest. and There was the wind that was blowing and birds at the top of trees were singing. Hero had his head lifted through the sky, with his face full of joy as he was enjoying the song of birds by watching them fly from one tree to another. Suddenly, Hero started breathing deeply as he was feeling the smell of another supernatural being, then Hero turned to his left because he had felt that the smell was coming from the other side. Immediately anger appeared on Hero's face, as he was staring at Prince and Prince's friends.

Suddenly, Hero made a noise with his mouth, and his blue eyes became dark blue, and he turned into a tiger. He started running through Prince angrily, and Prince had turned into a tiger, too and he was running through Hero with the anger in his eyes. Some tigers were running behind Hero and Prince, then both Hero and Prince started fighting angrily. Some other tigers fought between them too, while others fought with their supernatural bodies.

During the fight, two of them stabbed each other with tree branches, and they fell on the ground. ~~Suddenly,~~ Hero and Prince stopped the fight as they had noticed that two of their brothers were on the ground bleeding from their mouths and bellies. And they all rushed through their two brothers who were on the ground. They were all surrounded with their brothers named, Mark and Alex who were lying on the ground. Hero and Prince had the sadness on their faces as they were looking at Mark and Alex who had the tree branches in their stomachs. Those who had the shape of tigers turned into their supernatural bodies, and they were all still looking at their brothers on the ground silently. Then, Hero and Prince turned their heads looking at each other and still without saying a word, Hero had his eyes wet with tears.

Then, Hero and Prince walked towards their brothers. Hero bent close to Mark who was his friend, while Prince bent close to Alex who was his friend, too. Hero was looking in Mark's eyes with tears that were flowing down his cheeks, while Prince was looking in Alex's eyes with tears that were flowing down his cheeks.

Hero held the left hand of Mark and said, "Please, Mark, stay with us."

Mark looked into Hero's eyes and said, "It's impossible."

Hero said, "Do not worry, we will take you to the hospital."

Mark said, "It's too late."

Hero looked into Mark's eyes with his mouth opened but unable to pronounce a word, while Mark was breathing with difficulty. Then, Mark said, "I have a favor to ask you."

Hero replied, "You know well that you can ask me whatever you want."

Mark said, "I want you to stop the war with Prince and make peace with him." Hero looked at Mark with a surprised face without saying a word.

Mark said, "Please, I want to go in peace, and I want that my death to bring peace our world." Hero was still looking at Mark silently.

Mark said, "It's my last wish and it would help me to go in peace."

Hero said, "My heart is full of anger now, and the only thing that is in my head is revenge. I want Prince and his friends to pay for your death. But, if your last wish is to make peace, I promise you that I would fight for peace in this world." Then, Mark thanked Hero. Hero apologized to Mark, and he told him how much he was so sorry. Prince and Alex were looking at each other.

Prince put his right hand on Alex's bloodied belly and he looked into his eyes and said, "Please, do not abandon us."

Alex said, "Of course, I would not abandon you all, but I would go to another world to watch all of you."

Prince said, "Please, do not say that, because we all want you to stay in this beautiful world with us." Alex replied, "The time has come for me to go meet our ancestors."

Prince said, "I am sure that you still have a lot of time in this world with us."

Alex said, "I know that it's hard for you, but you must accept that my mission in this world is over, and the time has come for me to go."

Prince said, "I am so sorry."

Alex said, "You do not have to be sorry." He added, "I am glad that I am going by this way."

Prince asked, "What do you mean?"

Alex replied, "I have something in my heart."

Prince said, "I do not understand."

Alex said, "The last beating of my heart is asking for peace."

Prince said, "Still, I do not understand."

Alex coughed twice and said, "My heart is asking for peace in the tiger world. My heart is asking that Hero and you have to stop fighting and make peace with each other."

Suddenly, Prince's face changed. He was full of anger, and he said, "You cannot ask me to make peace with Hero, because right now, I am full of anger and the only thing I want to do it's to kill Hero and all his friends to avenge your death."

Alex said, "Please, forget about getting revenge because I want my death to be useful, that my death brings peace in the tiger world."

Prince said, "Sorry, I cannot because Hero and his friends must pay for your death."

Alex asked, "Do you want me to go in peace?"

Prince answered, "Yes, of course."

Alex said, "Make peace with Hero, then I would go in peace."

Prince asked, "It's your last wish?"

Alex answered, "Yes, it's my last wish."

Then, Prince promised to Alex to fight for peace, and that as long as he is alive, he would always fight for the peace in the tiger world. He would make sure that this kind of war between the inhabitants of the tiger world would never happen again.

Then, Prince and Hero turned their heads looking at each other, with the tears flowing down their cheeks without saying a word. Everyone was looking at them with teary eyes. Suddenly, Hero saw the lights go out from Mark and Alex's eyes, and those lights turned into two tigers that were the phantoms of Mark and Alex. Hero and Prince moved through the ghosts of Mark and Alex that were lying on the ground. They stared at the two tigers that were on the ground, and Hero noticed that the two tigers that were on the ground were bleeding through their bellies.

Hero understood that Mark and Alex had their phantoms inside their bodies when they stabbed at each other with the tree branches. Hero understood that the tree branches had killed the ghosts of Mark and Alex and he watched with tears in his eyes how the phantoms of

Mark and Alex closed their eyes. Hero and Prince put the fire on the dead body of Mark and Alex. They all watched the dead bodies of their brothers burned with silence and with the tears flowing down their cheeks. After fifteen minutes, Hero and his friends carried the ghost of Mark, while Prince and his friends carried the ghost of Alex. They all left the forest with the dead phantoms of their brothers.

The world of tiger was mourning, and the inhabitants were crying over the death of their two kids who were Mark and Alex. Although, the fact that the tiger world was crying for the death of their two kids in peace, and respect the rules of their tradition. There was anger inside them, even if they could not express that anger. Because, one of the rules of the tradition in the tiger world requires everyone to respect the moment of sadness like mourning by staying quiet in respect supernatural beings who had gone to join the ancestors. By avoiding everything that could turn into anger, discussion or fight.

The tiger world was divided in two for the first time in his history. The death of Mark and Alex had divided the tiger world, because one side there was Hero, his friends and the family of his friends, and on the other side, there was Prince, his friends and the family of his friends. Both sides were accusing each other of being responsible for the death of Mark and Alex. Some supernatural beings were very angry with Hero and Prince, because for them, it was Hero and Prince who were responsible for the death of Mark and Alex. The mess that was going on in the tiger world was a war of ego.

The ghosts of Mark and Alex were buried according to the rules of tradition of the tiger world. Three days following the burial of Mark and Alex were prayers, and the rituals according to the traditions for the phantoms of Mark and Alex join the ancestors in peace. All the inhabitants of the tiger world spent three days to the sacred place to pray and do the rituals as tradition required that when one of them died, the ancestors have to forgive all their sins and to welcome the ghosts of Mark and Alex close to them. During those three days, all activities were forbidden as tradition required. Although, the fact that the tiger world was divided into two, everyone was trying to hide their anger and talk to each other at the sacred place. The sacred place was not a place to keep the anger except for Hero and Prince who had not talked to each other. Hero and Prince spent the time just looking at each other without saying a word with their faces full of anger.

After three days, the ritual ceremony for Mark and Alex was over. Philip called a meeting to the sacred house with all inhabitants. All inhabitants of the tiger world were in the sacred house listening to Philip who was calling for the peace in the tiger world, and who was asking to Hero and Prince to stop their useless war that divided the tiger world. Thanks to this war, they had already lost two of their kids and they did not want to keep losing children. Hero and Prince will not stop the war, they would keep losing their kids. Then, Hero speak, and apologized for everything that happened to the tiger world because of the war between him and Prince. Hero apologized to the families of Mark and Alex for the death of their kids, and he promised to everyone to stop the war between him and Prince, by saying that Prince was not his enemy but instead his brother.

Suddenly, the smile appeared on everyone's face fade as they all heard the speech of Hero who was calling for the peace between Prince and him. Everyone looked surprised at Prince who was walking through the stage where Hero was talking. They were all wondering why Prince was going to the stage? The stage was only reserved for the king. Then, Prince reached the stage, and he turned to face everyone. He started to speak by apologizing to all inhabitants of the tiger world, mostly to the families of Mark and Alex, and by saying that the war between him and Hero was over. That the death of Mark and Alex had taught him a lesson. So from now on, he would fight for peace in the tiger world. Everyone started clapping with a smile on their faces.

of them were saying that the death of Mark and Alex had brought peace in the tiger world. Prince went on by saying that his enemy was not Hero, and that Hero was his brother, and that their enemies were not far from them. Suddenly, there was a surprise on everyone's faces and they were all wondering which enemies Prince was talking about? Their eyes opened wide. They were all looking at the wall that was in front of them with the amazed faces, as Prince was using his magic to make the photos appear on the wall. Prince face to the wall and there was the light that was getting out from his eyes and going through the wall and that The light was shining on the wall and turning into pictures.

Everyone was looking at the pictures that were on the wall with expressionless faces, and without exactly understanding what was going on, except that Hero understood exactly what was going on, and the meaning of the pictures that Prince was using his magic to appear on the wall. They all noticed that on those pictures, there were supernatural beings who were fighting, and some of them had marks of the supernatural beings of the tiger world. They were seeing a lot of animals like the tigers, birds, panthers, lions, snakes and other animal species on the wall. The other pictures were showing the corpses, blood, and the animals that were the phantoms of supernatural beings who were dead.

But they were completely lost, because they had a lot of questions going on in their mind, like what was the meaning of those pictures? Where Prince got those pictures? Why there were supernatural beings from the tiger world? Who were the other supernatural beings on those pictures who did not have the marks of the tiger world? Which race of the supernatural beings had the phantoms like lions, snakes, panthers, birds and other animal species? What was the message that Prince was trying to send them?,

Unfortunately, none of them could answer those questions, even Hero had started not understand what was going on. There were a lot of pictures on the wall that Hero didn't know the meaning of. Most of them started to get scared, even Philip was very afraid by looking on those pictures on the wall. They were all thinking that they were in danger. But, one thing that they all noticed was that those pictures on the wall were the old pictures, of the supernatural beings. Those pictures could be their ancestors?

Prince turned and looked at everyone with all eyes focused on him. had closed their mouths even Prince himself, but the hearts of most of them were beating with fear as they were all waiting for Prince to explain to them what was going on. After three minutes, Prince broke the silence. He said that the death of Mark and Alex was a message that their ancestors were sending to them, and that their world was in danger. Prince turned and looked at the pictures and he pointed his finger through the pictures by looking at everyone. He told them that the pictures were what had happened more than a century ago. And that it was the race of natural human beings who was responsible for all the tragedies that the race of supernatural beings had lived.

Prince continued to talk to them that it was time to get their revenge on the race of the natural human beings, and that if they did not fight now, it would be the natural human beings who would destroy them as natural human beings had done more than a century ago. That it was the right and duty of the supernatural beings to protect their race because they were all born for a mission as they had all read in the holy book and that that mission was to eradicate the entire race of natural human beings. Prince ended his speech by saying that it was time to go to the world of natural human beings to fight them. And everyone turned their head by looking at each other with astonished faces, without really understanding what was going on. There was a huge silence in the room, they were just looking at each other without uttering a word, although, the fact that some of them had open mouths, but no word was coming out from it. Prince broke the silence and said that he wanted the authorization of Philip to go into the world of natural human beings.

Suddenly, everyone was very surprised again, as they had heard Hero who had joined the idea of Prince by saying that he was going to the world of natural human beings with Prince to destroy the race of the natural human beings. Hero joined Prince on the stage, and Hero looked at the wall when the light in his eyes started getting out and going through the wall. Immediately, the eyes of everyone opened widely and the fear appeared on everyone's face s., as they were looking at the pictures that Hero had made appear on the wall through his magic. In the pictures, they were seeing the tiger world that had become the desert and other pictures on the wall were showing the end of the race of supernatural beings.

Then, Hero turned and looked at everyone by telling them that the death of Alex and Mark was a message that their ancestors were sending to them, by telling them that the time of their mission had come. Hero pointed his finger at the pictures that were on the wall by looking at everyone and by telling them that the pictures on the wall will be the future of the tiger world. They do not have another choice but to fight now if they wanted to preserve the race of the supernatural beings. And that if they did not fight now, they would be eradicated by their enemies as the images on the wall were showing to them.

There were no other solutions, because the only solution was the war against the race of natural human beings. The eyes of everyone were focused on the pictures that Hero had used his magic to make appear on the wall, and most of them were shaking of fear, as they were all seeing the end of their life through those pictures. Then, Hero and Prince started to convince everyone that it was time to declare the war to their enemies, and that the images on those pictures were exactly what had happened in the past, and what will happen in the future. As the magic of Prince was linked with the past, and the magic of Hero was linked with the future, and both Hero and Prince told everyone that the only way to prevent the tragedy that they were seeing on the pictures was to destroy the race of their enemies now. could not change the destiny of the past, but they had a chance to change the destiny of the future by fighting their enemies to protect their race before their enemies destroy their own.

Suddenly, the friends of Hero and Prince joined to agree with their idea by saying that they were going in the war against the race of natural human beings, too. The time of their mission had come, and that they were ready for their duty as the holy book asked them to be ready to fight at any time to protect their race.

Then, the supernatural beings started asking questions to Hero and Prince like why there were not the race of natural human beings on those pictures? As it was the natural human beings who were responsible for the tragedy that had happened a century ago. Who were the other supernatural beings that they were seeing in those photos? Who were the supernatural beings who had the phantoms like the lions, snakes, birds and other animal species? Why were the supernatural beings fighting for themselves? Who was responsible for

## SUPERNATURAL BEINGS

the death of the supernatural beings that they were seeing in the pictures? Why was it that the supernatural beings were killing each other? And if there were still other identities of the supernatural beings who had the phantoms like the other animals that they were seeing on the wall? Hero told them that he could not answer those questions, because all those questions were related the past, and his magic was related to the future so he could only answer the questions that were related the future. Hero added that those questions were the same questions that was going on in his mind, but he could not find the answers either. Prince answered them. He said, the answers to their questions were linked to the sad part of the history of the race of the supernatural beings.

And that it was the reason why the ancestors had not told them about the history that was linked to those questions in the holy book, because their ancestors wanted to protect them from the sadness and the suffering of what had happened in the past. He cannot answer all those questions because the answers were based on the secrets that their ancestors did not want them to know. But after their war against the race of the natural human beings, he would write a sacred book where he would talk about another part of the history of the race of the supernatural human beings. In that sacred book, they would find the answers to their questions, and they would find out a lot of secrets that were linked to the history of the race of the supernatural beings that they did not know.

Everyone in the sacred house was completely lost, and now, they understand that their life, history, origins, past and future were full of mysteries and secrets.-They were very worried. Although, the fact that more than ninety percent of them were sharing the idea of Prince and Hero to fight the race of natural human beings, there were less than ten percent of them who were not sharing the same idea of Hero and Prince to declare war. Philip was sharing the idea of those minority of the ten percent who were against the war to the race of natural human beings. The fact that Philip and those less than ten percent knew well that the holy book and their tradition obliged them to fight the race of the natural human beings to protect their race. There were tension and anger in the sacred house, as Philip was against the idea to send Hero, Prince and their friends to the world of natural human beings to destroy them.

Hero, Prince and other supernatural beings tried to convince Philip to let them go to the world of natural human beings to fight. They argued that even the holy book told them that their mission was to destroy the race of the natural human beings. their parents, and grandparents had tried to destroy the race of their enemy but had failed. Philip told them that he knew well that they all had a mission, and that was to eradicate the race of the natural human beings, but by seeing the pictures of what had happened in the past, he was very afraid that the same story could happen. He was afraid too, that during the war against the race of the natural human beings, it's the race of supernatural beings who would be eradicated, as the images on the photos that Hero had shown.

Philip was completely opposed to the war against the race of the natural human beings, although the fact that Hero and Prince had tried to convince him by telling him that they were born with the special magic for that mission. The mission was to destroy the race of the natural human beings, to protect their race, but Philip completely refused to allow them to go to the world of the natural human beings. They spent the whole day and the whole evening in the sacred house to try to convince Philip without succeeding, and most of them left the sacred house angrily. It was the first time that they had spent almost a day in the sacred house to argue and the first time too that they had left the sacred house with questions in their mind that they could not answer, with anger, fear, doubt and insecurity.

It was morning and was cold outside. All the inhabitants of the tiger world woke up with headaches, and most of them had no sleep the whole night, because they had spent the night thinking about their meeting of last night from the sacred house. Jessica was in her kitchen, sat in the chair with breakfast on the table in front of her, and she was waiting for Prince to come eat his breakfast. After a few minutes, Jessica started to wonder where Prince was, and she started calling his name, but Prince was not responding. Jessica got up from her chair and walked 'till the front door of the bedroom of Prince.

## SUPERNATURAL BEINGS

pushed the door, and she walked a step inside the bedroom, when she suddenly scream with fear. As she had seen Prince who was lying on his bed with his eyes opened, with difficulties on his breathing, blood on the left side of his body and his neck that was folded to the right side. Jessica rushed through the bed and climbed on it, and she looked the eyes of Prince by shaking him and by shouting his name, asking him what was going on. Immediately, Jessica realized that Prince did not have his ghost inside him, and that he was in the state or condition where his phantom was in danger somewhere in the same state. Prince was barely breathing.

Then, Jessica started asking Prince where his phantom was, with tears flowing down her cheeks, and Prince was just staring in her eyes without saying a word. Jessica tried to move the left hand of Prince and she noticed that his left hand was broken. understood that his phantom had broken his left foot from before, and she tried to move his head, and she noticed that his head was not making any movement. She understood too that the head of Prince's phantom was blocked somewhere.

Jessica left the bedroom and rushed through the yard of her house by screaming and calling for help. After a couple of seconds, Jessica's house was full of supernatural beings, and they were all seeing Prince who was dying in his bed. They all understood that the ghost of Prince was dying somewhere. Most of them had tears in their eyes, and some of them were saying that they must go to the forest to search the phantom of Prince, while others were saying that they must go call Hero, because Hero could use his magic to find where the ghost of Prince was. They were all in the yard of the house trying to find a solution to save the phantom of Prince that was in danger somewhere. Suddenly, they all turned their heads to the left side of the yard, as they had heard one of them scream with a hand pointing by saying that Hero was coming.

They were all seeing a tiger that was running faster towards the yard, and they all knew that was Hero. tiger reached the yard and turned into his supernatural body who was Hero, and they told him that the phantom of Prince was dying somewhere. Hero turned and looked at the wall and the light got out from his eyes and went through the wall. The dread appeared on the faces of everyone, as they had all turned their heads through the wall and they were looking with some of them had their mouths opened but no word was getting out. While others' hearts were beating faster than normal, and most of them were shaking with fear, crying as they were all seeing the ghost of Prince that was dying in the bush through the pictures that Hero had made appear on the wall using his magic. Everyone's eyes were wide open as they were looking at the phantom of how Prince's ghost was bleeding to his left side and a rope had grabbed his ghost's neck 'till that he could not move, and they noticed too that Prince's phantom had breathing difficulties.

Hero turned into a tiger and started running through the direction of the forest. The rest of them turned into tigers, too, and they started following Hero in the cold forest. After less than three minutes, the tigers were in the forest running as fast as they could following Hero who was running faster through the direction where the ghost of Prince was dying. After fifteen minutes of running, Hero reached the place where the phantom of Prince was, and he succeeded to save the phantom of Prince, then the other tigers joined him and took the phantom of Prince to the hospital.

The supernatural beings were in the yard of the hospital where the doctors were taking care of the phantom of Prince, and there were questions that were going on in the heads of everyone, but none of them could answer even one of those questions. Some of those questions were why Prince removed his phantom from his body? What did the phantom of Prince was doing in the bush? And who had tried to kill the phantom of Prince in the forest? But only Prince could answer their questions, and they were all hoping that he would recover soon and explain to them what had happened. There was another question that was going on in the minds on each of them, and that question was frightening them, because they were all wondering if Prince was not attacked by their enemies? They were wondering if natural human beings came into their world? And they were very afraid of their security, mostly when they were thinking about their meeting of last night in the sacred house with all the pictures that they had seen on the wall coming from the magic of Hero and

## SUPERNATURAL BEINGS

Prince. There were still the questions when they left the sacred house last night, which were unanswered.

The days passed, and Prince was still in a critical condition. whole inhabitants of the tiger world were very worried about Prince, and they go to the sacred place everyday to pray and ask the ancestors to protect him. It was morning, Jessica was in the bedroom of Prince, and she was staring at Prince in his bed, how he was suffering and when Jessica turned her head, she noticed a sheet of paper on the table. Jessica walked unto the table and took the sheet of paper and opened it. Suddenly, the expression of her face changed as she was reading what was written on the paper, with the tears flowing down her cheeks. Jessica rushed through the door with the paper in her hand. She ran unto the palace, and she gave that sheet of paper to Philip. It was already afternoon. Philip called a meeting to the sacred house with all inhabitants of the tiger world, and he told them about the letter that Jessica had given him a couple hours ago. Philip explained to them the content of the letter. He gave the letter to them and by reading it, they understood that Prince had tried to kill himself, because Philip had refused to give them the authorization to go to the world of the natural human beings.

Prince explained in his letter that he was born for a mission, and that he was sent to the tiger world by his ancestors with magic for a special mission, to protect the tiger world and the race of supernatural beings. That if he could not achieve his mission, the only solution was his death. It's the reason he chose to kill himself, so that he can go meet his ancestors because he had nothing to do anymore in the tiger world if he could not protect its beautiful world and his inhabitants. Everyone understood now why Prince had tried to kill himself, because Philip had refused to give him and the other supernatural beings the authorization to go to the world of natural human beings, as they could not go without Philip's permission. According to one of the rules of the tradition of the tiger world, only the king had the right to decide to declare the war against the enemies of the tiger world, but another rules of the tradition of the tiger world says that the king could consult the ancestors to know if he should declare the war against the enemies or not.

, Hero and other supernatural beings could not declare war against the race of natural human beings without the authorization of Philip. One of the rules of the tradition says that the inhabitants of the tiger world could not decide by themselves to declare a war against the enemies, and another rules of the tradition says that the inhabitants of the tiger world could not get out of the territory of the tiger world without the authorization of the king.

So, Prince, Hero and other supernatural beings did not have the power to declare the war against their enemies without the authorization of Philip, or even to get out of the territory of the tiger world without the Philip's permission. And they could not break the rules of the tradition because it was a curse to break the rules of the tradition. There were also the consequences for those who broke the rules of the tradition like the death sentence, death by hanging, torture, destroying of the powers of vampirism, and losing your identity as a resident of the tiger world. Prince had tried to kill himself, because he could not break the rules of the tradition by declaring war against the enemies by himself or to leave the territory of the tiger world without the authorization of the king. Most of the inhabitants of the tiger world were very angry with Philip, because for them Philip was the one responsible if Prince had tried to kill himself, and they were all still praying by asking the ancestors to help Prince to recover.

After three weeks, Prince was completely healed, and everyone was very happy to see that Prince was doing well. It was an evening; Philip was walking in his garden staring at the moon that was shining in the sky. One of his employees came and told him that Hero and Prince wanted to see him. Philip told his employee to let Prince and Hero join him in the garden. After a few minutes, Prince and Hero joined Philip in the garden, and they started walking and talking about the past and the future of the tiger world. Prince and Hero told Philip that their destiny was to protect the race of supernatural beings by going into war against the enemies of the tiger world, and it was the reason why they were born with the special magic. still turned down the proposition of Hero and Prince to make the war against the race of the natural human beings although the fact that Prince and Hero told him that they were ready to break the rules of the tradition by declaring the war by themselves. leaving the garden, Hero and Prince told Philip that they did not want to be the witnesses of destruction the race of supernatural beings, and that if Philip did not change his mind in the next twenty-four hours, they were going to kill themselves.

The next day, it was early in the morning, and the sacred house was full of inhabitants. They were all staring at Philip who face them and had called a meeting. They all noticed that Philip was very tired, and that it was obvious that he had not sleep the whole night. Then, Philip told them that he had a conversation last night with Prince and Hero about the destiny of the tiger world, and that he spent the whole night thinking about their conversation. Suddenly, fear appeared on everyone's faces in the room, when they all heard Philip say that Prince and Hero had decided to kill themselves, if he did not give them the authorization to make war against the race of the natural human beings. All smiles were replaced with fear on the face of everyone, as they had all heard Philip say that he was going to consult the ancestors about the destiny of the tiger world, and it will be the ancestors who will going to decide if the race of supernatural beings were going to make the war against the race of the natural human beings. Everyone clapped their hands after Philip's speech who announced to them his decision to consult the ancestors, about the preposition of Prince and Hero to make war against their enemies. They all left the sacred house with smiles on their faces, with the hope that the ancestors would authorize the war against their enemies.

The next day, Philip entered the secret room to communicate with the ancestors, while the rest of the inhabitants went to the sacred place to pray and to ask the ancestors to give their authorization to Philip to wage war against their enemies. Days were passing, and Philip was still in the secret room and the inhabitants were still going to the sacred place to pray by asking the ancestors to hear their wishes. Although, the fact that they were a little bit worried as Philip had not yet come out of the secret room, as he had already spent three days in that room. Usually three days were exactly the time they spend in the secret room. But they were not afraid, because they knew that it was not the first time that Philip stayed in the secret room for more than three days. And that the first time that Philip had spent more than three days in the secret room, was about the case of the magician twins who were born in their world. had come out of that secret room with the good news, and most of them had hope that he would get out again from the secret room with the good news.

Hero and Prince had organized a training with their friends to get ready for their mission, and they were spending their time to train in the forest after they had left the sacred place. It was midnight, the tiger's world was asleep, and Hero was twisting and turning in his bed, trying to find a way to sleep but to no success. The fact that he was very tired. Suddenly, Hero started to feel a strange feeling, and he was wondering what was going on, then he got up from his bed and he turned on the lights, he walked 'till the table was in the room while he carried the remedy that was in the glass on the table for him to drink. Suddenly, the glass fell from his hand and broke on the floor as he lifted it through his mouth to drink then, his eyes opened widely, as he was staring at the remedy that he wanted to drink on the floor. The remedy that he wanted to drink was like a sleeping pill, and he wanted to drink it to sleep.

Suddenly, Hero started breathing deeply as he was feeling something strange inside his body, and he was trying to understand what was going on without success. He was feeling that one part of his magic was sending him a message. Hero was trying to control that part of his magic without succeeding, and it was the first time that he was feeling a message coming from that part of his magic. It was the first time too that he could not control his magic. Hero did not even know the existence of that part of magic in his body, then he turned his head through the wall and the light got out from his eyes and went through the wall. Hero looked at the wall with an amazed face as he was staring at the pictures that he had made to appear on the wall through his magic. Then, he turned his head through the table that was close to him, and he handed his hand and he took the mask that was on the table and he wore it. Suddenly, Hero's eyes became dark blue and he turned into a tiger, and he jumped out through the window of his bedroom.

# SUPERNATURAL BEINGS

It was a very warm afternoon. The weather was beautiful, and the sun was shining. was a small family, a young woman with her parents who were spending their holiday in the lake on their boat. The young woman had stood at the edge of the boat and she was fishing. Suddenly, a strong wind started blowing and the parents who were on the boat heard a loud scream with their faces full of fear, as they had seen their daughter fell into the water. Then the parents rushed into the boat driver by yelling and calling for help. The fear on the parents' faces turned into a surprise, and they were looking through the water with the astonished faces and the boat driver had the mouth opened, as they had all seen a young man with a mask on his face coming from nowhere which jumped into the water. They all rushed through the edge of the boat, and they looked into the water as they saw a young man who was swimming faster towards the young woman who was drowning.

The young woman's mother started trembling with fear, and she turned towards her husband and the boat driver. She screamed at them to call for help, as they were not seeing anymore both the young man and the young woman in the water. The boat driver went to call for help, while the couple was still looking into the water with their hearts beating with fear as their daughter and the young man had disappeared into the water.

After a couple of minutes, they saw that young man who was swimming by, holding their daughter, and they drove the boat unto them. Then, they helped the young man get out of the water with their daughter. The young woman's mom hurried to tie a small rosary that she had held in her hand on the ankle of her daughter, without even searching to know if her daughter was still alive or not. young woman was lying on the boat unconscious, with her eyes closed and the young man was pressing her chest trying to revive her, while her parents were staring at their daughter with tears in their eyes. After a couple of seconds, young woman started coughing, and water was coming out of her mouth, then she opened her eyes. She stared at that young man who was reviving her with the mask on his face, and both the young woman and the young man were staring at each other eyes.

Suddenly, the young man turned his head and got up. He started running away, and the rest of the people who were on the boat turned their heads and they were staring at that young man who was running away with surprised faces without understanding what was going on. Then, the rescues came, and they took that young woman to the hospital, despite the fact that she was out of danger.

Prince and other supernatural beings were training in the forest, and Hero wasn't there. None of them had seen Hero since that morning, and Hero had not even come in the sacred place for the prayers. But, none of them was worried about Hero, although the fact that they find it weird that he was not there. After a couple of hours, they had finished training, and Prince said that they had to go to Hero's house to find if he was doing well, and they all agreed. Then, they walked into Hero's house, and they met Sarah who was at home making food. Sarah made an astonished face when Prince demanded her where Hero was. Sarah answered Prince that she had not seen Hero since she woke up this morning, and she told them that she thought that Hero was with them. Prince told Sarah that they last seen Hero last evening in the forest for their training, and none of them had put their eyes on Hero again after they had left the forest. Then, they started to worry, and they were all wondering where Hero was. Prince turned and looked at the wall, the light got out from his eyes and went through the wall.

Suddenly the surprise appeared on their faces, except Sarah who had a face full of fear, as they were all looking at the pictures that Prince had made appear on the wall through his magic. They were all seeing Hero who had turned into a tiger and who was running in the forest. Then, they turned their heads looking at each other, and some of them had their mouths opened but none of them was saying a word, they were all completely lost. They did not understand what was going on. Sarah broke the silence by asking, what Hero was doing in the forest alone? Prince answered that they had no idea, and that only Hero can answer the question when Hero would reach home. Prince and his friends left by saying that they would meet Hero the next day.

## SUPERNATURAL BEINGS

Hero reached home at night very tired, and Sarah asked him where he was. Hero lied to her by answering that he spent his whole day running in the forest. Sarah asked him what he was doing in the forest, and why he did not spend his day with his friends as usual? Hero answered that he wanted to be alone, that he was very stressed with the situation that was going on in the tiger world. Philip who was still in the secret room. Immediately, Sarah noticed that the expression of Hero's face had changed, when she told him that Prince had used his magic to find him. Hero asked Sarah where Prince found him through his magic? Sarah answered that Prince found him in the forest, then she noticed that the smile had appeared on Hero's face when she told him that they saw him running in the forest in the shape of his phantom. Sarah noticed that there was something wrong, and that Hero was hiding something, but she did not insist on knowing what it was.

After a few minutes of conversation between Sarah and Hero, he told her that he was very tired and that he wanted to sleep. Hero walked unto his bedroom. He was completely lost while walking, with a lot of questions that were going on in his mind, and some of those questions were why he felt that exceptional feeling last night? Why did his magic warn him that the young woman was in danger? Why did he go into the world of the natural human beings? Who was that young woman? Why did he save that young woman in the lake? Unfortunately, Hero could not even answer one of his questions. He still did not understand why he had saved a natural human being, and he knew that he had no right to save a natural human being, because one of the rules of their tradition forbid them to help or save a natural human being. Hero knew that he had broken two of the important rules of the tradition of the tiger world, one by getting outside of the territory of the tiger world without the authorization of the King, and another, by saving a natural human being.

The fact that he did not know why he had saved that young woman, who was a natural human being, made him realize one thing, he was sure that he did not save that young woman by his own wish. Hero tried to use his magic to review the scene that had happened in the lake, but he failed because his magic was not linked to the past. Hero started to remember about the scene in the lake of how that young woman was drowning in the water. He noticed that something strange had happened in the water where the young woman did not even try to swim, and that it was as if she had lost all her strengths once she had fell in the water, as if there were bad energies that were pushing her into the water. As if there were some mysterious people who wanted to kill that young woman through their magic, and suddenly the expression of Hero's face changed, as he remembered that when he got out of the water with that young woman, the mom of the young woman hurried to tie a small rosary on her ankle. And he was wondering why the first thing that the mom of that young woman had done once he had got out of the water with her, to tie that rosary on the ankle of that young woman. Her mom could have checked first if her daughter was alive, if her she was doing well.

But unfortunately, Hero could not answer that question, one thing he was sure about, was that there was a mystery around that young woman. Hero also remembered about a weird energy that he had felt once he had put his feet in the world of the natural human beings, but he did not pay attention to that energy. Hero spent his whole night walking around in his bedroom, about the young woman that he had saved.

It was early in the morning; the inhabitants of the tiger world woke up with the birds singing and with a smile on their faces as they had heard that Philip had got out from the secret room. They should be in the sacred house within fifteen minutes. All of the inhabitants were getting ready to go to the sacred house, and most of them had the heart beating with fear, they thought the ancestors had turned down the preposition to make the war against their enemies, while the rest of the inhabitants had their heart full of joy that the ancestors had accepted the decision to make the war against their enemies. After fifteen minutes, the sacred house was full of inhabitants, and they were all listening Philip's speech with their hearts beating faster than normal. Hero was very afraid 'till he was shaking of fear, that the ancestors found out that he had broken two of the rules of the tradition of the tiger world yesterday, by saving a natural human being, and by getting out of the territory of the tiger world without any authorization from the king. Hero was scared that Philip was going to talk about it, and that he was going to be killed as he had betrayed his family by saving an enemy. One of the rules of the tradition of the tiger world says that, all traitors who would dare to betray the tiger world must be killed on the orders of the king, or on the orders of the ancestors. And Hero knew that he was already a traitor, as he betrayed his family by saving an enemy.

Immediately, the smile appeared on the faces of everyone except Hero as they had heard Philip say that the ancestors had accepted the war against their enemies. and except Hero in the room, The rest of the supernatural beings were jumping for joy to make the war. Suddenly, the worry appeared on their faces as they had heard Philip say that the ancestors had decided to send only the magician twins, who were Hero and Prince for that mission. They asked Philip why the ancestors had decided to send only Hero and Prince? Philip answered that he had no idea that the ancestors did not give him the reasons for the choice of Prince and Hero. Then, they started wondering how Prince and Hero were going to live in the world of the natural human beings alone? Who was going to make food for them? Who would heal them if they got sick? How ~~only both Hero and Prince were~~ will both of them be going to kill all the races of the natural human beings? How only two of them were going to live in that new world that they did not even know? And why was that decision of the ancestors?

But unfortunately, none of them could even answer one of their questions, and even Philip himself could not answer their questions, although, the fact that he had been in touch with the ancestors in the secret room. They all thought that the ancestors should send more supernatural beings in the world of the natural human beings, with the doctors and chefs among them because they knew that the bodies of the supernatural beings, and the bodies of the natural human beings were different. The supernatural beings could not eat the same food that the natural human ate, and the supernatural beings could not be treated or cure by the doctors who were natural human beings, or even take the same pills that the natural human beings were taking. The doctors of the natural human beings had no idea about the sickness of the supernatural beings or how their bodies worked because the doctors treated or healed them through their phantoms, while in the race of the natural human beings, the doctors treated or healed them through their bodies. There were noises in the sacred house, and most of them were very angry about the decision of the ancestors. The fact that they knew that their anger would not change anything, and that they should respect the decision of the ancestors, as the rules of their traditions obliged them.

Hero was calm in the room, with his heart beating faster than normal. He was completely lost, he did not understand why Philip did not talk about the natural human being that he had saved yesterday. There were a lot of questions that were going on in his mind and he was wondering if the ancestors did not talk to Philip that he had betrayed his family by saving an enemy? If the ancestors told about his betrayal to Philip, and Philip only forgot to talk about it? And if the ancestors did not talk about it to Philip, and for which reason did the ancestors decide to keep the silence about that betrayal? Unfortunately, Hero could not find the answers of those questions, he was sure of one thing that the ancestors knew about his betrayals because the ancestors were their gods, they knew everything that they did, and the ancestors watched them. Hero was still quiet, while Prince was trying to calm those who were disappointed by saying that everything would be alright, that the two of them would succeed to eradicate the race of the natural human beings by using their magic.

After an hour, the meeting was over and most of them left the sacred house with sadness on their faces, as they were not chosen by the ancestors for that mission, while Sarah and Jessica left the sacred house with worry on their faces as their sons were going for that mission without the doctors, chefs and other supernatural beings. Hero, Prince and their friends were together, and they were talking about the mission of Prince and Hero. They noticed that Hero was not involved in the conversation, that he was absent minded. Prince asked Hero if everything was going well? And Hero answered that everything was fine. One of them asked Hero what he was doing alone in the forest yesterday? Hero lied to them by answering that he was very bored at home, and he decided to go visit the forest where he spent the whole day running. Then, they continued to talk about the mission, although, they had noticed that Hero was very tired and thoughtful.

The whole inhabitants of the tiger world started to prepare the ceremony of the departure of Hero and Prince to the world of natural human beings. According to their tradition, when kids of the tiger world were going outside the territory of the tiger world or were going for a mission the whole inhabitants of the tiger world should make a three-day ceremony to ask the ancestors to protect the kids who were going outside of the territory for the mission. All inhabitants of the tiger world spent the whole night talking about the mission of Prince and Hero. It was early morning, the whole inhabitants of the tiger world, were in the sacred place, and they were praying by asking their ancestors to protect Prince and Hero for their mission.

The inhabitants of the tiger world spent three days, to make the ceremony to wish good luck to Hero and Prince for their mission. and Prince slept in a small house called the house of ancestors, during those three days, to receive all the blessings of the ancestors for their mission. Hero was no longer enthusiastic for that mission, and his thoughts were still focused on the young woman that he had saved, but he could not refuse to go to that mission. because it was his right and duty as a citizen of the tiger world to protect the tiger world in case of danger, even to die in the name of the tiger world. Everyone had noticed that Hero had changed, and they all thought that Hero was just a little bit nervous for his mission.

## CHAPTER 11

# THE MYSTERIOUS WITCH ENEMY

It was the fourth day, at midnight and there was the moon shining in the cloud and it was a little bit cold. Hero, Prince and some supernatural beings left the tiger world, and they had all turned into tigers. They spent more than six hours running in the forest until close to the borderline with the world of natural human beings. Then, they all stopped close to the borderline and they turned into their supernatural bodies. They all started staring at the world of natural human beings by talking among them.

After three hours, Hero and Prince hugged their brothers and sisters who were with them, then both Hero and Prince started to walk through the borderline, while their brothers and sisters were watching them. Then, Prince and Hero reached the borderline and they turned and looked at their brothers and sisters without saying a word. Their brothers and sisters were staring at them too, then, they made the gestures with their heads. And Prince and Hero understood the message that their brothers and sisters were telling them Prince and Hero turned their heads and they walked a step, then, they crossed the borderline and they put their feet in the world of natural human beings. Both Prince and Hero felt something strange, and they were feeling as if they were in prison, as they could not express themselves, then, they understood that there was something going wrong, that there was a danger. brothers and sisters were watching them, then Hero and Prince turned their heads and looked at their brothers and sisters, and they made gestures with their heads. brothers and sisters turned into tigers, and Hero and Prince turned their heads and they kept walking and they started running in the forest through the houses.

Hero and Prince were walking, and suddenly Prince stopped, and he turned his head towards Hero, and he asked Hero if Hero was feeling the same thing that he was feeling. Hero stopped, and he stared into the eyes of Prince without saying a word. Hero started to remember that he had felt the same thing a couple days ago when he had come to the world of natural human beings to save that young woman, just that he had not paid attention to that energy. Hero told Prince that their mission was not going to be easy. And Prince replied that they had an enemy. Hero said that they were in danger. Prince said that they must find out who was their enemy first. Hero replied that they would be unable to succeed their mission if they did not get rid of their enemy.

Prince said that they should get rid of that enemy as soon as possible. Hero replied that their enemy was very powerful. Prince said that once he had put his feet in the world of natural human beings, he felt that one part of his magic was blocked, that their enemy had mysteriously blocked one part of his magic. Hero said that some abilities of his magic were blocked mysteriously by their enemy, too. Prince said that their enemy had blocked the part of his magic that he used to destroy things, to provoke the disasters, to hurt and to kill, but that their enemy had not blocked the part of his magic that was linked to the past, that he used to find out things. Hero replied that the link of his magic with the future was not blocked by their enemy. Prince asked why the enemy did not block both their magic links to the past and the future? Hero answered that only their enemy could answer that question.

Prince and Hero understood that they were being controlled by a mysterious enemy, and that the mysterious enemy knew about their mission, and that the race of natural human beings was protected by that mysterious enemy. Now, their first mission was to find out who was that mysterious enemy and to get rid of that mysterious enemy. After a minute of conversation between Hero and Prince about their mysterious enemy, they decided to continue walking, still by talking about their mysterious enemy.

After an hour of walking, Prince and Hero saw an empty car that was parked in the street, and there was nobody around the car. They opened the car's doors and got inside the car. drove 'till close to downtown, and Hero told Prince that they should park the car, because they can be caught by the police downtown with the car. Prince parked the car in the street, and they got out of the car. They started walking and thinking what to do, where to sleep and how they were going to live in the world of the natural human beings. After twenty-five minutes of walking, they reached downtown and got inside a mall by visiting things, and seeing how natural human beings lived. were seeing that their life was completely different from the life of the natural human beings, and that it was warmer in their world compared to their world.

The evening was falling, both Prince and Hero had not yet found where to sleep, and Prince told Hero that he would use his invisible phantom to steal money at the bank, and they started walking in the street looking for the bank. There were people who were walking away from the sidewalk, screaming with fear on their faces, but Prince and Hero were not paying attention to those people. Prince and Hero had turned their heads away by looking for the bank. Hero was pushed by someone who was running, and he turned his head and saw a car that had lost out of control on the road. He noticed that the car was coming into them and he screamed at Prince to move on the sidewalk. Hero ran away, but Prince did not move on the sidewalk, and Prince turned his head, then, suddenly his eyes opened widely, with his face was full of fear as he was seeing that the car had lost control was getting into him.

Prince found himself on the ground, and the car passed near him. There was a young woman on Prince, and it was that young woman who had saved Prince by throwing him to the ground. Prince and that young woman were looking at each other's eyes. Then, young woman got up on Prince, and handed her hand to Prince by looking into his eyes. Prince held the hand of the young woman and she helped him to get up. They were still looking at each other, without saying a word. Hero was a few steps away from Prince and the young woman. Hero was staring at woman with an amazed face, and he noticed that the young woman who had just saved Prince, was the same young woman that he had saved a couple days ago in the lake. Hero was staring at the young woman with her blond long hair, blue eyes, and with a beauty mark above the left side of her lips. Hero was noticing that the young woman had the same rosary that her mom had tied on her ankle when he got out of the water with her, and he also noticed that the young woman had another rosary tied on her wrist. It had been almost a minute, when Prince and the young woman were still looking at each other without saying a word, then, the young woman broke the silence by asking, "Are you alright?"

Prince answered, "I am fine." And he added, "How about you?"

She replied, "I am alright." Then, she handed her hand to Prince and said, "My name is Angel."

Prince shook her hand and said, "My name is Prince." With a smile on his face.

Then, Angel looked at the way that Prince was dressed-up, and she smiled at him and said, "I love the way you dressed."

Prince smiled at her without saying a word, then, he said, "I love your beauty mark, that you have above on the left side of your lips."

Angel said, "Thank you." She added, "I love the beauty mark that you have below your chin, too." Prince said, "Thank you." And he added, "Thank you, too, for saving my life."

Angel smiled and said, "Next time, watch yourself very well, when you are walking."

Prince smiled and said, "I will."

Then, Angel's friend who was with her joined them. Angel and Prince wished each other a good evening, then, Angel and her friend turned and walked away. Prince turned his head through the direction that Angel and her friend were walking on, and he started staring at Angel who was walking away with a surprised face. Suddenly, Prince turned his head to his left, as he had felt a hand on his shoulder, and he saw Hero who was staring at him. Hero said, "Your enemy saved your life."

Prince cried out, "Enemy?"

Hero replied, "She is a natural human being, and all natural human beings are our enemies."

Prince replied, "Yes, my enemy saved my life."

Hero said, "She is very beautiful."

Prince said, "She has something unique."

Hero asked, "What do you mean?"

Prince replied, "Angel has something different from the rest of the natural human beings."

Hero said, "Still, I do not understand."

Prince said, "Angel has a smell that is different from the smell of the race of the natural human beings."

Then, Hero was staring at Prince with a silence and he remembered that he had smell the same scent the day he had saved Angel in the lake. Angel's smell was different from the smell of other people who were on the lake that day. Then, Hero asked, "Her name is Angel?"

Prince answered, "Yes, Angel is her name."

Hero asked, "What else did you notice about Angel?"

Prince replied, "Since, I put my feet in this world of natural human beings, I stared at many natural human beings, and I stared at Angel during couple of minutes, I felt that Angel is different from the rest ~~of natural human beings~~ of them, the fact that she is one of them."

Hero asked, "How was Angel different from the rest of the natural human beings?"

Prince said, "She has a beautiful beauty mark above the left side of her lips."

Hero said, "Since I am in this world of natural human beings, I met a lot of natural human beings with beauty marks."

Prince said, "I know that there are a lot of natural human beings with beauty marks, and even us who are supernatural beings, we all have beauty marks. But, Angel's beauty mark is different and unique."

## SUPERNATURAL BEINGS

Hero started to remember the beauty mark that he had seen on Angel, and he opened his mouth and he said, "Angel is very mysterious."

Prince said, "There is a mystery that we cannot explain."

Hero said, "When we put our feet in this world, we noticed that we have an enemy. And now we met a mysterious young woman named, Angel."

Prince said, "We must forget about Angel, and we will try to find out who is our enemy first, then, we will destroy the race of natural human beings." And he added, "Let's go find the bank now."

Prince and Hero continued to walk while talking about their unknown enemy. After a few minutes walking, they saw a bank that was opened, and they walked 'till the front of the bank. They leaned to a car that was in front of the bank. Both Prince and Hero were staring at the bank, then, a light got out from the eyes of Hero and it turned into his double, who was still him but his invisible side, and who was his invisible phantom. And that invisible phantom of Hero started walking through inside the bank, and he was communicating with his invisible phantom through a link of magic that was connected to his brain. It was his Phantom's invisible brain. Through that link of magic, Hero was telling his invisible phantom what to do, and his invisible phantom was walking inside the bank towards the counter. The bank was full of people but none of them was seeing the invisible phantom of Hero. because it was unseen to the eyes of natural human beings, and only the supernatural beings. The magicians, the wizards, the vampires, the zombies, natural human beings who have good or bad magic, and natural human beings who practice magic or who have vision, were the only people who could see the invisible phantom of Hero. None of those people who were inside the bank was a magician, a wizard, a supernatural being, a zombie or a vampire who can see the invisible ghost of Hero, because all the people who were inside the bank were the natural human beings without any power. Then, the invisible phantom of Hero reached behind the counter, and it took a handbag employee that was put behind the counter. The invisible phantom walked two steps through a big box that was close to him, and he opened that big box,–and started to remove the cash money that was in in it, he was putting the cash in the handbag that he had in his hand. The cash money that was in the box was the money that the employees were using to serve the customers, who wanted cash, and who were making cash deposits. After less than a minute, invisible phantom left the bank, and walked 'till outside face to Hero and Prince. He handed the handbag to Hero, and he took the handbag in his hand from his invisible phantom, then that invisible ghost turned into the light and got inside the eyes of Hero. Prince and Hero turned, and walked away.

After a few minutes, Prince and Hero walked inside a hotel, and face the receptionist, and wanted to reserve a room. receptionist asked them their ID, then Prince and Hero turned their heads by looking at each other, and they turned their heads again towards the receptionist. Prince told the receptionist that they had lost their ID. But the receptionist refused their reservation, by saying that they could not have a room without their ID. Hero glanced at the receptionist, and the light got out from his eyes went through the receptionist, and that light shone on the receptionist., the receptionist felt something inside her and the expression on her face changed, then, the receptionist looked at Prince and Hero and she asked their names. And the receptionist rented the room to She gave Prince and Hero a room accommodation without even asking for their IDs.

After a few minutes, Prince and Hero were in their hotel bedroom, and there were food and wine that were served to them, but they had not even taken a look of the food and wine that were served. Both, Hero and Prince were in the room and they were facing the wall trying to find out who was their enemy by using their magic. They were making the pictures appear on the wall through their magic. But unfortunately, the pictures that were appearing on the wall were empty, there was nobody on those pictures. After hours, Prince and Hero had still not found out who their mysterious enemy was, and they had started to get tired. All the pictures that were on the wall were still empty. They stopped making the light of their eyes, and they turned their heads looking at each other, without saying a word.

After two minutes, Hero broke the silence by saying that it seemed that their mysterious enemy was invisible. Prince replied that he did not understand why they were unable to find their enemy through their magic. Hero said that there was something going wrong, because if they were feeling the threat of their enemy, it meant that their enemy was alive, and that both their magics were linked to the present, so that they should be able to find out who was that mysterious enemy through their magic. Prince said that himself, he was completely lost because he did not understand the reasons why they were unable to find their mysterious enemy.

Prince told Hero that he was going to use his magic to find out the past of their mysterious enemy, and Hero replied to Prince that he was going to use his magic to find out about the future of their mysterious enemy. Prince and Hero turned and looked at the wall. The light started to get out from their eyes and went through the wall, but the photos that were appearing on the wall were still empty. Prince and Hero spent more than an hour making the pictures appear on the wall, but unfortunately, the pictures on the wall were still empty. Prince and Hero turned their head, and they looked at each other with a silence, and they were just completely lost. They did not understand what was going on, and they did not know what to say. Prince started walking in the room still with his mouth closed, while Hero was staring at the empty pictures that were on the wall with an astonished face.

After hours of thinking, Hero told Prince that they were going to change their plan, that they did not have a choice because their plan could not work if they had not found out who was their enemy and killed that enemy. Prince replied to Hero that he knew well that they would never succeed in eradicating the race of natural human beings, when they had not put their eyes on their enemy and killed that cursed enemy. Because, the race of the natural human beings was protected mystically by their enemy, then, Prince demanded to Hero what their other plans? Hero looked at Prince and he answered that he had no idea.

Prince continued walking in the room very nervous, and Hero lifted his head through the ceiling. Hero was staring at the ceiling, and there was silence in the room. After less than a minute, Hero turned his head, and he stared at the television that was turned on, when the expression of his face changed as he was listening to the news on the television. After three minutes, Hero turned his head towards Prince, and he was staring at him who had lifted his head through the ceiling. Immediately, Prince turned his head towards Hero, as he had heard Hero say that there was another idea to destroy the race of the natural human beings. Prince asked Hero what was that idea? Hero answered that they must study the body of natural human beings. because by knowing how the body of a natural human being works, it would be easier for them to destroy the entire race of natural human beings. By that way their mysterious enemy would not prevent them from putting an end to their race.

Prince asked Hero how they going to study the body of the natural human beings? Hero answered that he watched the news that it's back to school within three days of the university, and that they should find a place in the university to study. Prince asked Hero, how they were going to study at the university of the natural human beings, if they were not one of them? Hero answered Prince that they were going to use their magic to have places to stay in the university, and that they were going to study the sciences on the functions of the body of a natural human being. Prince said that that plan would not work, because it would be impossible for them to spend their whole day almost everyday with the natural human beings.

They were completely different from them, and that even their brains were different from the brains of the natural human beings. So, did not understand how they were going to study with natural human beings if they could not even think like them. Hero answered Prince that it was true that their brains were different from the brains of natural human beings, but they were the magician supernatural beings, and that they had the abilities to adapt their brains in any situation, even to think like the natural human beings. Prince asked Hero how studying the body of the natural human beings would help them to destroy the race of natural human beings?

Hero started to explain his plan to Prince, and Prince found Hero's idea very interesting, although, the plan was going to take them more time than what they had planned, and would make them spend more time in the world of the natural human beings. Prince and Hero spent the whole night talking about their plan 'till midnight, and they got out of their room. walked into the parking of the hotel, and they stole a car, then, they drove it into the campus of a university.

They parked the car in the parking area, and got out from the car. started walking through a building, and after a few minutes they reached on a door, and Hero grabbed the handle of the door, and turned it, and pushed it. They got inside the building, and they started walking in a hallway and there was the light that were getting outside from their eyes.

Hero turned his head to his left by looking at the wall with the light that was getting out from his eyes and shining on the wall, then, a photo appeared on the wall, and there was a door on that photo There was the number three-hundred-one on the door. Prince walked two steps towards Hero, and looked at the door and Prince told Hero that they were on the main floor, and that the office that they were looking for, was to the third floor, then, Hero turned his head and looked at the door that was behind him, and the number one-hundred-three was written on that door.

Hero told Prince that they should find the stairs or the elevator to reach the third floor. Prince replied to Hero that there was a security guard in the building, and that they have to find the position of the security men first. The light got out from the eyes of Hero and went through the wall, and the pictures appeared, then, Prince and Hero were staring at those pictures, as they were seeing the security men on some pictures, and on the elevator. They noticed that there were other security men close to the elevator. Prince asked Hero to find the way to the stairs. Then, the light got out from Hero's eyes, and went through the wall, and the way to the stairs appeared on the pictures. They noticed that there were still security men through that way. So they turned their head looking at each other, and Hero asked what they were going to do? Prince answered that they must find another way to reach the third floor.

Prince turned his head through the wall, and the light got out from his eyes and went through the wall. The pictures appeared on the wall, but those pictures were empty. By looking at those empty pictures, Prince and Hero understood that there was no other way to reach the third floor, except by the stairs and the elevator, where the security men were guarding. So, Hero told Prince that they needed a plan, and both started thinking on how to reach the third floor.

After less than three minutes, Prince told Hero that he should use his invisible phantom to reach the third floor, and they would return in the car. Then, the invisible phantom would do the work that they were going to do to on the third floor. Hero replied to Prince that his invisible phantom could not do the work, because his magic was not located in his invisible phantom, but instead in his body, and that to do that work, he needed his magic. Prince asked Hero, how his invisible phantom stole money from the bank, if his invisible phantom did not have magic? Hero answered that the brain of his invisible phantom was connected to his brain through a link of magic that was inside his body, and he communicated with his invisible ghost through that link of magic that was inside his body. Hero went on by saying that his invisible phantom just stole the cash money that was put in a big box from the reserve in the bank without changing anything, but that the work that they were going to do to the third floor was different, because he would need his magic if he was going to change the data in the system of the university.

Prince asked what they were going to do now. Hero answered that the only solution was to distract the security men, who were in the building. Then, Prince asked, how? And Hero answered that he was thinking solution. After a couple of seconds, Prince told Hero that he had the solution, he was going to do the sport with security men while Hero would go to the third floor for. Hero was did not agree with the idea of Prince, because the security men could shoot Prince, as they have guns. Prince told Hero not to worry, he would remove his phantom from his body, and that even if the security men shoot him, he would not die, because his ghost would be not in his body.

Hero walked two steps in front of himself, opened the door that was on his right side, and got inside a room, while Prince started walking in the hallway. After a few minutes walking, Prince turned to his left, and the light got out from his eyes. Prince started running in the corridor by knocking at the doors, and security men started to run to where the noises were coming from. Then, Hero got out from the room where he was hiding, and the light got out from his eyes and turned into his invisible phantom. His invisible phantom started running in the hallway, and he looked at the wall, where the light got out from his eyes and went through the wall. Hero was looking at the pictures that were on the wall, and he was seeing that the way towards stairs were empty, because the security men were running after Prince. Hero was seeing some pictures, too, that Prince was going to be surrounded by the security men. He started to communicate with his invisible phantom, by asking it to go help Prince. Then, Hero turned, and started running through the direction of the stairs.

Prince was in the parking area and he was trapped by the security men. Prince face the security men who pointed their guns at him asking him to raise his hands. Prince could not run away because he was leaning against a car. There were cars around and behind him. He got an idea to use his phantom, although, he knew that he was taking a risk as the security men had guns, and they could shoot his phantom. Suddenly, the security men started walking towards and he started to smile on them, as he was seeing the invisible phantom of Hero who was walking behind the security men.

A security man fainted on the ground, as he was knocked from behind by the invisible phantom of Hero, and other security men turned their heads, trying to know who had knocked their colleague, but they were not seeing anyone. Some security men started yelling as they were feeling that they were knocked by someone they were not seeing, and some of them were on the ground bleeding. Prince turned, and he started to climb on the car, and a security man shot him in the leg, but even though, he was shot in the leg, he continued to climb on the car, and he felt another bullet in his other leg. He started to run by jumping on the cars which was on the parking. Two security men who had shot his legs were looking how Prince was running by jumping on the cars with amused faces, without understanding what was going on, and they were wondering how Prince was running as if he was not hurt. Most of the security men were on the ground were bleeding, because the invisible phantom of Hero had beaten them.

Hero was in the office of the international students, and he was working on the computer. He was changing the data in the computer by using his magic, and there was the light that was getting out from his eyes, shining on the computer that he was working on. Hero had succeeded in putting his photo and the photo of Prince on the computer. He had changed two names in the faculty of sciences. But Hero did not put their family names in the data, he just wrote letter T as their family names, and his name in the data was a Canadian student, and the name of Prince in the data was an American student. Then, the door opened, Prince walked inside, and he asked Hero if he was done. Hero answered that he was almost done. Suddenly, both Prince and Hero heard the sirens of the police's cars, and they understood that the police were coming. Hero turned his head towards Prince, and he asked him if he still had his phantom inside him? Prince answered that his phantom was inside him. Hero turned off the computer that he was working on, and he carried the chair that was close to him. Hero walked close to the window, and he used that chair he had in his hands to break the window glass. Hero turned his head towards Prince, and he told him that they have to get out. Both Prince and Hero turned into tigers, and they jumped out through the window, and ran until the parking area, then, they turned into their supernatural bodies, and there were police cars everywhere in the parking area. They stole a car and drove away.

Hero told Prince that they needed two passports, a Canadian passport, and an American passport. Prince asked Hero why they needed passports? Hero answered that they would stay in the world of natural human beings like international students, and their passports would be their ID. Hero explained to Prince that when they would going to school, they would act as they did not know each other, because they should avoid attracting the attention on them. Prince asked who was the Canadian citizen, and who was the American citizen? Hero answered that he was a Canadian citizen, and Prince was an American citizen. Prince asked Hero how they were going to find a Canadian passport and an American passport? Hero answered that they would use their magic to find people who had a Canadian passport, and an American passport, then, they would change the information in the passports by using their magic.

After twenty-seven minutes of driving, Hero parked the car in the yard of a building, and Prince asked him where they were going? Hero answered that they were in front of the building where most international students of their university lived, and that among those international students, there were Canadians and Americans. Both Hero and Prince got out of the car, and walked until the veranda of the building, and the light got out from Hero's eyes, and went through the wall. The pictures appeared on the wall, and among those pictures, there were bedrooms and people who were sleeping in their beds. Prince asked Hero how they would steal the passports that they needed? Hero answered that he was going to use his invisible phantom to steal the passports. The light got out from Hero's eyes, and that light turned into the invisible phantom of Hero, and it walked until the door of the building. The invisible phantom opened the door. It started to climb the stairs. Hero and Prince were still facing the wall by staring at the pictures that were on it, and Hero was using his magic to communicate with his invisible phantom through his brain. After eleven minutes, the invisible phantom got out of the building with two passports in its hand, and it handed those two passports to Hero, then, it turned into the light and got inside the eyes of Hero. Hero and Prince left, and after a few minutes both of them were in their hotel's bedroom. They were talking about their plans for the day. Hero had used his magic to change the photos and the names that were in the passports, and he had put his photo and Prince's photo, also their names.

It was 9:00 a.m., There was already sun outside, the weather was going to be beautiful for the rest of the day. Prince and Hero went to the bank and they opened their bank accounts. They put cash money that the invisible phantom of Hero had stolen from the bank. Hero had used his magic to prevent the employees of the bank from asking them questions about where the money was coming from, by making the light get out from his eyes and that light shone on the employees. After the bank, both Hero and Prince went to buy a small house, then, they bought two cars for them. Hero and Prince spent the rest of the day driving to visit the world of natural human beings in each of their cars. They were very surprised to see how the world of natural humans was built, and the way they lived. They had also noticed that their culture and traditions were completely different from the culture and traditions of natural human beings, and that the rules of natural human beings were based on the law. The world of natural human beings was led by a president who was elected by people, and that they were educated to respect the law.

## CHAPTER III

# HERO THE TRAITOR

It was already evening. Hero and Prince sat in the chairs in the living room of their house, and they were face to face. They were talking about their day, about how they found the world of natural human beings. Hero said that except the climate, they would have no problem living in the world of natural human beings, because they used to live in the cold and trees, and now they were living in the heat and civilization. Prince agreed and said that they would have a climate adaptation problem in the world of natural human beings, because they were going to stand the heat. in the world of natural human beings, none of them had eaten. After a few hours, Hero changed the conversation, and started talking about the school that they were going to start in two days. Hero was telling Prince how it was important for them to focus in school, because it was their only solution to destroy the race of natural human beings.

Prince asked Hero if he was alright? As he had noticed that Hero had become silent, and was acting as if there was something wrong. Prince asked Hero again if everything was fine? Hero did not answer Prince, and he was still quiet. Hero was feeling one part of his magic was sending him a message. After a couple of seconds, Hero got up from his chair, and rushed through the opened window. He turned into a tiger and jumped out through the window without saying a word. Prince had turned his head through the window where

Hero had got out, and with an astonished face, wondering what was going on.

Prince got up from his chair, and walked to the window. He looked at the window and did not see Hero. Prince turned and started walking to face the wall. The light got out from Prince's eyes, and went through the wall. Prince started staring at the wall with a surprised face. The pictures that were on the wall were showing that Hero was on the road in his car driving fast. Prince was wondering where Hero was going. Suddenly, the phone started to ring, and Prince turned to walked into the table. He picked up the phone, and it was King Philip on the other line, then, Prince started talking with Philip.

Hero parked the car in the parking area of a nightclub, and got out of his car, then the light out from his eyes and turned it into his invisible ghost. Hero started walking through the door of the nightclub, while his invisible phantom was running through it. Inside the club was full of people, as it was the last weekend before the school opens, and the dance floor was full of people who were dancing. There was Angel who was dancing on the dance floor with her friends, and there were other people who were dancing, too. There were three people, two young men and one young woman with green eyes, long black hair, and the beauty marks above the left side of their lips who had surrounded Angel.

Angel was not paying attention to those three people who were dancing around her, and one of those two young men moved behind Angel, and he grabbed Angel through her hips by dancing with her. While the other man moved to face Angel by dancing with her, and the girl was dancing to the right side of Angel, and the one who was dancing behind Angel put his chin on Angel's shoulder. Suddenly, his green eyes became dark green, and he turned his head through Angel's neck and the light was getting out from his eyes and shining on Angel's neck, then, he opened his mouth and there were long canine teeth in his mouth. He moved his head into Angel's neck, and he suddenly fainted on the floor when he wanted to bite Angel's neck, because he was hit from behind his head by the invisible ghost of Hero.

## SUPERNATURAL BEINGS

Then, the invisible phantom of Hero punched the one who was dancing face to face with Angel, and the people started screaming inside the club. There were people on the floor. The invisible phantom of Hero was fighting against those two men, and Angel was trying to run away, but it was impossible because the crowd was preventing and blocking her. Then, Angel felt that she was grabbed by someone, so she turned her head and she noticed that the young woman who was dancing from right side had grabbed her hand, and that young woman was pulling Angel towards her. Angel started shouting with her face full of terror, as she was seeing that the young woman who had grabbed her hand had the long canine teeth in her mouth. Immediately, Angel felt that she was grabbed from behind by someone else, and Angel was shaking her head, because she was feeling that the one who had grabbed her from behind wanted to bite her neck as she was feeling a mouth on her neck.

Hero appeared to Angel and punched the young man who grabbed Angel from behind, before that young man bites Angel's neck. The girl who had held Angel's hand bent and picked up the bottle of wine that someone had fell on the floor. She hit the bottle on Hero's head, and it hurt his forehead. Angel screamed as she had seen the blood was flowing on Hero's forehead. Hero grabbed the hand of Angel, and tried to run away with her, but he noticed that Angel was grabbed again by the girl, so he punched her in the mouth. The girl lost her balance, and let go of Angel's hand. Hero started running towards the door with Angel, as he held Angel's hand. Hero was pushing people who were on their way, while his invisible phantom was fighting against the two young men and the young girl who wanted to bite Angel's neck. The invisible phantom of Hero was fighting against those three people to prevent them from running or catching up with them. The people who were in the club were yelling, and some of them were on the floor bleeding, they were all trying to find a way to get out of the club.

Hero still had held Angel's hand, while they were running in the parking area of the club. They reached Hero's car, and he wanted to open the car door, when suddenly an eagle landed to face them. Angel screamed with fear, as she had noticed that the eagle had landed to face them had turned into a young man. Hero pulled Angel behind him, and she had grabbed his clothes while shaking with fear.

Hero and the young man was looking at each other. Hero noticed that the man who facing him was one of the two men who was inside the club and those who wanted to bite Angel. After a couple of seconds, young man broke the silence by saying, "Give me that young girl who is behind you, and I will not kill you." Hero replied, "I will not let you kill her." young man said, "You are not here to protect her." Hero looked at him without saying a word. The young man started walking through Hero angrily, and Angel was behind him breathing deeply with a fearful heart. The young man lifted his hand to fight Hero, and immediately, the light got out from Hero's eyes and went through the man, and the light turned into the tiger. The expression of Angel's face changed, and she was scared as she had seen the tiger was fighting with, but she did not see the light that had got out from Hero's eyes.

Hero turned and grabbed Angel's hand and they rushed towards the car, then, Hero opened the car door, and Angel got inside the car. Then, he drove away together with Angel. She was screaming in the car, by asking Hero to drive well, and she had turned her head towards Hero. She was yelling at him by saying that they were going to get into an accident if he kept driving like a crazy man.

Angel noticed that Hero had no balance, and he was not even looking in front of him, or where he was driving through. Also, he was shaking, and acting as if he was fighting with someone. Angel could hear Hero shouting a low cry as if someone was beating him. She was completely lost because she did not understand why Hero was acting like that. But they were lucky that the road was empty, and that there were no other cars on because Hero was driving without controlling his direction.

Suddenly, Angel opened her mouth widely by shouting, as she had seen an eagle landing on the hood of the car, and the eagle turned into a human body. She noticed that the one who was on the hood of the car was the girl who had held her hand in the club. The girl was hitting the windshield of the car with her hand, while Hero continued driving and Angel screamed when parts of the windshield glass were falling on her, and the girl kept breaking the car's windshield, then grabbed Angel's clothes as she was trying to pull Angel out. While Angel was yelling with a scared face, the light got in the eyes of Hero, and immediately went through the hood of the car. The light turned into a tiger. The girl who grabbed Angel's clothes by trying to pull her made a loud scream, and she let let go of Angel, as she had been bitten on her hand by the tiger. The girl started fighting with the tiger on the hood of the car, while Hero was continuously driving and the tiger was on that girl. and that girl was preventing the tiger from tearing her skin with his claws, then she grabbed a small part of the glass that was close to her, and she stabbed one of the tiger's feet.

Hero made a scream, and Angel turned her head towards Hero as she had heard him scream. She was looking at him with a worried face, as she was seeing that Hero was bleeding on his shoulder, and Angel was completely lost, she was not understanding why Hero was bleeding at his shoulder. Angel was staring at Hero with her mouth opened but unable to utter a word. She was seeing that Hero was still acting as if he was fighting, and there were a lot of questions that were going on in her head as to why Hero was bleeding? Who hurt him? How did he get hurt? What happened? Why was he behaving in the car as if he was fighting with someone? But unfortunately, she could not answer even one of her questions.

Fear appeared on Angel's face, and her heart was beating faster than normal, as she was seeing Hero with breathing difficulties, as if someone had held him through his nose to prevent him from breathing or if someone was smothering him and had grabbed him through his neck.-Angel noticed that Hero wanted to scream, or open his mouth but he had difficulties to do it, as if someone was closing his mouth, or if someone had put a hand on his mouth to prevent him from opening it. Hero was acting as if he was beaten by someone. Then, Angel turned her head in front of her, and saw that the tiger was fighting against two people who were the girl and a man on the hood of the car. girl had grabbed the neck of the tiger with one of her hands, and she had closed the tiger's mouth with her other hand, while the man was trying to beat the tiger.

Angel yelled, as they got into an accident, because Hero had hit the car on a pole that was on the sidewalk. The two people and the tiger who were fighting on the car's hood fell on the ground. Then, the light got in Hero's eyes, immediately that same light got out from his eyes and went through the ground where those people were fighting with the tiger. The light turned into the invisible phantom of Hero, and it started fighting against the man and the girl. Hero turned his head towards Angel, and he looked at her by asking, "Are you all right?" Angel looked at Hero without saying a word. Hero said, "Do not worry, you will be fine." And he added, "Let's go now to your home." Hero drove the car from behind, and drove it away. Angel was still looking at Hero without saying a word, and she was noticing that the behavior of Hero had not changed, he was still acting as if he was fighting, but that this time it was not worst, and he was trying to focus on the wheel and trying to control the car.

Hero asked Angel where she was living, and where was the way of her house? Angel was still looking at him with her mouth closed, and Hero turned his head towards her. He looked at her without saying a word, then the light got in his eyes. Angel noticed that Hero had turned to left, he had regain his balance, and he was not anymore acting as if he was fighting. She started screaming at Hero to drive slowly, they were going to make the accident again. But Hero did not pay attention to her, and he was just driving faster, although she was still shouting at him to drive slowly.

After a couple of minutes, Hero parked the car in front of a house. Angel noticed that she was in the yard of her house. She wanted to open the car's door to get out, but Hero prevented her from opening the car's door by holding her hand, as he had seen two eagles were flying around the car. He had understood that those eagles were there for Angel. She had turned her head to Hero, and they were looking at each other eyes without saying a word. Both of them had their mouths opened, but no word was coming out from it. Hero still had his hand on Angel's hand, and their hearts were beating faster than normal. After a couple of seconds, they turned their heads from behind, as they had heard a noise coming it. remarked that it was an eagle that had hit the car's glass, and Hero noticed that

## SUPERNATURAL BEINGS

fear appeared on Angel's face as she had seen the eagle was flying around the car. Hero looked at Angel's hands, and he remarked that she had not worn her rosary.

Hero removed his phone from his pocket, and handed the phone to Angel. and Angel She took the phone from Hero without saying a word, and she started to dial a number, then she put the phone on her ear. Hero heard Angel talking to her mom, and she was telling her mom what happened in the club. She was telling her mom too that she had forgotten to wear her rosaries, and that her rosaries were in her bedroom. After less than three minutes, Angel's mom named Rebecca got out of the house. She walked towards the car where Angel was and Angel opened the car's door, and she handed her hand to Rebecca and she wore the rosary on Angel's wrist, then Rebecca gave another rosary to Angel, and she bent, and wore that rosary on her ankle. Then, Rebecca held Angel's hand, and she helped Angel to get out of the car. closed the car's door without even saying a word to Hero, even Angel had got out of the car without a word to Hero.

Hero was in his car watching Angel and Rebecca who were walking towards the door. had grabbed Angel through her shoulder, and Hero was noticing that Angel was turning her head looking away with fear on her face as she was seeing the eagles that were flying. Then, Rebecca opened the door, and she got inside the house with Angel. They closed the door behind them, and Hero noticed that the eagles that were flying around the car had flown away. Then, the light got inside the eyes of Hero, and he drove away.

Prince was still on the phone talking with Philip, then, he turned his head towards the door as he had heard footsteps coming through the door. Suddenly, the expression Prince's face changed. There was worry on his face as he was looking at Hero, who was walking towards his bedroom with blood on his forehead and shoulder. Immediately Prince hung up the phone, and he rushed to face Hero. Prince and Hero were looking at each other's eyes, and Hero's heart was beating with fear that maybe Prince found out through his magic what he did. Prince was looking at Hero with an amused face, while Hero was just afraid that Prince was aware that he had broken the most important rule of the tradition of the tiger world, by saving a natural human being, and that he had betrayed their mission.

Prince broke the silence by asking Hero what happened? Hero understood that Prince was unaware of what happened with Angel, so he answered Prince by lying that he got hurt by the campus' security men. Prince asked Hero what he was doing at the campus? Hero answered that he had forgotten to put some information about them in the data of university's system, and he remembered about it when they were talking about the school. That's why he went to the university to put the information that was missing. Prince asked Hero why he did not tell him, so that they can go together? Hero answered that he hurried up, he did not know that there was a huge security at the campus, and that if he had not put the information in the data, it would be impossible for them to go to school. Prince asked Hero how he got hurt? Hero answered that there was a huge security at the campus, and that he was caught by the security men. He fought against them, but he succeeded to put the information that he wanted to put in the data at the university. Prince said that it was obvious that the university changed his security system, by strengthening the security as they were there two days ago.

Then, Prince looked at the injury that was on the forehead of Hero, and he said that he was lucky that the wound he had on his forehead was not a real wound, as the wound was not linked to the ghost of Hero. Prince turned his head Hero's shoulder, as Hero was bleeding there, too. Suddenly the expression of Prince's face changed, as he had understood that the phantom of Hero was hurt by seeing the wound on his shoulder, then he cried out, "How did they hurt your phantom?" By looking at Hero with an astonished face. Hero answered, "My phantom was out of my body when I was fighting, because I was it to fight them." Prince asked, "Why was it that you did not use your invisible phantom to fight them, because you should be safer by using it, as they could not fight your invisible phantom, because they could not even see your invisible phantom as they were all natural human beings without any magic." Hero replied, "I made a mistake by using my phantom to help me to fight them." Prince asked, "How are we going to heal that wound on your shoulder?"

Hero said, "It would cure alone, because there is no doctor in this world where can treat the wound on my phantom."

Prince and Hero continued the conversation for eleven minutes and again, Hero told Prince that he was very tired, that since they had set their feet in the world of natural human beings, they had not been able to sleep. Hero added that he wanted to take a shower to clean the blood that was on him, and get rest for a couple of hours before they start their day. Both of them shook their hands, and each went to his bedroom. After five hours, Hero was lying in his bed with his eyes opened, and there was still blood on him. By looking at him, it was obvious that he had not taken a shower as he had told Prince a couple hours ago. Since Hero had got inside his bedroom, he had not stopped thinking about what had happened in the club, and he did not believe what he had done. He did not realize that for the second time he had saved the same girl named Angel. Hero was quite lost, he did not understand what was going on, he had no idea of why he had saved Angel again, he had no idea of why his magic had warned him that Angel was in danger. Hero was wondering if it was his instinct that was driving him to save Angel, but at the same time he knew that he had an animal instinct, and he was wondering how his animal instinct could push him to save a natural human being.

Hero knew that he had the same number of senses as all supernatural beings, and he knew too that his last sense, which was the tenth sense was linked to his magic, and that it was his magic who was always pushing him to save Angel. He was wondering if it was his tenth sense who was warning him when Angel was in danger, and if it was his tenth sense who was pushing him to save Angel? But Hero could not really answer those questions He wanted to use his magic to see again the images of the fight that had happened in the club up to Angel's house, but unfortunately, he could not, and he started to remember what had happened. Hero remembered that the two young men and the young woman who wanted to kill Angel had the beauty marks in common, as they had the black long hair, with green eyes and the beauty marks above the left side of their lips. Also, they had the eagles' ghost. And that when they wanted to turn into the shape of their phantoms, their green eyes were becoming dark green.

Hero understood that those three people were not the natural human beings or the vampires, but they were instead the supernatural beings. He had also noticed that the young woman had magic, she was trying to use her magic during the fight. Hero started to wonder why those supernatural beings were interested in Angel? And why among all the natural human beings, those supernatural beings were only interested in Angel? But unfortunately, he could not answer those questions. Hero remembered the day where he and Prince were trying to convince the inhabitants of the tiger world to make war against the race of natural human beings, and Prince had used his magic that day to make the pictures appear on the wall. There were the animals like the lions, panthers, birds, tigers, and other animal species on those pictures, and those animals were the ghosts of supernatural beings, but among all those animals, there were no eagles. The fact that Hero did not know the history of those animals that were on the wall, he was wondering why among those animals, there were no eagles. He was wondering if the supernatural beings who had the eagles as their ghosts had not existed at that time, and where do they come from now? But unfortunately, Hero could not answer his questions and he was very confused, he did not understand what was going on.

Hero knew that it was impossible to find out the answers of his questions, and that the only way for him to find out was to know the history of the race of supernatural human beings, and to know the story of the tragedy that had happened more than a century ago. Hero knew that it was impossible for him to know through his magic, the history of the race of supernatural beings, and the story of the tragedy that had happened more than a century ago because his magic was not related to the past. Hero could not ask Prince for help because he knew that through the magic of Prince, he could know the history and the story of what had happened to the race of supernatural beings in the past. Hero knew that even if he really wanted to know the answers of his questions, it was a big risk to ask Prince for help, because he was afraid that Prince could find out that he traitor who betrayed his family to protect an enemy. was very afraid about what was going to happen when Prince and the tiger world would

## SUPERNATURAL BEINGS

find out that he was becoming a traitor who betrayed his own family to save an enemy.

Hero knew that he was in danger, and he was in trouble, too, that he had new enemies who were his own family, and that he would fight both enemies who were the race of natural human beings, and the supernatural beings of the eagle world. Hero knew well that he had taken a risk since he had declared the war against the race of supernatural beings by saving Angel, and that he would be alone against the supernatural beings of the world of eagle. There was an important question that was going on in his mind, and that question was, why had his destiny changed? As he was born with a destiny and that destiny was to destroy the race of natural human beings, not to save them as he was doing with Angel. But unfortunately, he could not answer that question.

Suddenly, Hero turned and looked at the door, as he had heard the noises coming from the door and he saw the door opened, his heart started to fear that maybe Prince found out through his magic what had happened in the club, as he was watching at Prince who was walking towards his bed silently. Hero took a deep breath when Prince smiled at him by asking him if he had rested well, then Prince also asked Hero why he did not clean the blood on him. Hero answered that he did not take the shower, because there were no clothes to change as they had not yet bought new clothes. Prince told Hero that it was already 3:00 p.m., they should go out to buy clothes, books and some stuff to get ready for school the next day. Then, Hero got up from his bed and went to the washroom to clean the blood on him.

After six minutes, both Hero and Prince were out shopping. Hero was trying to stop thinking about what had happened in the club, and to focus on the conversation with Prince, but Prince had noticed that Hero was always away during their conversation. Prince asked Hero if everything was alright. Hero replied to Prince that everything was fine. Both Prince and Hero spent the whole day out, to buy stuff, and they bought a new car for Hero as Hero had hit his car on the pole early this morning while he was trying to save Angel.-They spent the night talking about school, which will start the next day.

# CHAPTER IV

# THE MYSTERIOUS SUPERNATURAL BEING IN CLASS

It was 9:00 a.m., it was crowded at the university and the halls were full of students trying to find their classrooms. Hero was sitting at the last table in the class, and his eyes were focused on the door. He was staring at the students who were walking in the classroom. Suddenly, the expression of Hero's face changed, he was looking with an amused face, and his eyes were wide open, as he was staring at Angel who had stopped in the classroom and staring at him too, with a surprised face.

  Angel's eyes were looking at Hero, then Angel started to breathe deeply, as she remembered about the eyes that she had seen when she had opened her eyes on the boat in the lake, the day she had drowned in the water. Immediately, Angel opened her mouth trying to talk, but her mouth was shaking that a word could not get out, still with her eyes focused Hero's eyes, as she was remembering the eyes of the one who had saved her in the club a day ago. She remembered how she and that person were staring at each other in the car in front of her house. Angel noticed that the one who had saved her in the lake had the same eyes with the one who had saved her in the club, now, she understood that it was the same person who had saved her on both situations and that she was staring at the person right now. Then, Her heart started to beat faster than the normal, and she started walking towards Hero trembling still, with her eyes focused into his. Hero was still staring at her with the same expression on his face, as he was seeing her walk upon him.

Suddenly, Angel met with a friend named Bella, and she had frizzy hair, green eyes with a long chin. Then, Bella took Angel in her arms, and she started talking to Angel. She was trying to tell Bella that they would talk later, that she was in a hurry but Bella was not listening to her. Bella just kept talking to Angel, although, she was not listening to her. Angel moved her head and looked where Hero was sitting, then she cried out, "Where is he?" As she did not see Hero in his seat. Bella looked at Angel with an astonished face and asked, "Who?" Angel replied, "That young man with blue eyes that I was staring." Bella asked, "Which young man?" Angel looked at Bella without saying a word. Bella asked, "Are you alright?" Angel replied, "I am fine." She added, "We will talk later." Bella said, "I did not finish talking to you yet, what was I saying?" Angel said, "I have to find that young man." Bella smiled and asked, "Did you find a new lover?" Angel turned her head by looking in the classroom without answering Bella, and Bella was still trying to talk to Angel, but Angel was not paying attention to her.

Angel turned and started to run towards the door, as she had seen Hero who was getting out of the door. She was running as fast as she could among the crowd in the classroom, as there were students who were getting in, while other students were getting out. Angel succeeded to get out of the classroom, and turned to her right. did not see Hero, then she turned to her left, and she saw Hero at the end of the corridor who was taking another way. Angel started running to the left side of the hallway in the middle of people to catch Hero. And after a few minutes, Angel was on the other side of the building looking for Hero, but unfortunately he was already gone. She spent her whole day looking for him without success.

The days were passing by, and Angel was coming to school everyday, but she was not taking classes because she was spending her whole day looking for Hero. Most of the days, Angel was the first person to arrive at the campus, and she was staying at the entrance of the campus watching all students and instructors who were getting in the campus, with the only hope to see Hero. Sometimes Angel was the last student to leave the campus, because she would search the whole campus with the hope to find him. Angel was becoming more and more tired. around her, her parents and her friends had noticed it, and Angel was not sleeping anymore, she was spending her whole time thinking about Hero, as if she was haunted by him. Angel had completely changed since she had met Hero in her classroom, she was not eating anymore, and her parents were worried about her. When her parents asked her what was going wrong, she lied to them by answering that she was stressed about school. parents tried to advise her to drop out of school, and wait for next year she was just sixteen years old, and that all her friends were still in high school, and that she could return to high school. Even if she had graduated in high school, as she was very smart, the world of the university was very stressful. But Angel refused to drop out in school, and told her parents that everything would be fine.

Hero had stopped coming to school, but he was using his invisible side, who was his invisible ghost, to attend his classes. No one was seeing the invisible side of Hero in the classroom or in the university. was leaving home every morning, and was spending his time between the trees that were close to the university. When there was nobody around the place where Hero was, he would turn into his identity phantom that was the tiger and he would climb the trees. Hero was spending his days on top of the trees, and knew that Angel was looking for him. He was aware of everything that was happening inside the university, because he was communicating with his invisible phantom through his brain and the brain of his phantom. Hero was wondering why he was running away from Angel. He could not answer that question. Hero did not understand why he was in the same classroom with Angel, because mostly, he was the one who had chosen his classroom, but if he knew that Angel was in his classroom, he would choose another classroom. did not know that Hero was not coming to school, as Prince was very focus on his studies. was enjoying his courses, and was spending his time at home like in school to read the books on the functioning of the body of the race of natural human beings. After a month, Angel had still not started going to school, and she was still looking for Hero, and she was determined to find him.

It was 11:00 a.m., Angel walked inside the library of the university looking for Hero as usual, and there were students in the library, some of them had their heads focused on their books on the tables in front of them, while others were talking. Then, Angel turned to her left, and the expression on her face changed, and she was looking with a surprised face while staring at Prince who sat and was reading a book. Then, Angel walked towards Prince, and she stood up to face him, by staring at him, then, she cried out, "Prince?"

Then, Prince lifted his head and saw Angel facing him, then he got up with a face full of smiles, and handed his hand to Angel and said, "I am glad to see you again."

Angel shook Prince's hand with a smile on her face and said, "It's a pleasure to see you again, too." Prince asked, "Are you a student here?"

Angel replied, "Yes, I am a student here." And she added, "But, I have not yet started."

Prince said, "It's been a month that school started. So, I do not understand why you have not started yet."

Angel said, "I am looking for someone."

Prince asked, "Who?"

Angel answered, "I do not know his name."

Prince cried out, "What?" by smiling at her. And he added, "You are looking for someone that you do not know of?"

Angel smiled and said, "Do not pay attention to what I say, because I am a little bit crazy those last times."

Prince said, "You should start school, and stop looking for a ghost or a supernatural being."

Angel cried out, "A supernatural being?" By looking at Prince with an astonished face.

Prince said, "I called that mysterious unknown man a supernatural being, because you know nothing about him, even his name you do not even know."

Angel asked, "How did you know that I am looking for a man?"

Prince answered, "You used the word his." And he added, "We use that word for men."

Angel said, "You are right." And she added, "I think I am getting really crazy."

Then, both Angel and Prince sat down, and they started talking. their conversation, they found out that they were studying on the same program. They were taking the same courses. After an half hour, Prince got up from his chair by telling Angel that he was going to go back to his class, and he demanded her to start school the next day, because she was already late with the courses. Angel got up from her chair by replying that she was going to start school now. Prince asked Angel what she was meaning by that? Angel smiled by answering that it meant that she was going to class. They started to walk-outside of the library while talking, and Angel told him the number of her classroom to Prince, and he told her the number of his classroom, then, they decided to see each other at the end of their class.

It was evening, Angel's parents were in their living room, and they were talking about the attitude of Angel, then, they turned their heads through the door as they had heard the door of the living room opened. Suddenly the expression of their faces changed, and they were looking with the amused-faces as they were seeing Angel who was walking inside with a smile on her face. She walked towards her parents and she kissed them, and it was the first time that she was kissing her parents since she had started school. Her parents asked her, if she was doing well? Angel answered that she had a great day, that she met a wonderful friend named Prince, and she spent the time with him after class. Angel walked into her bedroom, that she was tired and that she wanted to get some rest. Her parents looked at each other with surprised faces, without saying a word, what had happened to Angel, and why she suddenly changed, but they were glad that she was doing well.

Hero was lying in his bed, and was not able to sleep. He was thinking of Angel, and he was aware that Angel and Prince had spent time together after school, because his magic had attracted his attention by warning him that Angel was in danger, and when he had used his magic to know where Angel was, he had found out that Angel

## SUPERNATURAL BEINGS

and Prince were spending time together. Hero did not why his magic had warned him that Angel was in danger when she was with Prince, and he was wondering why his magic had chosen to warn him about Prince, and not about other people who talked with Angel every day, as Hero knew that Angel had a lot of friends. Hero could not answer his question. He was quite lost. Also, Angel had already met Prince before, and she even had saved Prince when they both first met, but on that day his magic did not warn him about a danger. The question was, why this time his magic chose to warn him about the meeting between Prince and Angel? Still, there was no answer to his question. Although, Hero knew the reasons why Prince was in the world of natural human beings, he did not understand why when Prince was with the other natural human beings his magic did not warn him about any danger, as Prince was spending most of his time with the natural human beings. Prince was talking to natural human beings as he was studying with them, but his magic had never warned him about them. His magic had just warned him about Angel who was also a natural human being like the others.

The question that was going on in Hero's mind was, why among all the natural human beings who talked to Prince, or who spent time with Prince, his magic had only chosen Angel to warn him that she was in danger? And not someone else or other people. But again, Hero could not answer. Even if Hero knew that there were the supernatural beings of the eagle world who wanted to kill Angel for the reasons that he did not know, he was still wondering why Prince was a danger for Angel, and not on other people. Hero did not know what to do, and he was thinking to start class the next day by using his visible body, but he did not know if it was a good idea, and he spent his whole day thinking.

The next day, it was 9 am. Hero sat in class, with the same place where Angel had seen him. It was the same place that his invisible phantom was sitting when he was using it to attend classes. Hero was staring at Angel who sat three tables in front of him, and Angel was talking with Bella who sat close to her. Then, the instructor walked inside the class. After a minute, the instructor started to teach the course by walking in front of the class. The instructor noticed that there was a student that she had never seen in her classroom. instructor stopped teaching, and she looked at Hero by asking, "Are you a new student?" Hero got up and answered, "Yes, I am." Suddenly, Angel turned her head from behind, as she had heard a voice that was familiar to her, then, immediately her eyes opened widely as she was staring at Hero, and by seeing the expression on Angel's face, it was obvious that she had not seen Hero since she was in class. Most of the students had turned their heads through Hero, looking at him as he was answering the questions of the instructor.

Angel had her eyes focused on Hero, and she was very nervous, her whole body was a little bit trembling. Bella was staring at Hero too, with a smile on her face. Suddenly, Angel opened her mouth by looking with an amused face, as she had heard Hero answered that he had arrived in the world of natural human beings last night coming from Canada, when the instructor had asked Hero why he had started school late. was very confused, and she did not understand why Hero was lying to the instructor. Then, after some questions, the instructor continued to teach her course, and Bella was always turning her head from behind looking at Hero. She was bothering and telling Angel that Hero was very handsome, but Angel was not paying attention to Bella was saying. was very troubled as she was thinking about the lie that Hero had told to the instructor, and she was thinking how she was going to behave with Hero, especially that she spent a month looking for him. Now, he sat just behind her and she did not know what to say, or what to think and how to behave.

After three hours, it was break time and Bella told Angel that they must go to introduce themselves to Hero to welcome him in school, but Angel refused by saying that she did not want to greet the new student. Although, Angel refused to greet Hero, Bella went, and made her acquaintance to Hero. They spent their break time together talking, while Angel spent her break time with Prince.

The days were passing, and Hero and Angel had still not said a word to each other. They had not even greeted each other, but they were always looking at each other. Even in class, Angel was always turning her head from behind, looking at Hero. Her eyes were always meeting with Hero's eyes, because he was always looking at her, too,

## SUPERNATURAL BEINGS

and some students had noticed that Angel and Hero were always looking at each other. Bella had asked Angel why she was always turning her head from behind looking at Hero, if she did not want to talk to him. Angel lied to Bella that she was not looking at Hero, and that she still did not want to know him. Bella and Hero were becoming very close although, Hero was not talking too much, and Bella find Hero very weird and mysterious the way he talks, act and behave. There was something in Hero that Bella g, did not understand, and that she could not explain. Hero was always trying to avoid Bella, but she was always after him because he was attracting her. was the only student that Hero was able to talk with and most of the students find Hero very strange except Bella. He had never said a word to someone else in the classroom, and he was always sitting alone. While Prince and Angel were already best friends, and always spending their break time together. Angel had noticed that Prince had never put something in his mouth, and that Prince was not eating during lunch time. When Angel asked Prince why he was not eating, he lied to her by answering that he grew up by eating just twice a day morning and evening, and it became a habit for him to eat just twice a day. The magic of Hero was always warning Hero when Angel was with Prince, so Hero was spending most of his time watching Angel through his magic, and Hero had still not yet found the answer to his question of why Prince was a danger for Angel.

It was morning, Hero was in class as usual. The instructor was introducing a new chapter, that was talking about the difference between the animals and the natural human beings. Hero was paying attention to the instructor who was trying to compare the animals and the natural human beings. The instructor had taken the tiger, as an example of an animal to compare to natural human beings. The instructor was comparing the behavior of the tiger and the behavior of a natural human being. Hero understood that he had the same behavior as the tiger, but he was not surprised about that, because he knew himself that he was not a natural human being.

Suddenly, unknowingly Hero cried out, "Wrong." As he had heard the instructor make a mistake, by saying something that was not true about the tigers. And everyone in the classroom turned their head from behind looking at Hero, and Hero got up from his chair, then, he started to explain where the instructor had made the mistake. The eyes of all the students were focused on Hero, they were all listening to Hero with the surprised faces, and it was the first time that Hero was talking in class. After a few minutes, Hero had done his explanation, and they were all amazed by the way Hero talked about the tigers, even the instructor, and some students were even wondering if Hero lived in the forest with the tigers. Then, the instructor continued to teach her lesson.

After a couple of hours, it was break time and Angel walked in the lunchroom, and she looked at the place where she usually sits with Prince, and she did not see Prince. She removed her phone from her pocket, and sent a message to Prince. Then, Angel walked towards an empty chair and sat, and she put lunch box on the table that was in front of her. started thinking with a worried face, and she was remembering about the explanation of Hero in class. Angel was trying to understand how Hero knew about the tigers, she was wondering how Hero knew the tigers as if he was raising the tigers at his home like parents raised their kids at home, but unfortunately, she had no idea about who Hero was.

Prince joined Angel, and he was facing and staring at her. He noticed that Angel was away, and he broke the silence by asking her, if she was alright? Angel looked at Prince, and she told him that she was fine. Prince pulled the chair and sat facing Angel, and put the package that he had on his hand on the table. Prince looked in Angel's eyes while asking what was wrong, because she was thoughtful. Angel looked at Prince and she was thinking how she was going to talk to him about the behavior of her mysterious classmate named Hero, then suddenly she changed her mind, and lied to Prince by saying that she was stressed of the exams for the next day. Then, she changed the conversation by asking Prince where he was? Prince answered that he was hungry, and went to a shop outside the campus to find something to eat. Angel was very surprised to hear Prince say that he was hungry, because it was the first time that he was looking for something to eat during lunch time. She asked him what he got to eat for lunch? Prince put his hand on the package that he had put on the table, and lifted the package to Angel, showing it to her, and smiling at her. Angel looked at the package in Prince's hand and asked what it was.

The expression on Angel's face changed, and she cried out, "Food for cat?" Looking at Prince with an astonished face. Prince smiled at her and said, "Yes, it's the cat's food." Angel said, "Don't tell me that you are going to eat the cat's food." Prince said, "Of course I am going to eat the cat food." Still with the same smile on his face while looking into Angel's eyes. Angel cried out, "What?" She was still looking at Prince with the same expression on her face, and she asked, "Are you seriously telling me, that you are going to eat the cat food?" Suddenly, the smile that was on Prince's face disappeared, as he had realized the mistake that he had been talking to Angel as if she was a supernatural being. He understood that he should correct his mistake, then Angel took a deep breath as she had heard Prince told her that he was joking. Prince lied to Angel by saying, this had to do with their class this morning wherein their teacher talked about a chapter between the difference of the natural human beings and the animals. Wherein their instructor took the tiger as an example of an animal to compare to a natural human being, compared the cat and the tiger by saying that both the cat and the tiger were almost similar.

Then, when the instructor talked about the cat, he remembered that his cat had no food and he had forgotten to buy the food for it yesterday. So, during break time he ran to a shop outside the campus to buy food for his cat. Angel smiled while asking Prince, how many cats he had in his house? Prince answered her that he had only one cat, and he loved cats, just that he had no enough to take care of them. But Prince was lying to Angel, and had bought that cat food for himself, he wanted to eat it, because his instructor lectured in class that the tiger and the cat could eat the same food. Prince wanted to taste the cat food as he was a tiger. Angel told Prince that she studied the same course in the morning in class.

Angel opened the box of the food that was on the table in front of her, and removed two forks from her school bag. She handed one fork to Prince. Prince refused to take the fork by saying that he was not hungry, but Angel insisted by saying that she wanted him to taste the food., It was a traditional food in the world of natural human beings, and she had come to class bringing the food, because she wanted him to taste it. She was sure that since he came into the world of supernatural beings, he never tasted it. Prince took the fork in Angel's hand, and pushed the box of food in the middle of them. She looked at Prince and said, "Let's eat." Prince was staring at the food without knowing what to do, and how he was going to eat it, while Angel had started eating.

Angel looked at Prince and said, "Taste it, you would like it." While Prince was still wondering how the food was going to get in his belly, got an idea, he told Angel that he was not feeling well, and he promised her that he would eat the next time. But Angel refused by saying that she wanted him to just taste it, even only once. was still trying to convince Angel without being successful, and he noticed that Angel had started to get angry, so he decided to try to please her. Then, smile appeared on Angel's face, as she had seen Prince take the food with his fork, and was trying to put it into his mouth. Prince was putting the food to his mouth, his lips were shaking, and suddenly the food fell on the table once the food had touched his lips.

Angel smiled at Prince, as the food had fallen on the table, then she asked Prince to try again, but Angel had not noticed exactly what had happened for the food. Prince put his fork in the food, and he picked up the food with his fork, then he lifted the fork into his mouth and suddenly, the smile on Angel's face disappeared, fear appeared on her face. As Angel was looking at Prince with a face full of panic as she was seeing Prince who was trying to put the food in his mouth with difficulties. that his lips were shaking as he was putting the food into his mouth, and suddenly, she cried out, "Oh, my god." As she had seen the food that Prince wanted to put in his mouth fell again, and her mouth stayed open as she was staring at Prince and he was looking at her too expressionless. between them, after a minute, Angel got up and cover the box food. She picked up her bag and the food box, then walked away without saying a word to Prince. He got up from his chair and started following Angel by trying to talk to her, but Angel was not paying attention to him.

## SUPERNATURAL BEINGS

Prince followed Angel to the door of her classroom without saying a word to him, and Angel get inside her classroom while looking at Hero, who was looking at her too, as usual. Hero knew what had happened because he had followed Prince and Angel through his magic. Angel sat in her place, and looked at Bella. She noticed that Bella was sad, and she asked Bella what was wrong? Bella answered Angel that she argued with Hero because she got mad when-he did not want to answer a personal from her. Angel turned her head from behind, and she stared at Hero who was looking at her, too. less than a minute, Angel turned her head towards Bella, and she told her that she had better forget Hero, because he was not a man for her. Bella told Angel that even if Hero was mysterious, she was in love with him, and Angel replied to her that for her own sake, she must stop loving Hero. Bella and Angel spent the rest of the day together, and Prince had tried to talk to Angel after school, but Angel had ignored him. She had not even uttered a word to him, and Prince went to his house with a face full of sadness as Angel had refused to talk to him.

It was evening, Prince sat in the living room with the book on his knees, while he had the phone in his hands, he was sending a message. Hero walked in the living room coming from the kitchen and going to his bedroom. Prince was looking at Hero who was walking into his bedroom. Prince called Hero, and he turned his head and looked at Prince. Prince told Hero that he wanted to talk to him, and he walked towards his chair. Hero sat in a chair, and both of them were looking at each other. Prince asked Hero if everything was alright? Hero answered that everything was okay. Prince told Hero that he wanted to talk to him about their way of living, that they were living like strangers in the house, they were not talking and not seeing each other. Hero was always in his bedroom as if he was running away from him. Hero replied to Prince that he was having some hard times since he had put his feet in the world of natural beings. It was as if he was another person, as if he was not himself. Prince asked Hero what he meant by it. Hero replied that it was as if his destiny had changed.

Prince told Hero that still he did not understand. Hero stared Prince in silence. Hero knew that he could not talk honestly to

Prince about what was happening to him, and he started to think about what to say. Then, he opened his mouth and told Prince that his heart was full of anger each second that he was seeing a natural human being. If he could, he would have already destroyed the race of natural human beings since the first second that he had put his feet i on their land. And that it was impossible to stare at the natural human beings every day, knowing what they had done to our ancestors in the past. Prince told Hero to be patient, and that he was feeling the same anger inside him every time he was looking at a natural human being through the window of his house. It was harder to spend ten hours everyday with the natural human beings. Prince told Hero that they must be patient not to forget that they were in the world of natural human beings for a mission, and that they must focus on their mission. Prince asked Hero how school was going? Hero answered that school was doing well, even if he was not enjoying it, but there was no other choice, because studying the race of natural human beings was their only solution to eliminate them. Prince told Hero that they just have to be calm, because they could not make a mistake by failing their mission.

Prince asked Hero if there was a natural human being who Hero was close with? Hero answered him that there was a young woman in his classroom named Bella who he was sometimes talking with, and the young woman was acting as if she was in love with him. Suddenly, Prince burst into laughter and Hero was staring at Prince who was laughing, wondering what was so funny to put Prince in humor and laugh. Prince said that it was a good and fun news he had heard since he was born, a natural human being who was in love with a tiger. Prince looked at Hero and said, what if you love her too, how were you going to sleep with her? Your body and her body would never be in contact, because your body would reject her body. Prince went on by saying that today, he had tried to eat a food coming from a natural human being named Angel, but once he had tried to put the food into his mouth, his body started to reject the food, and the food fell once it touched his lips. Hero smiled and said that Prince had just needed to remove his phantom from his body and eat the food without a problem.

Prince looked at Hero with an amused face without saying a word. Then, he smiled to him and said that Hero had just saved him by giving him an amazing idea. If he had thought about that idea, he should have eaten Angel's food, and it should have avoided her being angry with him. Prince added that tomorrow he was going to remove his ghost from his body and eat Angel's food. Angel was very angry with him, as he had made her food fall, and since yesterday Angel left in the library angrily. She had not talked to him again, even if he sent her messages, she did not reply. Hero looked at Prince and said that it seemed that he was giving too much attention to woman named Angel. Prince looked into Hero's eyes, without saying a word, and they were looking at each other's eyes in silence.

After fifty seconds, Prince broke the silence and said that Angel was special and unique among all the natural human beings he met. Only Angel had attracted his attention, there was something in Angel that was attracting him through her, but he could not explain it. Prince went on by saying that he loved to spend time with Angel, and that when he was with Angel, he forgot everything, he forgot that he was with her enemy, he forgot the reason why he came in the world of natural human beings, he forgot that he was a supernatural being and that she was a natural human being.

Every time when Angel was sad, he was sad, too, her sadness was affecting him, and when Angel was happy, he was happy, too, and that his mood was depending on the mood of Angel, and that he hated to be far from her. He hated to spend his weekend without seeing her. And that he was feeling a strange feeling inside his body when he was near her. His body was reacting as if there was a butterfly that was flying inside it when he was talking with Angel, and his heart was beating faster than normal when he was looking in Angel's eyes. Hero looked into Prince's eyes and asked if Prince was in love with Angel? Prince stared in Hero's eyes for a couple of seconds without saying a word. Prince broke his silence and said that he did not think he was in love with Angel. But that Angel had something inside her that was attracting him, but still, he did not know what the thing was, and why was she attracting him. and even worse he could not explain exactly how that thing was attracting him.

Hero asked Prince if he was in love with the mysterious thing that Angel had inside her? Prince took a deep breath and answered that yes, he was in love with that mysterious thing that Angel had inside her, because when he was close to Angel that mysterious thing inside her was making his heart beat with love. Hero was looking at Prince in silence, and he was not completely surprised, by what Prince told him about Angel, because Hero himself knew that there was a mystery around her. There was something who was making Angel different from the rest of natural human beings. Hero was wondering what Angel might have of different from the rest of natural human beings, and what was that mysterious thing that Angel had inside her that was attracting Prince., he could not answer those questions, like a lot of questions that were still in his mind without the answers. Prince looked at Hero and asked why silent? Hero answered that he was just surprised, by what Prince said about Angel and that he did not know what to say. Prince told Hero that he thought that Hero should laugh at him by saying that he was crazy.

Hero told Prince that his-story about Angel was strange. Prince said that he was in love with something that Angel had inside her, and if Prince tell this story to someone else, that person would say that Prince was crazy. Prince replied that himself, he was sometimes wondering if he was not crazy, or if he was not making some fixations on Angel, or if Angel really had something inside her. Hero looked at Prince by asking if Prince could kill Angel? Prince put his left hand on his forehead, and-started to rub his forehead and his head was a little bit bent, as if he was thinking, then, Prince removed his hand from his forehead, he looked in Hero's eyes by answering that yes. He could kill Angel. but did not know if he could kill the mysterious thing that was inside her, if she really had it.

Hero opened his mouth to start talking, but suddenly, his mouth stayed open with no word coming out. Hero was warned by his magic not to say what he wanted to say. Prince looked at Hero by asking if Hero was alright, as Hero was looking at him with his mouth opened. Hero answered that he was fine. Prince asked Hero what question he wanted to ask before his mouth stayed open. Hero replied to Prince that he wanted to ask Prince if he had found some-

## SUPERNATURAL BEINGS

thing about their mysterious enemy. ~~And~~ Prince replied that still, he had no idea about their mysterious enemy. But Hero had lied to Prince, because the question that he wanted to ask him was not about their mysterious enemy, but instead about the reasons why Angel was always wearing the rosaries. Hero wanted to ask Prince if he knew the reasons why Angel had the rosaries on her wrist and on her ankle, but the magic of Hero prevented him from asking that question to Prince. Hero did not understand the reasons why his magic prevented him from asking that question to Prince, and it was the first time that Hero's magic was controlling his conversation because his magic had never prevented him from saying a word or to ask a question. Hero was very amazed because he did not even know that his magic could control his words.

Prince and Hero spent almost the whole night talking about their mysterious enemy, and they also talked about their exams for the next day. During their conversation, Hero had asked Prince how they were going to eat, because since they had put their feet in the world of natural human beings, they had not put something in their mouths. And that if they kept staying there without feeding their phantoms, their ghosts would become tired and their ghosts would get sick for lack of food. Prince had told Hero that the only solution they had to feed their phantoms, was to send their phantoms into the tiger world for their phantoms to eat, as their ghosts could not eat the food of natural human beings. Hero had agreed with the idea of Prince to send their phantoms into their world, that their ghosts would get food to eat. Both of them went to bed at 3:00 a.m.

It was 9:00 a.m., all students were in class taking exams, except for Hero who was not in class. Angel was not really focused on her exams, she was always looking at the door to see if Hero was getting inside the classroom. She was also turning her head from behind to see if Hero was in his place. She was wondering where Hero was, and she was thinking that maybe Hero had run-away from the exams. After fifteen, Angel had bent her head looking at her exam's paper, and she was writing on it. She lifted her head looking in front of her as she had heard the footsteps, and she was staring at Hero who was walking in the classroom. Most of the students had their eyes looking at Hero who was walking towards his place, then, the instructor followed Hero with the exam's paper. Hero sat in his place, and the instructor gave him his exam's paper turned and left. Hero removed the pen from his bag, and turned his head through Angel's place. He noticed that Angel was looking at him. Both of them were staring at each other. After nine seconds, Hero bent his head into his exam's paper that was on the table in front of him, and he started to write on it while Angel was still staring at him. After a minute, Angel turned her head and she continued to write on her exam's paper.

After eleven minutes, Hero got up with his exam's papers in his hand, and started to walk through the desk of the instructor. Angel, Bella and some students had turned their heads towards Hero, looking at him. And the instructor saw Hero who was walking towards her, and demanded Hero to return to his place. She would come see what he needed, and suddenly, the students who were focused on their exam's papers turned their heads towards Hero, as they had heard Hero told the instructor that he was done. All students' eyes were focused on Hero, and there Angel's mouth opened and they were all wondering how Hero had done the exams in less than fifteen minutes. Hero gave his exam papers to the instructor, and checked on them. The instructor looked at Hero with an amused face as she had noticed that Hero was really done. Hero left the classroom. And the students continued to do their exams, but Angel had lost her concentration on the exams, she wanted to go out to meet Hero.

After an hour, Angel got up from her chair, and took her exam papers. She walked to the desk of the instructor, and gave her the exam papers, and she left the room. Angel was walking in the hallways of the campus, and she was looking for Hero. She suddenly met Prince, and he tried to talk to her, but she was still walking away without paying attention to him who was walking after her. After a few minutes of persistence, Angel turned her head to Prince, then they started talking, and Prince apologized about what had happened with the food yesterday.

Then, Prince invited Angel to the restaurant, but she turned down his invitations and said that she wanted to walk. Prince proposed to walk with her, and she accepted the proposition. They started to walk together while talking, but Angel was walking because she was looking for Hero. After an hour, both Prince and Angel were still walking, and Prince asked Angel where exactly they were going. Angel answered Prince that there was no destination, they were just walking. Prince and Angel were walking on the veranda of a classroom while talking, and suddenly Prince became quiet, and stopped walking. He was breathing deeply, as he was smelling a smell coming from a supernatural being, and he that there was a supernatural being around.

Angel was looking at Prince with a worried face by asking him if he was fine, but Prince was not replying to Angel. Prince concentrating on himself by trying to find out where that smell was coming from. Prince turned his head through the window of, and suddenly, the expression of his face changed. He was looking with an astonished face as he was seeing Hero who was doing exercises on the board, and there were students who were paying attention to what he was doing. Angel noticed that Prince was looking through the window, and she turned her head through to see what he was staring at, then the expression of her face changed, as she was seeing Hero who was explaining the exercises to some students. Angel was very amazed to see Hero who was explaining the exercises to the students, and she was staring at him with a heart that was beating faster than the normal, while saying in her mind, "I got out without finishing my exams, because I wanted to see you, I walked in the campus more than an hour looking for you, while you are here explaining the exercises to the students." Prince turned his head towards Angel, and he told her that they should go, but Angel refused by saying that she was interested in mathematics that Hero was doing on board, that her next exam was mathematics.

Prince told Angel that he was good at math, that they have to go find a room, and he would explain to her about it. Angel replied to Prince that there was no enough time to go find a room because they were going to class in a couple of minutes. But Angel was lying to Prince that she was interested in math because she was instead interested in Hero, she just wanted to stare while Hero was working. Angel was staring at Hero's face without an expression, there was no smile, no sadness and no happiness on Angel's face, but by looking at her, we could notice that she was enjoying seeing Hero explaining math.

Hero turned his head through the window, and saw Prince and Angel. Both Angel and Hero started staring at each other. And students who were in the room turned their heads looking at Hero and Angel. were surprised by the way that Angel and Hero were looking at each other, even Prince. Hero turned his head to the board, and he put the marker that he had in his hand at the edge of the board, it was the marker that he was using to write on the board. Hero started walking towards the door, and a student came to see him and that student showed Hero an exercise in the book by asking him to explain the exercise.

Hero stared at that student and remarked that the student was his classmate, then continued to walk through the door without saying a word. And the students had turned their heads looking at Hero who was getting out of the classroom, with the amused faces without understanding what suddenly happened to him as he walked out of the classroom without uttering a word. Hero did not pay attention to the student who asked him for help, mostly he was so nice to them a couple minutes ago, and Hero was the one who had decided to help them to explain the math, without them asking him, as he had seen them doing math on the board. He walked in the classroom, then he started explaining to them.

Even Angel was looking at Hero with an astonished face without understanding why he was behaving like that, and only Prince who had the smile on his face as Hero had refused to help that student. Hero got out of the classroom, and started walking into the corridor of his classroom. Angel had turned her head looking at him., Angel asked Prince to go in the classroom and to help those students with solving the math as Hero had abandoned them. Prince refused by saying that his next exam would start soon. Angel told Prince there was still fifteen minutes before the next exam start, and that he could use even eleven minutes of those fifteen minutes to explain math to those students, but Prince refused by saying that he had a headache and that he did not want to talk because he did not want to increase his headache before his exams.

Angel walked towards the door of the classroom without saying a word to Prince, she got inside the classroom walking into the board, and took the marker that Hero had left on the edge of the board. Angel started to write on the board by continuing the exercise that Hero had left behind, and the students had turned their heads through the board by looking at Angel. of them were very surprised. Angel turned, through the students and started to explain them the math solution. Prince was looking at Angel through the window with an ~~amazed~~ amused face, as Angel was explaining the math solution to the students. Prince did not realize the way that Angel explained, as he was noticing that she was very smart. Prince was wondering who Angel really was, and he started having doubts about the real identity of Angel, because it was obvious for him that a natural human being could not be as smart as Angel.

After fifteen minutes, all the classmates of Angel were in the classroom taking exams, except for her who was not in the class yet. After nine minutes, Angel walked inside her classroom while staring at Hero who was writing on his exam papers as she walked unto her place. The instructor came and gave Angel the exam papers. After two minutes, Hero got up with his exam papers in his hand, and started walking to the desk of the instructor. All students were looking at him with surprised faces, wondering how did he finish the exams of two hours by just eleven minutes. No one exactly who Hero was. And for most of the students, Hero was not answering the questions that were on the exam papers, because it was impossible to write the answers of those questions in less than fifteen minutes. Hero was walking towards the instructor while looking at the her, who was looking at him too. Then, the light got out from Hero's eyes and went and shone it to the instructor, Hero stopped walking and he turned to his left side. He walked three steps and put the sheet of paper in front of a student without saying a word. He turned, and continued to walk towards the instructor.

The whole classroom was very astonished by what Hero did, knowing that the instructor was looking at him. students turned their heads and looked at each other in silence, with the amused faces, while other students had their mouths opened but no word was coming out. They did not believe what Hero had just done. They all looked at Hero on how he gave his exam papers to the instructor, and he left the classroom without the instructor asking him about the sheet of paper that he had put in front of that student. They were all wondering why the instructor did not ask Hero about that sheet of paper because they all thought that the instructor had seen how Hero had put that sheet of paper in front of the student. But the instructor had not seen how Hero had put that sheet of paper because the light that had got out from Hero's eyes and shone on the instructor had prevented from seeing how Hero put the sheet of paper in front of the student. And none of the students had seen that light that had got out from Hero's eyes, so the students could not understand what was going on, and why the instructor had not asked Hero about that sheet of paper that he had put in front of a student.

Then, the instructor noticed that the whole class was looking at her, and she looked at the students with a surprised face. she asked, what was going on, why they were all looking at her, and students turned their heads and started to look at each other in the room without saying a word. Most of the students turned their heads into their exam papers, while other students were looking at the student that Hero had put the sheet of paper in front of him. were wondering what was written on that sheet of paper. And the student that Hero had put the sheet of paper in front of him had not yet touched that sheet of paper. He was staring at that sheet of paper with fear on his face, wondering why Hero had put the sheet of paper in front of him, and what was written on it. Then, student remembered that he had asked Hero for help a few minutes ago in another classroom, when Hero was explaining them the math, but Hero had ignored him, so the student started to understand what that sheet of paper could be. The student took the sheet of paper and looked at it, suddenly he smiled, as he noticed that Hero had done all the exercises of the exams on the sheet of paper, and he started to copy the answers.

All the students of the classroom of Hero finished their day with doubt in their heads, they did not understand how Hero had finished his exams in less than fifteen minutes. of them were sure that he had answered his exam because they had seen the sheet of paper that Hero had put in front of their classmate, and they had noticed that Hero had written all the answers of the second test on that sheet of paper. understood that Hero was really doing his exams, but they did not understand how Hero was doing them in less than fifteen minutes. Angel had understood that Hero had put that sheet of paper in front of that student to apologize, as Hero had ignored that student, when that student had asked him for help.

After few weeks, Hero was still the mysterious student that nobody knew, and the only thing that his classmates were sure about Hero was that he was a very smart student, because he had gotten one hundred percent on all his exams. instructors had told the marks of Hero to the students, like the students wanted to know if Hero was really doing well in his exams. Hero had found out that Angel was very smart, he had used his magic to find out the marks of Angel on the tests that they had taken a few weeks ago. Hero was very surprised by seeing that there was only one test that Angel did not get one hundred percent. The days were passing, Angel and Hero still had-not said a word to each other, and they were still just looking at each other, in silence. Angel and Prince were in a relationship, and they were spending most of their time together. Angel was very happy being close to Prince. He was removing his phantom from his body every time he wanted to eat the food of natural human beings, and when he wanted to kiss Angel. Hero was very worried about Prince and Angel's relationship, because he knew that Prince had a plan, and that he was going to use Angel for his plan. was sad because she had confessed her feelings to Hero, but Hero had replied to her that he was not a good person for her.

It was evening, Hero and Prince were in the living room of their house, and each of them had the book on their knees. They were sharing their ideas about the race of natural human beings, about what they had studied so far about the functions of the natural human being's body. Hero was explaining to Prince what he had found out about the natural human being's body, when suddenly Hero became silent, as his magic was taking him somewhere. Hero concentrated, and he was following his magic.

Suddenly, Hero was seeing through his magic the three supernatural beings of the eagle world who had tried to kill Angel, who were talking with a young man, and those three supernatural beings were giving money to that young man. Prince was looking at Hero by asking him if he was fine, but Hero was not paying attention to Prince, because he was focused on his magic. Hero looked at Prince and he told Prince that he was not doing well, that they would keep studying the next day. Hero got up from his chair, took his book and walked to his bedroom. Hero started walking towards his bedroom, and the conversation between those supernatural beings and the young man was already over. Hero had not listened to their conversation because his magic warned him about the conversation when when it was about to end.

The only thing that Hero had seen through his magic was, how one of the supernatural beings was giving money to the young man. And Hero had noticed that the young man was a natural human being, and there were a lot of questions that were going on in his mind, like, what were these supernatural beings and the young man were talking about? Why did those supernatural beings give money to the young man? Who was that young man? Why did his magic warn him about that meeting between them? But unfortunately, Hero could not find the answers to those questions. And even his own magic could not find out what these supernatural beings and the young man talked about, because his magic was not linked to something that had already happened. Hero spent his whole night walking inside his bedroom, trying to find the answers of the questions that were in his head, and trying to know why those supernatural beings had met that young man.

It was 8:00 a.m., Hero was in class, and he was listening to the instructor who was teaching a course about the race of the natural human beings. Suddenly, Hero felt a violent headache, he closed his eyes, and he felt that his magic was taking him somewhere. Then, he opened his eyes and looked in Angel's place and he noticed that Angel was not in class. Hero got up from his chair, and started walking faster through the door, and all the students had turned their heads looking at him with surprised faces while wondering what was going on with him. The instructor was asking Hero where he was going, but Hero was not paying attention to his instructor. Hero got out of the classroom, and started to run so fast in the hallways of the campus. People who were walking in the corridors had turned their heads looking at Hero with amused faces, wondering what was going on with him.

Hero was running through a balcony, he turned his head and looked around him. He noticed that there was no one around, and his blue eyes became dark blue so he turned into a tiger. Then, the tiger jumped through the balcony, and started running in the parking area, reached a car, and the tiger turned into the body of a supernatural being who was Hero. He opened the car's door, got inside, and drove away. Hero was on the road, and was driving so fast with his foot on the accelerator. ~~and~~ He was not paying attention to the traffic lights, and was doubling all the cars that were on his way. After twenty-one minutes of driving, Hero turned to an empty road, and was driving through where his magic was taking him. were trees at the edge of the road, and after nine minutes of driving, he turned to his right side, and started driving among the trees. Hero saw a house that was surrounded by trees, but it was impossible to drive through that house, because there were trees everywhere that were preventing him from driving.

The light started to get out from Hero's eyes, and was shining in the car, and the car got up from the ground. Hero was driving in the space among the trees, then he went, and he hit the door of the house with the car. ~~The~~ car broke the door, and there was the front of the car inside the house. The rest of the car was outside the house. So, the car was in the middle of the door, then Hero opened the car's door, and got out. He suddenly heard a voice cry out, "Hero?"

Hero turned his head in the room, and saw Angel who was tied to the chair. There was someone who was bending and facing Angel, and that person was trying to remove the rosaries that were on the wrist and ankle of Angel. There were four other men in the room. And they had all turned their heads towards Hero, looking at him with surprised faces. Angel was looking at Hero with her mouth opened, and it stayed open a couple of seconds ago as she had called the name of Hero. Looking at Angel's face, she could not believe that Hero was facing her, and she was wondering what he was doing there.

Hero looked at the young man who had bent close to Angel, and said, "Do not even dare to touch her." Then, one of the men in the room removed a gun from his jacket, and he pointed the gun to Hero by asking, "Who are you?" Then, Angel started screaming the name of George to not shoot Hero, to drop his gun. And Hero was looking for the man named George who had pointed the gun at him. He noticed that George was the man that he had seen through his magic last night. The one who was talking with the supernatural beings, then Hero lifted his head, and remarked that the windows of the house were opened. Angel was still begging George not shoot Hero.

Then, George turned his head to Angel by saying, "You betrayed me." Angel replied, "I did not betray you." George said, "If you did not betray me, what this young man named Hero is doing here? I told you last night that nobody should be aware that we were going to meet here today." Angel said, "I did not talk to him." George said, "Stop lying." And he added, "I would kill both of you." Angel kept begging George to let Hero go. And another man looked at George and asked, "What to do now?" George looked at that man who had asked him the question and answered, "We will not change our plan about Angel, because they asked me not kill her, just to remove the rosaries that she's wearing, and leave her tied in the chair in this house. But we will kill this man named Hero, because we do not want a witness." Hero looked at George and said, "You had better order your men to untie Angel, and to not touch the rosaries that she's been wearing on her wrist and ankle." George laughed and said, "It may be true that your name is Hero, but you are not a superhero or a superhuman to save Angel." Hero replied, "Do not waste my time because I hate to see Angel suffer." George burst into laughter and said, "I can see that you are the new lover of my ex-lover, and you want to impress your sweetheart by saving her in the hands of her ex boyfriend who is me, by pretending to be a superhuman. But, what you forgot it's not like you are the Superhuman by Thierry Kouam, who has a lot of things such as magic, powers, the advance on time, and even the bullets cannot kill a superhuman, but you do not have all those things because I am going to kill you with the bullets that would get out from this gun." Hero looked into George's eyes angrily and said, "You have eleven seconds to release Angel." George looked into Hero's eyes and said, "I would help you to count, one, two, three, four, five, six, seven, eight, nine, ten, and eleven."

Suddenly, the light got out from Hero's eyes, and went through Angel, then everyone turned their heads to the left side of the room, as they had heard a loud scream coming from that side, and they were looking with terror on their faces, as they were seeing the man who was bending to face Angel, and who wanted to remove the rosaries on her wrist and ankle was crying on his back. They were all wondering what had happened to him for they found the man on the left side of the room. They did not understand how that man who was in the middle of the room had landed on the left side of the room, and hitting his back against the wall as if someone had carried him and threw him against the wall. The light that had got out from Hero's eyes had turned into his invisible phantom, and the invisible ghost had grabbed the man and threw him against the wall.

Then, they all turned their eyes towards Hero, and they were looking at him. George tried to point his gun to Hero, but suddenly Angel screamed as she had seen Hero who had jumped on George. Hero had jumped from where he was, and he had thrown George on the floor, before George pointed his gun at him. George was trying to fight with Hero, but he was too weak to fight him. Hero had punched George, and he had thrown the gun of George away. Hero got up from the floor, while George was on the floor bleeding on his mouth, and his nose. Hero walked towards Angel, and he started to untie Angel while other men were helping George to get up from the floor. Hero held Angel's hand and helped her to get up from the chair. He noticed that Angel was feeling some pains on her wrists and ankles as she was tied to her wrists and ankles. Hero looked in her eyes, asking her if she could walk, and Angel made the gestures with her head by saying, yes.

Both Hero and Angel turned through the door, while he had held Angel's hand, and they started to walk, but George and the other men walked towards them. Those men were looking at Hero and Angel, then George turned his head looking at those men who were close to him by asking them to kill Hero. Those men started to walk through Hero and Angel, while Angel was begging George not to kill Hero. Hero punched the first man who was after him, then he let go of Angel's hand by asking her to move behind him. Hero started fighting against those men, and Angel was watching the fight with an amused face, as she was very surprised to see how Hero was very strong, and how he was beating all these five men alone. Angel started yelling as Hero had grabbed the neck of one of those men, and was having breathing difficulties as Hero was pressing the neck of that one with one of his hands. Hero turned his head towards Angel as she was screaming his name, and saw the fear on Angel's face. Angel was asking him to not kill the man. Hero lifted that man that he had held by the neck, and he threw him against the wall, and the rest of men were on the floor bleeding, crying in pain.

Hero rushed towards Angel and grabbed Angel's hand. Both of them started to walk through the door, and their eyes suddenly opened widely, as they had seen three eagles flew inside the house through the window. Those eagles landed to face them, except Hero, the fear appeared on the face of everyone in the room, even those who were on the floor. As they had seen that those three eagles that had landed in the room had turned into two men and a woman. Angel started to walk from behind with her face full of dread, and her whole body was trembling. The people who were on the floor were trying to get up, but they were feeling the pains in their whole bodies, because Hero had almost broken their bones. Hero was looking at the three supernatural beings who were facing him, and they were the same people who had fought with them a couple weeks ago in the club. Then, George got up and he looked at those three supernatural beings, he cried out, "William?" With his mouth who was shaking. The supernatural being that George had called his name turned his head towards him and looked into his eyes and asked him to remove the rosaries that Angel had on her, then Hero looked at George by telling him to not touch Angel. The light got out from Hero's eyes and went through where Angel was, and the supernatural beings noticed that the light that had got out from Hero's eyes had turned into the invisible phantom of Hero, and they understood that Hero had removed his invisible ghost to protect Angel. And the woman who was between the supernatural beings started to walk through where Angel was, and other two supernatural beings started to walk through Hero.

Hero started to fight with two supernatural beings who were facing him, and his invisible phantom was fighting against the woman who was close to Angel. All the natural human beings who were in the room were looking with the amused faces as they were watching the fight, they were surprised by the way that the supernatural beings were fighting. But they were looking at the woman who was fighting close to where Angel was, without understanding what was going on, and they were wondering whom that woman was fighting with, as they were not seeing the invisible phantom of Hero. Hero was stronger than the two supernatural beings that he was fighting against, and the supernatural being named William screamed at George to grab Angel and to remove the rosaries that Angel had on her. Hero shouted at George to not even dare to touch Angel, then George turned, and he ran through the door by dragging his legs and George's friends followed him by dragging their legs too, and there was only Angel in the room who was watching the fight.

After three minutes, those supernatural beings turned into eagles and they flew through the window, as they had understood that it was useless to keep fighting as George and his friends had run away, because they needed George and his friends to remove the rosaries that were on Angel. The invisible phantom of Hero turned into the light and got inside Hero's eyes, and Hero went, and he grabbed Angel's hand, and they rushed into the car, and got inside the car, then Hero drove away.

Hero was driving on the road, there was silence in the car, and Angel had turned her head through Hero looking at him as he was driving, then she broke the silence by asking Hero how he found her? And how did he know that she was in that house? Hero did not answer the questions of Angel, and she asked again twice but still Hero did not answer, then Angel turned her head in front of her, and she saw a package of food close to her, and she took that package and she noticed that that package was opened, and she looked at Hero and asked, "What is inside this package?" Hero answered, "It's my food." Angel cried out, "What?" And she asked, "Your food?" By looking at him with an astonished face, she opened that package and looked inside. She looked at the package, and there was a picture of the cat on the package. looked at Hero and asked, "Are you eating the cat food?" Hero turned his head and looked at her without saying a word. He understood that he had made a mistake by telling her that it was his food. It was Prince who had given that package of food to Hero to taste it. Angel was reading what was written on that package, and she turned her head towards Hero by telling him that it was written on that package the food was for cats, and that human beings could not eat that food. But Hero was not paying attention to Angel, and he was just kept on driving, while Angel was looking at him with her mouth opened without knowing what to think. but There was a question that was going on in her mind, and that question was, who Hero was?, she could not answer that question.

Then, Hero parked the car in front of a drugstore, and asked Angel to wait in the car, he got out of the car and he walked inside the drugstore, while Angel was left inside the car, with a lot of questions that were going on in her mind. After a few minutes, the car's door opened, and Hero got inside the car with a small bag in his hand, then he drove away. Angel was just looking at him as he was driving through her house, then Angel asked Hero who he was? Hero stayed silent, and he said in his mind that he must think about something to distract Angel to prevent her from asking him some questions. Then, Hero put his foot on the accelerator, and Angel started to yell at him to drive slowly, but Hero was not paying attention to her. He was driving among the cars by doubling the cars that were on his way without respecting the traffic lights. While Angel was still shouting at him with her face full of fear, asking him to stop the car, that they would cause an accident, and Hero was not even looking at her, he was just driving by pretending to not listen to her.

After nine minutes, Hero parked the car in the yard of Angel's house, and he got out of the car with the small bag that he had got from the drugstore with, then he walked into the other side of the car, and he opened the car's door, then he helped Angel to get out of the car. He put Angel's hand around his shoulder, then he asked Angel to lean on him, they started to walk through the door, but Angel had difficulties in walking because she was feeling all the pains on her ankles. Hero carried her in his arms, and he started walking. They were looking at each other in the eyes, Hero suddenly screamed a little because he had hit his foot on the stairs and Angel laughed. They were still looking into each other's eyes. Angel said, "You should watch your way, as you are climbing the stairs." Hero asked, "Did you hate when I am looking at you?" Angel answered, "Of course, I love it when you look at me, just that I do not want you to hit your foot again." Hero said, "Do not worry." Angel said, "You have beautiful eyes." Hero replied, "Thank you." And he added, "You have beautiful eyes, too."

Then, they reached the front door, and Hero put Angel on the floor. They looked at each other, then Angel told Hero that there was nobody in the house. Hero asked her if she did not have the key. Angel replied that her key was inside her school bag, and that it was inside the house. Hero asked her how she got out of the house without her key, and she answered that her ex-boyfriend named George called her last night by telling her that he had an important thing to talk to her about. George came early this morning with his car, and he took her with his car. did not know that George was going to kidnap her. She thought that they should just talk for a couple of minutes, and after that she should return to the house. she got out of the house, her parents were still in the bed, and her parents locked the door when they left the house, that she was already in school. Hero asked her what they were going to do, and she answered that she had no idea. Then, Hero handed his hand through the door. He grabbed the handle of the door, he turned it, and he pushed the door. Angel turned her head through him by looking at him with an astonished face as he had opened the door, and by looking at Angel's face, it was as if she was watching a miracle. Hero carried Angel and he walked inside the house with her. He put her on the sofa, and he pulled a chair and sat on it facing her. He bent his head and he lifted the feet of Angel and he put her feet on his lap then, he took the small bag that he had got from the drugstore., He removed an ointment from the bag, and started to rub the ankles of Angel with the ointment. While Angel was looking at him without saying a word. Hero was just focused on rubbing the ointment on her ankles, then Hero looked at her and he asked, "How are you feeling?"

Angel answered, "I am feeling in pain."

Hero said, "You would be fine after."

Angel said, "Your colors, your hair and your beauty mark."

Hero asked, "What is wrong with my eye colors, my hair, and my beauty mark?"

Angel replied, "You have the same eye colors, the same hair and the same beauty mark as my boyfriend." Hero looked at her without saying a word.

Angel said, "It's like as if my boyfriend and you are twins or are coming from the same family."

Hero said, "It's just a coincidence, a lot of people look alike."

Angel said, "I do not think that it's a coincidence." Hero asked, "What do you mean?"

Angel replied, "It's like you have the same genes as my boyfriend."

Hero asked, "What do you mean?"

Angel answered, "my boyfriend and you have the same ancestors."

Hero said, "I already met a lot of people who looked like me, and we are not from the same family."

Angel said, "I know that a lot of people look alike, but there is something inside me that tells me that you and my boyfriend are kinship."

Hero said, "I do not know your boyfriend."

Angel said, "Tomorrow it's Saturday, and I am going to the cinema with my boyfriend. I want you and Bella to join us. There, I would introduce my boyfriend to you."

# SUPERNATURAL BEINGS

Hero said, "I have something to do tomorrow."

Angel said, "I hope we can go another day."

Hero looked in Angel's eyes and he told her that he had a favor to ask her. Angel asked him what was the favor. Hero told her that he did not want someone to know about what had happened today. Angel replied if Hero did not want her to talk to her parents about her ex boyfriend wanting to kill her, but Hero answered that he did not want someone to know that he was the one who saved her. Angel looked in Hero's eyes, asking him why she should not talk to someone that he was the one who saved her, and Hero looked at her without saying a word. After a few minutes, Hero broke the silence by asking Angel if he could trust her? Angel answered yes, and Hero told her to keep silent about what happened today, that nobody would be aware that he saved her. After a few minutes, Hero had done rubbing the ointment on Angel's wrist and ankles, and they were looking at each other in silence. Then, Angel opened her mouth and she told Hero that she was hungry, and he asked her what she wanted to eat, that he could go out to find her something to eat. Angel replied to him that they must go to the kitchen to make something to eat. Hero got up from his chair, and he helped Angel to get up from her chair, then she leaned on him and he helped her to walk towards the kitchen. sat in the chair and she demanded Hero to make her sandwiches. Hero was standing facing her, and he was just staring at her without saying a word. asked him to open the fridge and to remove the bread and vegetables to make the sandwiches, and that if he wanted some meat, he could remove the meat from the fridge, but not to put the meat on her sandwich.

Hero walked to the fridge, and opened the it. He was staring inside the fridge, while Angel was just staring at him. Then, Hero closed his eyes, as he was trying to concentrate. He was trying to put his hand in the fridge, and his hand started shaking once his hand was getting inside the fridge. When he succeeded to put his hand inside the fridge, he suddenly removed his hand. Angel was still staring at Hero with an amused face, without understanding what was going on with him. Hero put his hand again in the fridge, but once when his hand got inside the fridge, he immediately removed his hand.

Angel asked him if he was all right? Hero turned, and he looked at Angel without uttering a word. Then, Angel got up and grabbed the chair. walked to where Hero was, and she looked into Hero's eyes, then she removed the vegetables and bread out of the fridge. She asked him if he wanted to eat meat, and Hero did not reply to her. Then, she removed the meat out of the fridge, and removed the knife from the drawer. She handed the knife to Hero by telling him to use the knife to cut the vegetables, and that if he wanted to eat meat, he had to put the meat on his sandwiches.

Hero took the knife in Angel's hand without saying a word. He turned, and walked a step through the counter, and he stopped in front of the counter where Angel had put the vegetables, bread and meat. Hero was in front of the counter with the knife in his hand, and he was touching the vegetables as if he was afraid of the vegetables. Angel was looking at him as he was touching the vegetables, and she was noticing that Hero was removing his hand from the vegetables once he had touched them. Angel moved close to Hero and she took the knife in his hand and she asked him to move, then she started to cut the vegetables. She asked him if he wanted sandwiches or hamburger, but he did not reply. Angel continued to make the sandwiches, and hamburger while Hero was standing up close to her, looking at her silently.

After a few minutes, Angel was done making the sandwiches and the hamburger. served the sandwiches and the hamburger to Hero, and she served herself a sandwich with a bowl of carrots. asked Hero what he wanted to drink, and Hero looked at her without saying a word, then she asked him if he wanted to drink wine, still Hero did not say a word. served a glass of juice, a glass of water and a glass of wine close to the food of Hero, and she served herself a glass of water, then she sat in front of her food and she started eating the carrots. While Hero was still standing up close to the counter, and he was staring at her how she was eating the carrots without saying a word. He was amazed by the way that Angel loved the carrots, because all time that he had watched her through his magic, she was eating, it was always the carrots that she was eating. Then, Angel turned her head and looked at him and she told him to sit and eat.

## SUPERNATURAL BEINGS

Hero told her that he was leaving, and she replied to him that she had made the sandwiches and hamburger for him, and he had not even tasted them. Hero told her that her friend was coming, and she asked him which friend, and he answered her that-her friend would be there soon. Hero started walking through the door, and Angel turned her head and looked at him with an astonished face, and with her mouth opened as he was walking through the door. Angel got up from her chair, and she walked to the yard of the house. She stared at Hero who was driving away without knowing what to think about him, and she suddenly saw Bella in her car who was driving through her house. She started to stare at the car, then she remembered that Hero told her that her friend was coming. And she understood that Hero was talking about Bella, but she was wondering how Hero knew that Bella was coming, but unfortunately, she could not answer that question.

Bella parked the car close to Angel, and got out of the car. They went inside the house, and Bella asked Angel why she was not in class, and Angel lied to Bella by answering that she was sick. Bella told Angel how Hero had left the classroom this morning without saying a word, without even taking his school bag, and that it was still in the classroom. Angel understood that Hero had left the classroom to come and save her. She wanted to talk about it to Bella, but she remembered that she had promised Hero to keep silent. Then, both Angel and Bella spent the rest of the day talking. Most of their conversation was based on Hero, and each of them had questions about Hero that they could not answer. It was evening, Hero was in his bedroom lying in his bed, and he was thinking about what had happened. He understood that the supernatural beings who wanted to kill Angel had paid George to kidnap Angel, and to remove the rosaries that were on her wrist and ankle. Hero remembered that once when George and his friends had run away, after three minutes the supernatural beings ran away too. He remembered too, that when he was fighting against supernatural beings, one of the supernatural beings demanded George to remove the rosaries on Angel's wrist and ankle. And that when he left Angel, the supernatural beings did not follow him, as these supernatural beings had followed him after the club the day that he had saved Angel. Then, Hero understood that Angel was protected by the rosaries that she's been wearing, and that it was the reason why the supernatural beings who wanted to kill her had paid George just to remove those rosaries on her. Hero started to wonder why those Supernatural beings could not remove the rosaries that Angel was wearing by themselves, but he could not answer that question, and he spent the whole night trying to understand why those supernatural beings could not themselves remove the rosaries that Angel wore.

The following day, it was 2:00 p.m., The weather was beautiful, and there was no sun outside as usual. Prince and Angel parked the car in the parking area of the cinema, and they got out of the car and they held their hands while started walking towards the cinema entrance. They were talking and laughing, and the wind was blowing Angel's long hair. After a few minutes, Prince and Angel were sitting in the movie theater, and their eyes were focused on the screen that was in front of them. The movie theater was almost full. And the movie was starting, when suddenly Angel's eyes opened widely as she was watching the tigers on the screen that was in front of her, and she noticed that the movie was about the tigers. She was watching the tigers that were running. Prince was enjoying the movie with a smile on his face, while Angel was looking with a surprised face how the tigers were running, jumping and fighting, and how their eyes were changing when they get angry. Angel's mouth opened, with her face full of fear and started to remember about the fight that had happened yesterday between Hero and those men who wanted to kill her.

Angel remembered how Hero had jumped on George, and how Hero was fighting, also about Hero's eyes and the expression that was on Hero's face when he was angry. Angel noticed that Hero had the same characteristics as a tiger, that Hero was fighting like a tiger, then Angel got up from her chair. She turned, and she started to run towards the door, and Prince was still enjoying his movie. He had not even noticed that Angel had left. Then, Prince felt a hand on his shoulder coming from behind, and he turned his head from behind and the man who had touched his shoulder told him that her friend had left the room.

Prince turned his head to his left where Angel was sitting, and he noticed that Angel had left. He suddenly got up from his chair, and he started running towards the door. After less than a minute, Prince was standing up in the parking area and he was turning his head looking for Angel, then he saw Angel far to the other side and he screamed her name twice, but Angel did not turn. looked around him and he noticed that there was nobody in the parking area, and he started running, then his eyes became dark blue and he turned into a tiger. After less than a minute, the tiger was behind Angel and the tiger turned into the body of a supernatural being who was Prince, and Angel turned from behind, as she had felt a hand on her shoulder coming from behind. She looked at Prince, and he noticed that Angel's face was full of panic. Prince asked Angel, why she had left the movie theater? Angel answered Prince that she was scared of the movie, and Prince was looking at Angel on how she was shaking, and he walked a step facing her, then he took her in his arms. He told her how he was sorry, that he did not know that she was afraid of the tigers, and that next time he would choose a good movie. Then, they walked to the car, and they got inside on it, and Prince wanted to go to the restaurant, but Angel said that she wanted to go home. Prince noticed that Angel was thoughtful, that there was something that was bothering her, and he did not ask her what was going wrong, so he just drove her to her home.

Angel spent her whole weekend in her bedroom, and she had refused to see Bella and Prince who had come to visit her. She was in her bedroom thinking about Hero. Angel was remembering everything that Hero had done as Hero had saved her in the lake, as he had saved her in the club, as he had saved her in the house where she was kidnapped. How he was fighting, about his behavior in the kitchen when she had asked him to make the sandwiches, and about the movies on the tigers. There was a question in her mind and that question was, who was Hero? And Angel spent her whole weekend trying to answer that question.

It was Monday morning. Hero was walking in the yard of his house, and was walking towards his car. a few steps of walking, he reached his car and grabbed his car door. Suddenly, he started to breathe deeply and the light got out of his eyes and went away. There was fear on Hero's face, and he removed his phone from his pocket. He started to dial the number of Prince and suddenly, he stopped once he had understood that he was putting Angel in danger by calling Prince. Then, Hero did not know what to do, he was seeing the danger in the tiger world, and he knew that the tiger world was going to be attacked in a couple of minutes by the supernatural beings of the eagle world. Hero knew that he was responsible if the tiger world was going to be attacked by the supernatural beings of the eagle world as he had prevented the supernatural beings of the eagle world to kill Angel, and that it was a way for the supernatural of the eagle world to get revenge on him by attacking the tiger world. Then, Hero did not know what to do, he had already sent his ghost to the tiger world, to help his family to fight against the supernatural beings of the eagle world.

He wanted to go into the tiger world, but he knew that it would be impossible to arrive in the tiger world on time. Then, Hero got inside the car, and started the engine, and he started to drive without knowing exactly where he was going. Hero was very afraid, and he knew that the attack of the supernatural beings of the eagle world in the tiger family was going to help his family to find out about his betrayal. Hero was very worried about Angel, and he knew that now she was in danger and that he would not anymore be able to protect her, as his family was going to find out about his betrayal, and that the ancestors would order Philip to destroy his vampirism powers that were his strengths to prevent him to keep fighting to protect Angel, and that he was going to be killed on the orders of his ancestors.

Angel was in the classroom, and she was not paying attention to the instructor who was in front of the class teaching the course. She was always turning her head from behind in the place where Hero was sitting and looking if Hero was in class. Angel was always looking at her watch that was on her hand, looking at the time and she was wondering why Hero was not yet in class. It was already 11:00 a.m., and she was wondering where Hero was, because it was the first time that at 11:00 a.m., he was not in class yet. There was Hero's school bag in his place, and with his book opened on his table that he had abandoned last Friday, as he had left the classroom to go and save Angel. She had her head turned from behind, when she felt a hand on her lap and she turned her head towards Bella, as she had understood that it was Bella who had touched her lap, then she noticed that Bella was looking at the door, and she turned her head towards the door and the expression of her face changed as she was looking with the amused eyes at Hero who was walking in the classroom. Hero walked to his place and he sat. Hero had his eyes focused on the instructor, listening to what the instructor was saying, and Angel had turned her head from behind looking at him, then Angel turned her head towards the instructor, and she started to pay attention to what the instructor was saying.

After fifteen minutes, some students heard the noises coming from behind, and they turned their heads from behind and suddenly their eyes opened widely, as they were seeing Hero who was shaking in his place. The other students who were still listening to the instructor noticed that the instructor had stopped talking, and that the instructor was looking at the last table of the classroom with a surprised face, and those students turned their heads from behind. The surprise appeared on their faces as they were looking at Hero. The whole classroom had turned their heads from behind, and they were all looking at Hero who was acting as if he was fighting, and some students were looking at Hero with the amazed faces and mouth opened, while others were looking at Hero with fear on their faces. Suddenly, the eyes of everyone opened widely, and the horror appeared on everyone's faces, as they had heard Hero scream. They saw blood that was flowing from Hero's hand, and some of them noticed a wound on Hero's hand.

Then, Hero got up from his chair, and he started to run through the door by holding his wounded hand, and everyone turned their heads looking at Hero who was running towards the door. Their hearts were beating faster than the normal, and the hearts of some of them were beating with fear, while others were shaking of fear. Then, the students turned their heads and they were looking at each other in the room with panic on their faces without saying a word. Most of them were breathing deeply, and by looking at their faces, it was as if they were terrorized, and none of them was realizing what had happened. Even Angel, who had already seen Hero in that situation, was very surprised like the rest of the students, and it was like a miracle for all of them, because none of them could explain what they had just seen.

After less than a minute, there was still silence in the classroom, and the fear on the face of students' faces had not yet disappeared, then Angel got up from her chair and she walked to where Hero sat. Angel was standing up in the place of Hero, and she was staring at the blood that was on the Hero's stuff with an amazed face, and all the classroom had their eyes turned towards Angel. Then, an idea came in Angel's mind and she took Hero's book that was opened on his table and there was Hero's blood on that book, and she walked to the instructor with that book. Angel looked in the eyes of the instructor, and she asked the instructor if there was a difference between the blood of an animal and the blood of a human being. And the instructor answered her, yes, that there was a difference between the blood of an animal and the blood of a human being. Angel turned, and she walked to Hero's seat, and she put the book that she had in Hero's bag, and she grabbed Hero's school bag in her hand, and she turned, then she started to walk towards the door with Hero's bag, while everyone was looking at her with an astonished face and wondering where she was going with Hero's bag. The instructor asked Angel where she was going, but Angel did not pay attention to the instructor and she got out of the classroom. Angel walked towards the parking, and she got inside her car then, she drove away.

Hero was in the washroom of the university, and he was hitting himself against the wall. He could not control himself, and a student walked inside the washroom, singing., the eyes of that student opened widely. And that student was looking with a frightened face and with the mouth opened, as he was seeing Hero in the bathroom who was moving by hitting himself against the wall as if Hero was fighting against people, then that student turned, and ran away. Hero had seen that student, and his magic warned him that he was in danger in the toilet. Hero ran through the door and he got out of the toilet, and he started to run in the hallway by hitting himself against the lockers that were in the corridor and falling on the floor.

And the students who were in the hallway were looking at Hero with amazed faces, wondering what was going on with him, and they were afraid to go help Hero when he was falling on the floor, when he was trying to get up from the floor, then some students ran away. Despite the difficulties, Hero had succeeded to reach the parking area. He was close to his car and he heard the noises coming from behind him, and he turned his head through where the noises were coming from, and he saw the security men of the university who were running after him. Hero understood that the students had told the security men about him, and Hero opened his car door and he got inside the car, and he drove away. Hero was in the car driving with difficulties, and it was impossible for him to concentrate on the wheel, and he was driving in all directions. The cars on the road were honking at him. Suddenly, Hero lost direction and he hit a car that was parked on the sidewalk. He stayed in the car by breathing deeply, and he was taking control of himself, he was not anymore acting as if he was fighting, but he was very tired. Looking at Hero, it was obvious that his phantom had stopped fighting, and that the fight was over in the tiger world, but Hero was feeling all the pains in his whole body.

Suddenly, Hero's magic warned him of a danger, and he started hearing the sirens coming from the ambulances and police cars. understood that the people had called the police and ambulances about the accident that he did, then he started the engine of his car and he drove away. Angel was in the hospital where her mom was working as a doctor, and she was in the office of her mom. She was talking with her mom, and there was Hero's school bag on the desk of her mom, and Angel asked her mom to do a test on the blood that was on the school bag. Rebecca was asking questions to Angel, like who the blood on the school-bag belonged? And why she wanted to take the blood test? But Angel refused to answer the questions of her mom, and she was just begging her mom to take that test.

Then, the light got inside the office through the window that was opened, and that light turned into the invisible ghost of Hero, and that invisible phantom took the school bag that was on the desk and walked towards the door with that school bag in his hand. Angel and Rebecca turned their heads towards the door as they had heard the noises coming from the door. Both of them were looking at the door with the amazed faces, as the door was opened, and they turned, and they looked at each other. Angel asked Rebecca who opened the door? Rebecca replied that she had no idea, then Rebecca turned her head towards her desk, and she asked Angel where was the school bag, and Angel turned her head towards the desk. And suddenly, Angel's eyes opened widely, as she was staring at the desk and she understood that it was Hero who had taken his school bag, but she was wondering how Hero had taken ~~his school's bag~~ it, without her and her mom seeing him, and what time Hero got inside the office to take his school bag. Rebecca looked at Angel, asking if everything was alright. Angel turned his head towards her mom, and she replied to her mom that everything was fine, and she told her mom that they would see each other at home. Angel rushed through the door before her mom opened her mouth to say a word.

Hero was in his bedroom lying, and he was feeling all the pains on his whole body and those pains and the wound that was on his hand were coming from his ghost, because his phantom got hurt during the fight in the tiger world. Hero's phantom was sent to hospitalized to the tiger world, together with the other phantoms that got hurt during the fight and the doctors were taking care of those phantoms. The tiger world was in shock, and the inhabitants of the tiger world did not understand why they were attacked by the supernatural beings of the eagle world, and they were very afraid. There were a lot of questions that were going on in their mind, like who was really their enemies? Where those supernatural beings of the eagle world were coming from? And why were they attacked in their world by the supernatural beings of the eagle world? But, none of them could answer even one of their questions.

## SUPERNATURAL BEINGS

They were all happy that none of them was killed during the fight, despite some of them were injured, and they were hoping that those who were hurt would recover soon. were very worried about Hero who would be suffering somewhere in the world of natural human beings, as Hero's ghost had been wounded during the fight, and they had all noticed that during the fight their opponents were concentrated on the phantom of Hero. And that their opponents were trying to kill the phantom of Hero, but unfortunately for their opponents, Hero's phantom was very strong. Hero's phantom had killed two of their opponents. And they were very glad that Hero had sent his ghost to help them to fight against their enemies. They were wondering why Prince did not send his ghost to help them to fight against their enemies. And they spent the rest of the day talking about the fight that had happened, and some of them were very afraid. They were hoping that their ancestors would talk to them through their king, the reasons why they were attacked by the supernatural beings of the eagle world.

It was evening, Prince and Hero were in the living room. Hero had worn a t-shirt with a long sleeve to hide the wound that was on his hand, and Prince had noticed that Hero was looking very tired, and that there were marks on Hero's forehead as if he had a fight. Prince noticed too, that the marks that were on Hero's forehead were not coming from Hero's body but instead from Hero's ghost. Prince asked Hero what happened about the marks on his forehead? And Hero lied to Prince by answering that his phantom got those marks from the tree branches in the forest, when his phantom was going to the tiger world to find something to eat. Then, Prince started talking to Hero about the new chapter that his instructor started in the class today, and that he really liked that new chapter because that new chapter talked about the guinea pig, and that the new chapter would help them. Hero asked Prince how that new chapter was going to help them? Prince answered that the new chapter would help them to understand very well the functioning of the body of a natural human being, and that they would be able to take some tests by using a natural human being. Prince added that he also found out a product that was dangerous for the race of natural human beings, and he was going to try that product on his guinea pig, and that he already had a plan for. Hero asked Prince what was his plan? Prince answered that he was going to use Angel as a guinea pig to make the test, and to try that product on her to understand very well the functioning of the body of a natural human being. Hero asked Prince why he was going to use Angel as a guinea pig, if he was in love with her? Prince answered that he was not in love with Angel, but that he was instead in love with the mysterious thing that Angel had inside her.

Prince added by saying that Angel was a natural human being, and that he would never be in love with a natural human being, because to be in love with a natural human being, it would be a betrayal for the race of supernatural beings. Prince went on by saying that he hated himself every time when he removed his phantom from his body to kiss Angel, and every time when he would look in her eyes and smile at her and lied to her that he loved her. Hero asked Prince when he was going to use Angel as a guinea pig? Prince answered that he had not set the date yet, that he was going to use Angel as the guinea pig, and it would depend on the chapter on the guinea pig, because he wanted to understand very well that chapter before practicing it on Angel. Prince told Hero that they were going to start to work together very soon, after that he would use Angel as a guinea pig. Both of them must start to spend more time together to work on destroying the race of natural human beings. chapter on the guinea pig would help them to answer all the questions about the body of the natural human being, and after that chapter it would be the time to start the destroying of the race of natural human beings.

Hero did not say a word to Prince, but Hero's heart was beating with fear, he was very worried about Angel, and he was afraid that he would not anymore be able to protect Angel. Prince and Hero spent the rest of the night talking about the traditional feast of the tiger world that would be held in less than six weeks. Prince told Hero that they must leave the world of natural human beings three days before that feast starts. because they must prepare for the feast with all the inhabitants of the tiger world. Both of them went to bed at 3:00 a.m.

# CHAPTER V

# THE WAR BETWEEN THE SUPERNATURAL BEINGS

The days were passing. Hero was not able to go to school and he was spending his entire day at home, but Prince was not aware that Hero was no longer going to school. The phantom of Hero was still in the hospital of the tiger world, and the doctors were still taking care of his phantom. Hero was doing well and his ghost was recovering very well. was spending his entire days at home to think and try to understand what was going on. Hero was trying to understand why his future had changed, why his destiny had changed, why he had become an enemy for his own family, but what he did not understand was the fact that his ancestors were silent about his betrayal.

Philip had spent three days in the secret room to ask the ancestors the reasons why the tiger world was attacked by the supernatural beings of the eagle world. when Philip got out of the secret room, he announced to the inhabitants of the tiger world that the ancestors said that this attack was a mistake, and that they were not the enemies of the eagle world, and that in the future they were going to make a team with the supernatural beings of the eagle world to fight their enemies, and eradicate the race of their enemies. Hero had followed the speech of Philip through his magic, and he was very surprised. He did not understand why the ancestors did not talk to Philip that it was his fault the tiger world was attacked by the supernatural beings of the eagle world. Hero did not understand why the ancestors did not talk to Philip about his betrayal. had attracted the attention of Hero in the speech of Philip, and he was thinking about Philip's words. As Philip had said that the ancestors said that the supernatural beings of the eagle world, and the supernatural beings of the tiger world were going to make a team in the future to fight against their enemies and to eradicate the race of their enemies. Hero started to be afraid, and he knew that the worst was going to happen.

Then, he started thinking about how to protect Angel, even if he knew that it was going to be almost impossible to keep protecting her, especially when the supernatural beings of the tiger world and the supernatural beings of the eagle world would be united to destroy the race of natural human beings. Hero was not really worried about his case, because he knew that sooner or later his family was going to find out that he was a traitor, and he was going to be killed, but Hero was worried about Angel. He was wondering who was going to protect her after he was being killed. Hero was spending his time thinking.

It was Friday morning. Angel and her classmates were in the classroom taking exams, and some students had lifted their heads. They were looking at the door as they had heard footsteps and they were looking with the amused faces as they were seeing Hero who was walking towards his place. The instructor went, and gave the exam paper to Hero, and the whole classroom had turned their heads towards Hero looking at him with surprised faces, and some of them had fear on their faces. It was the first time for Hero to return to school since he had left the classroom bleeding. was staring at the Hero's school bag, and she was noticing that it was the same school bag that had mysteriously disappeared in the office of her mom. was not really surprised because she knew that it was Hero who had taken it, but she was still wondering how he had taken his school bag in her mom's office. And the day spent without a problem, despite some students spent their day with worries inside them, and Angel wanted to talk to Hero their lunch time but unfortunately, Hero had disappeared before lunch time. It was evening. Angel was in her bedroom, and she was in front of her computer. She was making some research

## SUPERNATURAL BEINGS

about the tigers, and the reasons why she was reading the documentaries about the tigers, it was because she was trying to understand who Hero was.

It was morning. Prince was in front of the door of Hero's bedroom and he was knocking at the door. Hero got up and went to open the door. Then, Prince asked Hero to help him to tidy the house as Angel was coming at 1:00 p.m. He was going to use Angel as his guinea pig. Suddenly, Hero's eyes opened widely, with his heart beating with fear as he was staring at Prince. But Hero did not say a word to Prince, except on agreeing to help Prince to tidy up the whole house. Both of them started tidying up the house, and there was a smile on Prince's face as he was working, while Hero's face was empty of expression. Hero knew that he was going to prevent Prince from using Angel as his guinea pig, even if it was going to be his last time to save Angel. Hero was happy that he was doing well. His ghost was completely healed and was inside his body. The hours were passing, and Hero was becoming more and more anxious, especially that his magic was warning him about a danger. Prince had ordered food and wine at home for Angel.

It was 12:00 p.m., Prince and Hero had already finished cleaning the house. Prince was in the living room waiting for Angel, while Hero was walking in his bed room thinking about how he was going to save Angel and preventing Prince to use her as a guinea pig. Hero's heart was beating faster as time was passing, and Angel was in danger as he had not yet found the solution about how to save her. Then, Hero got an idea and that idea was to go talk to Angel about Prince and the reasons why Prince was in a relationship with her. Hero felt that his magic was sending him a message. He turned his head through the wall and the light got out from his eyes and went through the wall and read, "No." He understood that his magic was against his idea to talk to Angel about who Prince was. Hero was wondering why his magic was refusing him to talk about the truth to Angel, and he was becoming nervous as he was thinking about how to save Angel. His magic could not talk to him on how to save her, because the only thing that his magic could do was to warn him about a danger not to give him the solution. Hero turned his head through the wall, and looked at the clock that was on the wall. He noticed that it was already twelve, passed forty-five minutes and he understood that Angel should be there in less than fifteen minutes, and that he no longer had time. Hero looked at the wall and the light got out from his eyes and went through the wall, then he saw Angel in her car through the pictures that were on the wall, and he was noticing that Angel was driving to his home.

Suddenly, Hero turned his head through the window that was opened, and his blue eyes became dark blue, then he turned into a tiger and he jumped out through that window. The tiger ran towards the car, and turned into his supernatural body, then Hero got inside his car and drove away.

Hero was driving faster like a race driver without paying attention to other cars that were on the road. He was driving on the opposite road that Angel was driving on. After eleven minutes of driving, Hero noticed Angel's car on the other side of the road through his magic, and he lowered the window of his car. The light got out from his eyes, and went out through the window, and that light turned into the invisible phantom of Hero, and that invisible phantom started to run towards Angel's car. After a couple of seconds, that invisible ghost reached Angel's car. Angel was still driving. Then, that the invisible phantom bent, and the invisible ghost lifted Angel's car and threw the car in the space. The invisible ghost turned into the light and he went into the space and got inside Angel's car. And people who were in the streets had lifted their heads through the sky, looking at Angel's car that was turning into the space with fear on their faces. Hero was in his car, still driving, and his magic warned him that he was in danger. He suddenly removed his other ghost from his body called again identity phantom to prevent his identity ghost from being hurt in the accident that was going to happen, so the two ghosts of Hero were out of his body.

There were loud screams of people. There were voices of sadness, and the fears in those screams, as they had seen Angel's car that had fallen on Hero's car. Tears were flowing down the cheeks of most people in the street. All the cars on both sides of the road had stopped, and for everyone it was obvious that the people who were in those both cars that had crashed were dead. They did not understand what had happened for the car was thrown into the space.

After less than a minute, the ambulances arrived. Stretcher men were trying to remove Angel and Hero from the cars that had crashed, and there were camera men who were filming the scene of the accident, and the journalists who were making the report. everyone's eyes were opened widely as they were seeing Angel who was carried on the stretcher, and she was not hurt, and there was no blood somewhere on, was just unconscious. Angel was not hurt because the invisible ghost of Hero had protected her in the car when fell on Hero's car. Angel was taken to the hospital. And the people were looking at Hero's car with fear on their faces. of them had tears who were flowing down their cheeks, as they were seeing the rescuers who were breaking Hero's car to remove him inside, because his car was folded. They all thought that Hero was dead, and even the journalists were making the report with sad voices. After less than six minutes, everyone's eyes were opened widely, and the voices of journalists had changed, as they were all seeing Hero who was getting outside of his car by himself. Even the rescuers who were breaking the car had stopped, and they were also looking at Hero with amused faces. Looking at the faces of most people, it was as if they were dreaming, and there were some people who had panic on their faces as they were looking at Hero. His body was full of blood, because Hero had a lot of injuries. And everyone could not believe that Hero had survived in that accident, and for all of them it was a miracle. Hero was taken to the hospital against his will. was in the ambulance and the car was going to the hospital, and the stretcher men were preparing the bandages to take care Hero's wounds. Suddenly, the car started shaking as a stretcher man wanted to take care of Hero's wounds. Everyone in the car started to lose balance like the car was shaking, and stuff was falling in the car. driver was losing the control of the car, and the driver wanted to stop the car, but it was impossible because the car was not stopping.

Except Hero, no one else was understanding what was going on, and it was Hero who was using his invisible phantom to shake the car, because Hero did not want the stretcher men to make the bandage on his wounds. And suddenly, the back door of the car opened, and Hero jumped out of the car. and The light got inside Hero's eyes, and he ran to the sidewalk and he opened the door of a car that was parked on the sidewalk. He got inside that car then, he drove away. Before the stretcher men asked the driver to park the car, Hero was already gone.

Prince was walking in the veranda of his house, angry with his phone in his hand. He was wondering where Angel was, and he had tried to call Angel, but her phone was off. Then, Prince saw three eagles that were flying through his house, and the expression of his face changed as he was feeling that the eagles that were flying through his house were not the natural eagles. Then, those eagles landed on the veranda facing Prince. And suddenly, eyes became dark blue, and he turned into the tiger. The tiger was looking at the eagles, while the eagles were staring at the tiger.

Then, the three eagles turned into two young men and a young woman, and the tiger was still looking at them angrily ready to fight. One of the two men looked at the tiger and said that they were not there to fight, but instead to talk. And the tiger turned into the supernatural body who was Prince. They were looking at each other, then one of those supernatural beings introduced himself to Prince by saying, "I am William." And William turned his head to his left and said, "He is Matt." Then, William turned his head to his right, and he said, "She is Sol." Prince asked them what they wanted, and William told Prince that he had been betrayed by Hero, that Hero was fighting to protect the race of natural human beings. Prince did not believe what William told him, and William asked Prince to use his magic to find out the truth.

After a few minutes of hesitation, Prince invited them inside the house, and they walked to the living room. Prince turned his head through the wall, and the light got out from his eyes and went through the wall. Suddenly, eyes opened widely as he was staring at the wall, and there were the pictures of Hero on the wall who was fighting against William, Sol and Matt in the club to save Angel. William asked Prince to find more pictures Hero's betrayal through his magic, that Hero had betrayed the tiger world before Hero leaves

## SUPERNATURAL BEINGS

the tiger world to come into the world of natural human beings for his mission. William also told Prince that if Angel did not come to her appointment, it was because she had been into an accident, and that it was Hero who had caused the accident to prevent her from coming. Then, Prince turned his head and looked at William. He turned his head again through the wall and the light got out from his eyes and went through the wall, and the pictures appeared on the wall.

Prince was staring at the wall with his face full of anger, as he was seeing everything that Hero had done, how Hero had saved Angel in the lake, how Hero caused the accident of Angel and by looking at Prince, it was obvious that Prince did not believe what he was seeing on the wall. There was silence in the room, and after three minutes, Prince turned his head towards William, and he asked William why they were interested in Angel? William answered to Prince, it is to use his magic to find out the birth of Angel. Then, Prince turned his head through the wall, and the light got out from his eyes and went through the wall. Prince opened his mouth by breathing deeply as he was seeing the birth of Angel through the pictures that were on the wall. Prince started to understand the reasons why Angel got his interest, and why he enjoyed spending time with Angel, and why he was in love with that thing inside Angel.

Prince turned and looked at William, Sol and Matt in silence, while they were looking at him in silence, too. Prince asked them who knew about the secret of Angel. William answered to Prince that except some supernatural beings of the eagle world, nobody else was aware of the secret of Angel, that even Angel herself and her parents were not aware of that secret. Sol said that even Hero who was fighting to protect Angel had no idea of Angel's secret. Prince asked them how Angel's secret was possible? Sol answered that it was a long story. Prince told them that did not understand why the ancestors of the tiger world did not talk about the betrayal of Hero, because the ancestors watched everything that all the supernatural beings of the tiger world did, and that the ancestors of the tiger world communicated with the inhabitants of the tiger world through their king named Philip. added that he talked with Philip many times, and

Philip told him that the ancestors said that everything was alright, and that the ancestors were watching him and Hero.

The ancestors were happy by the way that he and Hero were preparing their mission. Sol looked at Prince by saying that no one could answer that question, except the ancestors themselves who knew the reasons why they did not talk about the betrayal of Hero. replied that he and Hero were sent for this mission to eradicate the race of natural human beings by the ancestors of the tiger world. Sol told Prince that before the ancestors chose Hero and Him for the mission to eradicate the race of natural human beings, Hero had already betrayed the tiger family by saving Angel in the lake. Prince was completely lost, and he was wondering why the ancestors had chosen Hero for that mission, knowing that Hero was a traitor? Why did the ancestors not talk to Philip that Hero had broken one of the most important rules of the tradition of the tiger world by saving a natural human being? Why did the ancestors not order Philip to kill Hero? And why the ancestors were keeping their silence about the betrayal of Hero? Unfortunately, Prince could not answer even one of his questions, but he was sure that the ancestors were aware of Hero's betrayal. Prince opened his mouth and he asked William why Hero was protecting Angel? William answered that he had no idea that there was only Hero who could answer that question. Prince asked William what was their plan? William answered that the tiger world and the eagle world had the same goal, and that goal was to destroy the race of natural human beings. Prince asked them why the supernatural beings of the eagle world wanted to eradicate the race of natural human beings? William answered that the supernatural beings of the eagle world wanted to destroy the race of natural human beings for the same reasons that the supernatural beings of the tiger world wanted to destroy the race of natural human beings. Sol looked at Prince by saying that the natural human beings were responsible for destroying the race of supernatural beings in the past. Prince replied that he was aware of the story that had happened more than a century ago.

Then, Prince told them that he was ready to make a team with them, because together it would be easy to eradicate the race of natural human beings. William looked in Prince's eyes and he told Prince that the world of tiger was attacked a couple of days by the supernatural beings of the eagle world, and if they had attacked the tiger world, it was to get their revenge on Hero who was preventing them from killing Angel. Prince asked what had happened during the attack? William answered that they had lost two of their brothers during the fight, and their two brothers were killed by Hero. Prince asked if Hero was in the tiger world during the fight? William replied that the phantom of Hero was in the tiger world during the fight, and that Hero was fighting through his phantom.

Then, Prince looked at the wall, and the light got out from his eyes and went through the wall, and Prince was watching the fight that had happened in the tiger world through the pictures that were on the wall. Prince understood that the marks that he had seen on Hero's forehead were coming from Hero's phantom, and that Hero's ghost had got those marks during the fight against the supernatural beings of the eagle world. Prince realized that Hero had lied to him during all those times, and his anger started to appear on his face as he was seeing the ghosts of supernatural beings of the tiger world that were in the hospital, like those ghosts had got hurt during the fight. Then, Prince turned his head towards William, Sol and Matt. Prince opened his mouth to talk, and Sol looked in the eyes of Prince, and the green eyes of Sol became blue. Suddenly Prince closed his mouth, and William and Matt turned their heads and they looked at Sol, as William and Matt had understood why Prince had suddenly closed his mouth when Prince wanted to talk.

Prince, William, Sol and Matt spent the rest of the afternoon planning about how to destroy the race of natural human beings, and William asked Prince to help the eagle family to kill Angel, and Prince agreed to help them to kill Angel. Sol told Prince that the only thing that Prince was going to do was to try to convince Angel to remove her rosaries, or he should remove the rosaries from Angel by himself. Then, the supernatural beings of the eagle world would come and kill Angel by themselves, because it was impossible for the supernatural beings of the eagle world to kill Angel with the rosaries that she wore on her. Sol also told Prince that it was necessary to kill

Angel, because they would never succeed in eradicating the race of the natural human beings when they would not have buried Angel first. But, they all knew that it was not going to be easy to kill Angel, because she was protected by Hero, and Hero had two advantage on them, the first advantage was that Hero had an advance on the time like his magic was connected to the future, and the second advantage was the double ghost of Hero, so Hero could fight against many people at the same time, by using his identity phantom, and his invisible phantom.

It was evening. Angel was in the hospital, and she sat on the hospital bed while she was talking with her parents and Bella who had come to visit her, and Angel was doing well, but she was waiting for the results of her x-rays to make sure that she had not broken somewhere in her body. Angel has not remembered anything about the accident, the only thing she remembered was that she was on the road driving through Prince's home, and she woke up in the hospital bed. And there was the television that was turned on in the hospital, but they were talking without paying attention to what the television was showing. Then, a doctor walked inside the bedroom of Angel, and they all turned their heads looking at the doctor who was coming through them. The doctor walked close to her bed, and told Angel that he wanted to do a check up on her, and the doctor asked Angel to lie on the bed with her back. Suddenly, they all turned their heads towards Bella as they had heard Bella cry out, "Oh, my god." And they noticed that Bella had her head turned through the television, and they all turned their heads towards the television. Immediately, their eyes opened widely as they were watching the accident of Angel in the news. Then, Angel cried out, "Hero?" And she started to breathe deeply as she was seeing Hero who was getting out of his car during the accident. She was seeing Hero who was taken to the hospital in the ambulance. Then, Angel got off from her bed, and she started to run through the door without saying a word. Rebecca started running after Angel by screaming Angel's name. Angel was running in the hallway of the hospital, and people who were walking in the corridor had turned their heads looking at Angel and wondering what was going on with her.

Then, Angel stopped to a nurse who was walking in the hallway and Angel asked to the nurse where was the emergency department, and the nurse showed Angel where the emergency department was. Then, Angel ran to the emergency department, and she asked people who were working in that department that she wanted to see the young man who had been in the accident this afternoon, then she explained that it was her car that had crashed on the car of that young man. Then, a nurse asked Angel to wait, that she was going to call one of the ambulance men who was at the scene of the accident, and the nurse turned and walked away, while Angel was waiting with a worried face.

After a few minutes, a man joined Angel, and he told Angel that he was at the scene of the accident. He was one of people who had helped Hero to get inside ambulance, then the surprise appeared on Angel's face as she heard the man talks about how Hero had jumped out of the ambulance, and that Hero had run away in a car that he had stolen on the sidewalk. Angel turned and started walking away without uttering a word, and without even letting the man finish to talk to her. Angel was walking in the corridors of the hospital thinking without even knowing where she was going. Angel was not really surprised to hear that Hero had run away when he was in the ambulance, and she was wondering how Hero survived in that accident, especially that people had only broken his car to remove him inside, and she was also wondering how herself had survived in that accident, she did not even get hurt.

Angel started to remember the images of the accident that she had seen in the news a couple of minutes ago, and she remembered too, that at the moment of the accident, she was going to Prince's home and she was driving to the right side of the road. But, when she watched the accident on the television, her car was on the left side of the road, and her car had crashed into Hero's car. Hero was driving to the left side of the road, also her car was on Hero's car, like if her car had fallen on Hero's car coming from the sky. Then, there were a lot of questions that were going on in Angel's mind like, how her car left the right side of the road to go crash on Hero's car that was on the left side of the road? Why did she not remember something about the accident? How did the accident happen? And why among all the cars that were on the road, her car crashed on Hero's car? Angel understood that it was Hero who had caused that accident, and she was wondering why he had caused that accident, but she could not answer that question.

Angel stopped walking, and she was staring at a room, as she was seeing kids in that room who were sick, and some of those kids were suffering from disability issues, and she walked through the door of that room. She met a doctor on her way, and Angel greeted the doctor. She asked the doctor what the kids in the room were suffering from? doctor replied to Angel that she was in the department that takes care of kids who were suffering from all kinds of diseases, and whose families did not have money to pay for the treatment of their kids. They took care of those kids, thanks to the donation. Angel asked the doctor how to make the donations, and the doctor took Angel to the reception area. doctor gave a brochure to Angel with all the information on it, and she asked doctor if she could visit the department to see the kids. And the doctor agreed. He told her that he was going to call someone, who should show her all the rooms, but Angel replied that she could visit alone, and that she would not be long. Then, the doctor agreed, and left. Angel was walking in a large room between the beds, and she was staring at those kids who were lying on those beds. Angel turned her head from behind as she had felt a hand on her shoulder coming from behind, and she looked in the eyes of Prince who was looking at her, too.

Then, Prince opened his arms and Angel turned. She walked in the arms of Prince, and he had taken Angel in his arms and none of them was talking. After a couple of seconds, Angel turned her head and looked in Prince's eyes by asking him how he was aware of the accident? Prince answered her that he had watched the accident in the news. Angel asked him how he found her in that room? Prince answered her that when he reached the hospital, he noticed that everyone was looking for her, and he was very worried, then he started looking for her in the hospital, and fortunately, he found her. But Prince was lying, because he had used his magic to find Angel. Prince told Angel that they must go, because her parents were very worried, and Angel started to explain to Prince what she was doing in that room. But she noticed that Prince was not interested in the situation of those kids that she was talking about, then she told Prince that they have to leave. Both of them started walking through Angel's bedroom, and they met Angel's parents and Bella on their way who were looking for Angel. told Angel that they had received the results of Angel's x-rays and that everything was fine, that they could return home. Then, they all walked to the hospital bedroom of Angel, and she changed her clothes, then they all left the hospital.

Hero sat in the living room of his house. He had his eyes focused on the wall that was facing him, and looking at Hero, it was obvious that he was thinking, and was worried too. Hero knew that Prince was aware of his betrayal, because he had found out through his magic the meeting between Prince, William, Sol and Matt, but Hero did not know exactly of what William, Prince, Sol and Matt had talked about. Hero had listened to their conversation when the conversation has ended. Hero knew that Prince would call the tiger world to talk about his betrayal, but Hero was not worried about what was going to happen to him. He was very worried about Angel. Hero heard the footsteps in the house, and he understood that the time had come, and he got up from his chair. He turned his head towards the front door, and his eyes met with Prince's eyes. Hero noticed the fury in Prince's eyes, and they were staring at each other in silence., the anger appeared on Prince's face, and he started to breathe deeply. Suddenly, Hero's eyes became dark blue and he turned into the tiger, as he had seen Prince who had turned into the tiger. The two tigers started running through each other, then they started fighting. The tigers were fighting inside the house with the anger in their eyes. were jumping in the house breaking stuff, and they were running everywhere in the house fighting. After half an hour, both tigers were still fighting with the same energy and same rage, then they heard the sirens of the police cars that were coming towards their house.

They understood that the neighbors had called the police, like there were noises of the fight coming from their house. Then, one of the tigers jumped through the window, and hit the window's glass with his head and the glass window broke, and the tiger jumped out, and that tiger turned into the body of supernatural being who was Hero. He started to run away while his forehead was bleeding as he had broken the glass window with his head. The other tiger was groaning in the living room, then an eagle flew inside the house through the window where Hero had got out, and that eagle landed on the floor facing the tiger, and that eagle turned into the body of supernatural being who was Sol. The tiger turned into the body of supernatural being who was Prince. Both Sol and Prince were looking at each other, and Prince asked Sol what she was doing there. Sol answered Prince that she came to help him. Then, they heard the police who was knocking at the door, and Prince told Sol that they must run away. He did not want to answer the questions of the police. Sol replied to Prince to not worry, that it was the reason why she came. The police were kept knocking at the door, but Prince and Sol were just looking at each other with the silence.

Then, they heard the door open, and heard the footsteps in the house, as they turned their heads towards the corridor of the entrance to the house. They saw three policemen who were walking towards them, and they turned to face those policemen. And one of the policemen opened his mouth to talk, and Sol looked in the policeman's eyes, and her green eyes became blue, then the policeman closed his mouth. Then, Sol did the same thing by looking in the eyes of the other two policemen and her green eyes changed to blue, and all those policemen were just looking at the mess that was inside the house without saying a word. After a few minutes, those policemen turned their heads and left without saying a word, then Prince and Sol sat, and they started talking.

Angel was in her bedroom and sat in front of her computer. She was trying to understand who Hero was by doing some research about the tigers, the vampires and the immortal people thought that Hero belonged to one of those three families, first to the tigers because Hero was acting something like a tiger, mostly when he was fighting. Second, to the vampires because Hero was fighting against the vampires who wanted to kill her. Angel thought that the supernatural beings of the eagle world were the vampires as she was seeing them turned into the shape of the eagles. And third to the immortal, because Hero could not fight against all those vampires if he was a dying human being, and Hero could not survive in that accident that had happened if he was a dying human being. Angel had spent her whole night doing some research to try to understand who Hero was, while Hero was in a hotel room. He was following what Angel was doing through his magic, and it was funny for him to see that Angel was doing some research to find out who he was.

The next day, Prince, Sol, William and Matt had spent one part of their day together to talk about their plan, and Hero had followed their conversation through his magic while in the hotel bedroom where Hero was living. But Hero did not get all the information that he was expecting in the conversation of Prince, William, Sol and Matt, because he was expecting them to talk about the reasons why they wanted to kill Angel. But they did not talk about it, and they just talked about killing Angel and destroying the race of natural human beings. Something had attracted Hero's attention when he heard them talk how it was important for them to kill Angel if they wanted to destroy the race of natural human beings. That if Angel is alive it would be impossible for them to destroy the race of natural human beings. Only the supernatural beings of the eagle world could kill Angel, and Prince would make sure that Angel would not have her rosaries on her wrist and on her ankle at the moment when one of the supernatural beings of the eagle world would like to kill Angel. Hero also had heard them say that Angel was a natural human being. He was very confused, and did not understand what was the mystery that was on Angel.

They were a lot of questions that were going on in his mind like, why was it necessary to kill Angel before starting to destroy the race of natural human beings? Why with Angel alive, it was impossible to destroy the race of natural human beings? Why would the supernatural beings of the eagle world not kill Angel with the rosaries on her? Why only the supernatural beings of the eagle world would kill Angel? But unfortunately, Hero could not answer any of his questions.

Hero started to think that it was impossible to eradicate the race of natural human beings with Angel alive, as he had heard Prince, Sol,

William and Matt say in their conversation. It could mean that Angel could be the mysterious unknown enemy who had mystically blocked one part of his magic and one part of Prince's magic, to prevent them from destroying the race of natural human beings. three hours of thinking and using his magic, Hero understood that it was impossible for Angel to be that mysterious enemy s. The first reason was that Angel was a real natural human being, as he had heard Prince, Sol, William and Matt talked about, and that the mysterious enemy who was protecting the race of the natural human beings was not a natural human being. Every time he tried to find out who was that mysterious enemy through his magic, his magic told him that that enemy was not a natural human being, and even the magic of Prince had told him that the mysterious enemy was not a natural human being. Second reason, Angel was visible but according to Hero's magic the mysterious enemy was invisible. Third reason, Angel was living in the land of the natural human beings while the mysterious enemy is not living in the land of the natural human beings. The fourth reason was that Angel does not have any magic or special powers. The mysterious enemy is known to have it's magic and power. Hero's ghost had been detected by Angel's magic or power if she ever had. Also, Hero should know if Angel is different because he has the capacity to see if the person has magic or special powers regardless if he is a vampire, natural human being or supernatural human being. And the last reason was that Angel doesn't know that the supernatural being exists but the real enemy knew everything about the supernatural being. Because if Angel already knew the existence of supernatural beings then, she should have not made the research about the tiger, vampire, etc. She would have known the very first time that he saved her on the lake and at the club. Hero understood that if Angel was not their mysterious enemy, and that it was important for Prince, William, Sol and Matt to kill her before starting the project of destroying the race of natural human beings,. And that there was also a secret on the life of Angel, so Hero spent his whole evening and night to think about the secret of Angel's life.

The next day, it was 9:00 a.m., Hero walked in his classroom, he went to sit in his place, and the students had turned their heads looking at him, even the instructor, and they were all wondering who Hero was. As they had all seen Hero in the news, getting out of his car that had crashed with his body full of blood, then, the instructor took a deep breath and asked Hero if everything was fine? Hero replied that he was doing great.

Then, the instructor told Hero that she watched the accident in the news, and that he and Angel were very lucky to survive last Saturday. Hero looked at the instructor without saying a word, then he got up from his chair and he ran through the door without taking his school's bag with him. He got out of the classroom, and everyone had just looked at him without understanding what was going on. Angel turned her head in Hero's place, she started to stare at his school bag that was on his table, and got an idea. Angel got up from her chair, and she started to walk through the table of Hero by staring at his school bag, then the invisible phantom of Hero passed at Angel and took Hero's school bag.

Suddenly, Angel stopped walking as she had noticed that Hero's school bag that she was going to take had disappeared. was not really surprised, and understood that Hero knew that she was going to take his school bag to find the information about him. Angel turned, and walked to her table. The day was doing well for Angel, until she went to see the one responsible for the sport of the university named Charly. She told him that she wanted to organize a basketball game with her friends in the university. She told Charly that she wanted to sell tickets to raise funds for the kids who are handicapped and other disabilities in the hospital. But Charly refused. left Charly's office with sadness and disappointment on her face, and she did not return in class, she immediately went home without finishing her entire class at school.

It was evening. Angel was in her bedroom in front of her computer, and she was trying to find the information online about how to raise the funds for the hospital. Prince was in his house, and he was following what Angel was doing through his magic. Prince had not seen Angel during the day, he had called, and she did not pick up, but she had sent him a message by saying that she was not feeling well, and that she would call him the next day. Prince knew well that

Angel was not feeling well, because Charly who was responsible of the s university sport had turned down her proposition, about the game that she wanted to organize to raise the funds for the hospital. Prince was not anymore interested in school, and for the first time he had spent a day without opening his books, even during the day in class he was not paying attention to what the instructors were saying.

Prince was now focused on Angel, he had spent his whole day following her through his magic, to see if she was going to meet Hero. Prince wanted to make Angel believe that he was deeply in love with her, so Angel had become his goal. Hero sat in his bedroom at his hotel room. He was trying to find some information on how to help Angel in raising some funds and he was aware of what she was doing through his magic. Hero knew too that the proposition of Angel to organize the game to the university had been rejected, because he had followed Angel all day through his magic, and he had watched the meeting between Angel and Charly. Angel went to bed at 3:00 a.m., Prince and Hero closed their eyes a half hour after that Angel was deeply asleep.

It was 8:00 a.m., Hero walked into the university sport office, he sat and introduced himself to Charly as Chris. It was a fake name. Then, Hero told Charly about the game that Angel wanted to organize to raise funds for the hospital. He told Charly too, that he should accept the proposition of Angel to organize that game for the kids who were sick. And when Charly opened his mouth to talk, the light got out from Hero's eyes and went and shone on Charly, then he agreed to organize the game. He asked the contact number of Angel. Hero used his magic to find Angel's, then Hero wrote the email and phone number of Angel down a sheet of paper and gave it to Charly. Then, Hero left the office of Charly, and he went in class. Hero left Charly's office and went to his class. Angel was in class when she received an email from Charly. Her face was full of joy as she read the email and she noticed that Charly changed his mind and agreed to her proposal about the game to raised funds. During break time, Angel went to see Charly and talked about how they could organize the game and agreed that the game will be fixed on a Saturday. Angel's friends would play versus the university's team. Then, Angel and Bella were spending their day talking about the game and how to raise the funds. They tried to find players and Angel had asked Prince to play but he refused, saying that he hated basketball. She was a little disappointed with Prince's attitude knowing that he was not supportive to her fundraising project. The days had passed. Angel was so busy in preparing for the game for the fundraising until she was not paying attention anymore to her studies. She even forgot about her research about Hero. Prince was very angry about the fundraising project because Angel has put so much energy on it that she doesn't have any time on him anymore. For the first time they argued with each other. Prince was aware of everything that Angel was doing, because he was following her each second through his magic, and Hero was spending his time to follow Angel through his magic, too. Every night, Hero was watching basketball on television, and he was trying to understand the rules of the game.

It was the eve of the game for the fundraising, and Angel had laid in her bed to get rest, and she was so tired that she closed her eyes without knowing it, and there was the invisible phantom of Hero who was standing up in her bedroom, and who was staring at her. After three hours, the invisible phantom of Hero turned his head, and he saw the stuffs of Angel on her study table, then he walked till that table and he took the pen that was on the table, and he opened a notebook and he tore a sheet of paper, then he wrote on that sheet of paper. Then, he walked till close to the bed, without closing the notebook that he had opened on the study's table, and he put that sheet of paper close to Angel, then he turned, and he walked till the door, and he opened the door and he left.

After an hour, Angel opened her eyes, as she had heard her mom who was calling her by knocking at her door, and Angel wanted to get up from the bed when a sheet of paper that was close to her attracted her attention, and she took that sheet of paper and she looked at it, then she read, "You are so beautiful, and you are so sweet when you are asleep." And Angel started wondering where that sheet of paper was coming from, and who had written those words and who had put it on her bed. And she started to think if it was herself who had put that sheet of paper on her bed, and she remembered that it could not be her, because no one had given her that sheet of paper, and she looked at it again very well, by thinking that it could be Prince who had given it to her and she forgot, but she noticed that the writing that was on that sheet of paper was not the handwriting of Prince. Then, she got up from the bed, and she started to walk through the door to go open the door to her mom who was still knocking at her door, by calling her, then a book on her study's table attracted her attention, and she walked till her study table and she looked at her stuffs, and she noticed that someone had touched her stuffs.

And Angel looked at the notebook that was opened on her study's table, and she noticed that someone had torn a sheet of paper in that notebook, and she looked at the sheet of paper that was in her hand, and she noticed that the sheet of paper that was in hand had been torn from the notebook that was in front of her. And she started to look with attention to the writing that was on the sheet of paper that she had in her hand, then she cried out, "Hero?" With her eyes widely opened, as she had remembered the handwriting of Hero that she had seen in his notebook the day he had left the classroom by bleeding, as she had taken his stuffs that day to analyse the blood that was on his book, and she also remembered the writing that was on the sheet of paper that Hero had given to their classmate the day they were taken exam in class. And she noticed that the writing that she had seen in the notebook of Hero was the same writing that had seen on the sheet of paper that Hero had given to their classmate, and it was also the same writing that was on the sheet of paper that she had in her hand, then she understood that it was Hero who had put that sheet of paper in her bed. And she started to wonder how Hero got in her bedroom, and at what time he got in her bedroom, and she looked again at that sheet of paper in her hand, and she read again what Hero had written.

Then, Angel got an idea, and she pulled the chair and she sat, and she turned on her computer, then she continued to make the research on Hero, as she had stopped it, without paying attention to her mom who was still knocking at her door. And she spent her whole night doing research on Hero.

## SUPERNATURAL BEINGS

The next day, it was 1:00 p.m., Angel was sitting in the stadium stands in the middle of Prince and Bella, and the stadium was full of people and they were all waiting for the game to start. And there were also William, Sol and Matt who were sitting in the stadium stands, but they were hiding among the crowd and Angel could not see them. After a few minutes, the players started to walk in the stadium and the eyes of Angel, Prince, Bella, Matt, Sol and William were opened widely, as they were all seeing Hero who was walking in the stadium between the players and Hero was in the team of Angel's friends. Bella turned her head towards Angel, and she looked in Angel's eyes by asking, "Are you the one who invited Hero to play?" Angel answered, "No." And she added, "You know well that we do not talk to each other." Bella asked, "Who invited Hero to play?" Angel replied, "Only Hero can answer that question." And she added, "Do not forget that you are the only student who Hero talks with." Bella said, "Hero is so mysterious." And she added, "Let's watch the game. I would ask Hero later about the one who invited him to play."

Then, both Angel and Bella turned their heads through the stadium, and Prince had heard the conversation between Angel and Bella. Then, Prince used his magic to know who had invited Hero to play that game, and he found out through his magic that Hero had used his invisible phantom to get inside the office of Charly to write his name, on the list of the names that Angel had given to Charly. The game was going to start, and the eyes of Angel were focused on Hero. After three minutes that the game had started and the eyes of everyone were focused on Hero, they were all amazed by the way that Hero was playing, how Hero was faster, how he was not losing the ball, and the way that he was taking the ball to his opponents, how he was blocking all the balls that his opponents wanted to score, and how he was scoring all his balls. After a half hour of game, everyone was fascinated by the way that Hero was playing, even people who were not supporting his team were stupefied by the way that he was playing, and all the eyes were only focused on him, even the eyes of the supporters of the opposing team. And Hero had still the same energy that he had started the game with, he was everywhere on the stadium, and he was sometimes using his invisible phantom to prevent his opponents from scoring. When Hero was on the other side of the stadium, and that one of his opponents had the ball and wanted to score, the light was getting out from Hero's eyes and going through his opponent who had ball and who wanted to score, and that light was turning into his invisible phantom, and that invisible phantom pushed the ball away to prevent his opponent to score when his opponent was throwing the ball in the basket. And people thought that it was the opponents of Hero who had the difficulties to score, except Prince, William, Sol and Matt who knew who Hero was, and who knew that Hero was using his invisible phantom to prevent his opponents from scoring.

After an hour of game, the team of Hero had already scored more than one hundred goals, and Hero had scored one hundred-nine of the goals of his team, and the opposing team had not even scored a goal, and both teams had already made the replacements of all their players, except Hero who had not been replaced yet. There was the anger on the face of Prince, Sol, Matt and William as they were seeing Hero who was playing, and as they hearing the whole stadium clapping their hands each time when Hero had the ball in his hands, and they were angry when they were hearing the whole stadium scream the name of Hero at each time when Hero was scoring. There was joy on the face of people as they were watching Hero play, and William turned his head towards Sol by looking in her eyes, and he told Sol to make the team of Hero lose the game. And Sol answered William that it was impossible for her to make the team of Hero lose, because she could not look in the eyes of the teammates of Hero, as Hero's teammates were running everywhere in the stadium. And as Hero's teammates were all focused on the ball, and that the only way for her to make the team of Hero lose, it was that her eyes be in contact with the eyes of the teammates of Hero.

Angel was watching the game with a silence, and her eyes were still focused on Hero, and she was not clapping her hands or screaming when Hero was scoring the ball, she was just watching at Hero play, with her heart that was beating faster than the normal, and there were the images of tiger that was going on in the mind of Angel every time when Hero was jumping. As Angel was watching Hero play, she was remembering the stories on the tigers that she had read online, and all the videos of the tigers that she had watched online, and she was noticing that Hero was behaving exactly like a tiger, that Hero was jumping, running and moving like a tiger. It lacked three minutes for the end of the game, and Hero was replaced, and the whole stadium had got up, and they were all clapping their hands to Hero who was getting out, even Angel had got up and for the first time, Angel was clapping her hands as Hero was walking out of the stadium.

Except, Prince, Sol, William and Matt who did not get up, and they were not even clapping their hands, and they were just looking at Hero who was getting out of the stadium with the rage on their faces. Then, Angel started to climb down the stands by running among the crowd, and Bella was screaming the name of Angel by asking her where she was going, but Angel was not paying attention to Bella who was screaming her name. And Prince was still sitting in his place quiet, and he knew well where Angel was going. Hero was walking in the hallway, and he turned his head from behind, as he was hearing his name who was screaming by someone, and he was looking at Angel who was running through him, then he turned face to her as she was close to him. Both Angel and Hero were looking at each other eyes in eyes with silence. Then, Angel broke the silence and asked, "Who invited you to play this game?"

Hero replied, "It's your way to say thank you?"

Angel asked, "Who are you?"

Hero replied, "You screamed my name less than a minute ago."

Angel said, "I am not asking your name."

Hero asked, "What do you want?"

Angel answered, "I want to know who you are."

Hero said, "I do not understand your question."

Angel said, "You know well what I mean."

Hero said, "I am not a magician to know what is going on in your mind."

Angel opened her mouth to talk and the light got out from Hero's eyes and went through her, and Angel was trying to talk but her mouth was shaking, and no word was coming out from her mouth like that light that had got out from Hero's eyes was shining on her. And Hero was staring at Angel with a surprised face. Then Angel took a deep breath and she looked in the eyes of Hero by saying, "You are acting like a magician."

Hero asked, "What do you mean?"

Angel replied, "I am talking about your school's bag that disappeared in the office of my mom, and in the classroom."

Hero said, "I do not know what you are talking about."

Angel asked, "How did you put the letter in my bedroom last night?"

Hero replied, "Still, I do not know what you are talking about."

Angel said, "I did the research on the tigers, and I found out that you act exactly like the tigers."

Hero stared in Angel's eyes by saying, "You should start to make the research on yourself to try to find out who exactly you are first, before making the researches on me to know who I am."

Angel looked at Hero with a surprised face, by asking, "What do you mean by I should start to make the research on myself, to try to find out first who I am?"

Then, both Hero and Angel were looking at each other eyes in eyes with a silence, then Hero saw Prince who came through them, and Hero turned, and he walked away without pronouncing a word and Angel was staring at Hero who was walking away. Then, Prince came, and he took Angel in his arms, and Prince asked Angel if everything was going well? And Angel answered that everything was all right. Then, Prince told Angel that Charly was looking for her. Angel looked at Prince by asking who was Charly? Prince answered that Charly was the responsible for the sport of the university, and Angel told Prince that she was sorry, that there were a lot of things that were going on in her mind, that she even forgot who Charly was. Then, Both Angel and Prince walked till the stadium, and they met other people, and people were congratulating Angel for the fundraising game that she had organized, but Angel was not really focused on conversations with people. Angel's mind was focused on the conversation she had had a couple minutes ago with Hero, and she was remembering the words that Hero had told her, as she should start to make the research on herself to try to find out first who she was.

Angel was wondering what the meaning of the words of Hero were, and why he asked her to do the research on herself, but unfortunately Angel could not answer even one of those two questions. And people were talking about Hero, and they were asking Angel where Hero was, and they were asking other questions to Angel about Hero, but unfortunately Angel could not answer any of their questions, because herself she had no idea about who Hero was. Then, Charly joined Angel, and he told Angel that he wanted to meet with Chris, because he wanted Chris to be part of the basketball team of the university. Angel asked Charly who was Chris? Charly answered that Chris was the one who had come to his office, to convince him to accept the proposition she had made to him to organize the game to raise the funds for an hospital, and that Chris was also the one who had given him her contacts. And Angel replied to Charly that still she did not know who Chris was.

Then, Charly told Angel that Chris was the best player who was playing with her friends, and that everyone had applauded in the stadium. Then, Angel understood that Charly was talking about Hero, and she looked at Charly without saying a word, then she turned, and she started to run away, and Charly was looking at her running away with an astonished face, without understanding what was going on with her. Angel was running in the yard of the university without even knowing where she was going, then a car parked near to her and she stopped running and she stared at that car, and she saw Prince get outside of that car. Then, both Prince and Angel looked at each other without saying a word, and Prince walked till the other side of the car, and he opened the car's door, and he turned his head looking at Angel. And Angel walked till close of Prince and she got inside the car without uttering a word, and Prince closed the car door, and he walked till the other of the car, and he opened the car's door, and he got inside the car, then he drove away. After eleven minutes of driving, Prince and Angel had not uttered a word, then Prince broke the silence by asking, "What is going on with you?"

Angel asked, "What do you mean?" without even looking at him.

Prince said, "Since your accident, you are not the same person."

Angel said, "Maybe it's the effects of the accident."

Prince said, "Or maybe it's the effects of your lover."

Angel turned her head through Prince by asking, "Which lover?"

Prince replied, "You know well, who I am talking about."

Angel said, "The only lover I have it's you."

Prince said, "I noticed the way you look at him."

Angel said, "Still I do not know who you are talking about."

Prince said, "Hero."

Angel turned her head through Prince, and she looked at him without saying a word. And Prince said, "I thought that there was no secret between a couple."

Angel asked, "What do you mean?"

Prince asked, "Since, when you are in love with Hero?"

Angel answered, "Hero is my classmate."

Prince asked, "Are you in love with him?" Angel did not say a word. And after three minutes, Prince broke the silence and said, "Your silence means yes?"

Angel turned her head and she looked at Prince and said, "Please, let's have this conversation another day."

Prince asked, "Why not now?" Angel answered, "I need some time and I would explain everything to you." And Prince looked at her without saying a word, and after three minutes of driving, Prince parked the car in the yard of Angel's house, and Angel got out of the car without saying a word to Prince, and she walked till the door of her house, then she opened the door and she got inside, and she locked the door behind her, then Prince drove way.

Hero was in his hotel bedroom, and he was walking inside his bedroom like a crazy man, with a question that was going on in his mind, and that question was, who was Angel? Hero did not understand why his magic did not have the effect on Angel, when he had made the light get out from his eyes and shine on Angel during his conversation with Angel in the corridor of the university. Hero did not understand why that light that had got out of his eyes and shone on Angel did not change the thinking of Angel, because that light should have had an effect on Angel's brain, and Angel should change her thinking once when that light had shone on her. And Hero started to remember about the conversation he had had with Angel during the day in the hallway of the university, and he was remembering how Angel was reacting when that light was shining on her, how her mouth was shaking and how she had the difficulties to talk, but that light did not change her thought.

Then, Hero understood that there was a reason why the light that had got out from his eyes and shone on Angel did not change the thinking of Angel, but he did not know what that reason was. And although the fact that Hero knew well that Angel was a natural human being, he knew too that she had something different from the rest of the race of natural human beings that he did not know what it was. And the fact that the light that had got out from his eyes and shone on Angel did not have the effect on her, was proof that Angel had something different from the rest of natural human beings, even if she was a natural human being. Because, Hero had the power to change people's thinking, and if Hero had not succeeded to change the thinking of Angel through his magic, that meant that Angel was special. And Hero spent his whole night to think and to try to understand the reasons why the light that had got out from his eyes and shone on Angel did not have an effect on her.

The days were passing, and Angel was not anymore paying attention to school, although the fact that she was still going to school and she was spending her time to read the books about the tigers, the immortal and the vampires because she was trying to understand who Hero was. And by reading those books Angel had found out that Hero had nothing in common with the vampires and the immortals, but that Hero had a lot of things in common with the tigers, that his behavior was similar to the behavior of the tigers. Angel was wondering how it was possible that a human being could be a tiger, and she could understand that a human being could be a vampire or an immortal, but she could not understand that a human being could be a tiger. Angel was completely lost, and she was spending her time wondering why Hero had a lot of things in common with the tigers, but she could not answer that question. And Hero and Angel had not talked to each other again since they last talked in the hallway of the university, although the fact that they were seeing each other everyday at school. And the relationship between Prince and Angel was going well, and they were seeing each other everyday, and Prince was spending most of his evening with William, Sol and Matt to talk about their plan. But Hero was aware of everything that Prince, William, Sol and Matt were talking about, because he was following them through his magic.

It was 1:00 p.m., Angel and her classmates were in the classroom, and they had just returned from their break time, and there was a sheet of paper on each table that the instructor had put. Then, the instructor demanded everyone to find a partner and to do the exercise that was on the sheet of paper on their table, but that their partner would not be their table's neighbors. Bella wanted to get up, and Angel put her hand on Bella's hand, and she looked in Bella's eyes by demanding to Bella where she was going, and Bella answered that she was going to work with Hero, because she was the only student who Hero talks with. Angel asked Bella to wait, then Angel turned her head from behind, and she stared at Hero who sat alone in his place, and there was an empty chair close to Hero, and there was also the sheet of paper of the assessment in the middle of the table. Then, Angel got up from her chair, and Bella demanded to know where she was going, and Angel answered that she was going to work with Hero, and Angel walked till Hero's table, and she sat in the empty chair that was near to Hero. Angel turned her head through Hero, and said, "Hi."

Hero looked at her and said, "Hi."

Angel said, "I am here for the work that the instructor asked us to do."

Hero pushed the paper that was in the middle of the table in front of Angel without saying a word, and Angel looked at that sheet of paper in front of her, then she looked at him, and she said, "I am sorry."

Hero asked, "For what?" In a low voice

Angel answered, "For my behavior."

Hero looked into Angel's eyes and asked, "What do you mean?"

Angel answered, "You did a lot for me, and I have never said thank you to you."

Hero said, "It's okay." Then he bent his head.

Angel said, "I am aware that you are the one who had convinced Charly to organize that game for the charity."

Hero looked at her and said, "I just wanted to help you."

Angel said, "Thank you." And she asked, "What are you going to do this weekend?"

Hero replied, "Nothing."

Angel said, "We can hang out this weekend together."

Hero asked, "Are you asking me to go out with you this weekend?"

Angel answered, "Yes, I am asking you to go out with me this weekend."

Hero said, "Sorry, I already have a plan for this weekend."

Angel said, "You told me less than a minute ago, that you had nothing to do this weekend."

Hero said, "Sorry, I had forgotten that I had something to do."

Angel asked, "Are you going to be busy the whole weekend?"

Hero answered, "Yes."

Angel asked, "How about tomorrow?"

Hero answered, "We have class tomorrow."

Angel said, "We can miss class tomorrow, and spend the time together."

Hero asked, "Why not spend the time with your boyfriend?"

Angel looked into Hero's eyes with disappointment on her face and said, "I thought that we could be friends."

Hero said, "I am not looking for friends"

Angel said, "I think we should start to work."

Then, Angel turned her head through the sheet of paper that was in front of her, then she lifted her head through the instructor by listening to the instructor who was asking them if they had finished, and most students replied to the instructor that they had not yet finished. And the instructor told them that they had three minutes to finish. Then, Hero turned his head through the sheet of paper that was in front of Angel, and the light got out from Hero's eyes and shone on that sheet of paper that was in front of Angel and the writings appeared on that sheet of paper. Angel turned her head through Hero, and she looked in his eyes by saying, "We have less than three minutes to do our work."

Hero replied, "We already finished."

Angel asked, "What do you mean?"

Hero replied, "Look at the sheet of paper that is in front of you." Then, Angel bent her head through the sheet of paper that was in front of her, and her eyes opened widely as she was staring at that sheet of paper, and as she was noticing that Hero had already done the work, and she remembered that six seconds ago when she looked at that sheet of paper, there were not the writings on that sheet of paper. Then, Angel turned her head through Hero, and she looked in his eyes by asking, "How did you do it?"

Hero asked, "Did you still want to hang out with me this weekend?"

Angel answered, "Of course not." Then, Angel got up and she left.

The rest of the day finished well, and both Angel and Hero had not spoken to each other again. The next day was the last day of the week, and Hero was in the classroom sitting alone in his place, and most of the students were not yet in the classroom. Then, Bella walked inside the classroom, and she went, and she sat in the empty chair that was close to Hero and she started talking with Hero. After a few minutes, Angel walked inside the classroom, then she stopped immediately when her eyes saw Hero and Bella who were talking, and Angel smiled at Bella by greeting Bella, and Angel looked at Hero with an expressionless face that meant a face without joy and without sadness. Then, Angel kept walking, and she went, and she sat in her place. Angel spent all her day alone in her place, because Bella had spent her whole day in the place of Hero talking with him. But Angel had spent her breaktime with Prince.

It was 3:00 p.m., the end of the class, and it was less warm than usual although there was sun shining outside. The school parking lot was almost full of students trying to get their cars. And both Angel and Bella were walking in the school parking by talking, and Angel was surprised when Bella told her that she was going outside the next day with Hero. Angel asked Bella if Hero had accepted to go out, and Bella answered that yes, that Hero had accepted to spend his next day with her, but that Hero had turned down the invitation to the birthday party of Nany. And Angel asked Bella if Bella wanted to go to the birthday party of their friend called Nany with Hero? Bella answered that Yes, that she wanted to go to that birthday party with Hero, but Hero refused. Then, both Angel and Bella got inside Bella's car, and Bella drove away.

Hero was in his car driving on the way to his hotel, and Hero noticed a crowd on his left side, then he lowered the window's glass of his car, and he heard people who were screaming, then Hero parked the car on the left side of the sidewalk. Then, Hero got out of his car, then he saw people who had lifted their heads through a building, by looking with fear on their faces and by screaming as they were seeing a kid of three years old who had grabbed the balcony of the fourteenth floors to not fall on the ground. The rescuers arrived, and they were running through the stairs, and the others were taking the elevator to go save that kid, then Hero lifted his head and he saw that kid who had grabbed the balcony to not fall.

Then, Hero ran between the crowd, and he jumped through the building and he grabbed the balcony of the third floor, and people were looking at Hero with the amazed faces how he was climbing on the building. Some people had removed their phones, and they were filming Hero who was climbing on the building, and they were all surprised by the way that Hero was climbing on the building. In nine seconds, Hero had already reached the eleventh floor of the building, and suddenly people pushed a loud scream, and Hero saw that that kid was falling through the ground. And immediately Hero jumped in the space through that kid, as if he was flying, and he grabbed that kid in the space, and he fell on the ground with that kid. And everyone ran through where Hero had fallen, and they surrounded Hero and that kid who were on the ground, then Hero got up with that kid, Hero bent face to that kid and he looked in the eyes of that kid, then he asked that kid what his name was. That kid answered that his name was Raul. Then, Hero introduced himself to that kid by saying that his name was Hero. Then, Hero asked Raul if he was all right, and Raul made the move with his head by saying yes. Then, Hero handed his hand to Raul, and Raul shook Hero's hand, and Hero smiled at Raul and he told Raul that it was a pleasure to meet him, then Hero lifted his head and he started to walk through his car. And people had turned their heads through Hero looking at him as he was walking away, and some people were still taking the pictures of Hero, and Hero got inside his car, then he drove away.

Hero drove till his hotel by thinking about the kid that he had just saved, and he got inside his hotel bedroom, and he threw his school's bag on the bed, and he sat in the chair that was close to his bed by thinking. Hero was not understanding why his magic did not warn him about Raul, because he had found out that that Raul was in danger by himself, and it was just a chance if he had found out that that Raul was in danger, as he had noticed the crowd on his way, and he had heard the screams, then he had parked the car and he got out of the car to see what was going on. And Hero started to wonder why his magic warned him every time when Angel was in danger, and his magic did not warn him about Raul that he had saved less than an hour ago, and although the fact that he was close to Raul, his magic did not warn him. And although the fact that Hero knew well that both Angel and Raul were the natural human beings, he knew well too that there was difference between both Angel and Raul, and that that difference was the reason why his magic warned him every time when Angel was in danger, and his magic did not warn him when Raul was in the danger. But Hero did not know what that difference was, but the fact that his magic did not make him think that Raul was in danger, it was another evidence that Angel had something different from the rest of natural human beings. Then Hero got up from his chair, and he started to walk in his bedroom thinking what the difference there was between Angel and Raul, and he spent hours trying to find the answer to that question without succeeding.

It was evening, and people were in their houses sitting in front of their televisions as usual, and they were watching news, and suddenly the expression on their faces changed, and there was a surprise on their faces as they were watching Hero who was climbing on the building to save a kid. And by seeing the expression that there was on their faces, they were not believing what they were watching on television, and people screamed when they watched Hero fly in the space to hold Raul who was falling on the ground. And people spent the whole night talking about what they had watched on television, and most people had noticed that Hero was the same person that they had watched in the news a couple weeks ago got out of an accident car. And people started to wonder who Hero was, and they had been surprised when they had seen Hero get out of the car's accident alive, and now they were not understanding how he had succeeded to save that kid. And most people who had watched Hero play basketball were just saying that Hero was good at everything, that he was just a genius by watching him in the news how he had saved Raul. While most of the classmates Hero were not really surprised by watching Hero on television how he had saved Raul, and for them Hero was a mysterious human being. The inhabitants of the world of natural human beings spent the whole night talking about Hero.

It was early morning, there was a long line in front of all the kiosks of newspapers of the world of natural human beings, people were fighting to buy the newspapers, and there were the pictures of Hero in front of all newspapers. There were different photos of Hero in front of newspapers with the different headlines, like there were his photos climbing on the building, with the headline like, "Superhero." There were his photos in the space holding a kid with the headlines like, "Supernatural Being." There were his photos getting out of his car's accident, with the headline like, "Who is Hero?" There were his photos playing basketball with headlines like, "The magician." There were his photos getting out of the classroom with the blood on his hand, with the headline like "The mysterious." And there were his photos taking the assessment in class with the headline like, "The genius." The journalists had spent their whole last night investigating Hero close to his classmates, even Angel and Bella had been approached by the journalists to talk about Hero, but they had completely refused to say a word about Hero. People were buying newspapers like if they were buying bread for breakfast, and they were all surprised at what they were reading about Hero, despite the fact that there were not a lot of things in newspapers about Hero. Because, even the classmates of Hero who had accepted to talk to journalists about Hero did not say a lot of things about Hero, because themselves they were wondering who Hero was, and they had just told about the behaviour of Hero to journalists, how Hero behaved in class.

Prince was lying in his bed deeply asleep, and he got up as he had heard the doorbell rang, and he was wondering who it could be, because it was the first time that the doorbell of his house rang since he lived in that house. And he was wondering if the windows of the house were not open, because he was always letting the windows of his house open for Matt, Sol and William. Then, Prince wore a t-shirt and he started to walk through the door, and when he reached the living room, he noticed that the window was opened, and he understood that it could not be William, Sol and Matt at the door, then he imagined that he should be Hero, and he walked till to the door angrily and ready to fight.

Then, Prince opened the door and the expression of his face changed, and the anger that was on Prince's face turned into a smile, when he saw Angel face to him, then he moved from the door by asking Angel to enter, and Angel walked inside with the newspapers in her hands. Angel reached the living room, and she started to stare at the mess that was in the living room, and she turned her head towards Prince, and she stared at him by asking him where his cat was? Prince asked her which cat she was talking about? Angel replied to Prince that he told her a couple months ago in the lunchroom of the campus, that he had a cat.

Then, Prince remembered that he had told Angel that he had a cat, and he opened his mouth and he lied to her by telling her that his cat was dead. And Angel replied to him that she was sorry, and she asked him when his cat was dead. Prince answered that his cat died a few weeks ago, and Angel stared at the living room and she asked Prince why there was the cat in his living room, if his cat was dead a couple weeks ago. Prince answered that it should be the people who used his house last night who put the cat's food in his house, because he spent his whole night outside, and he got inside the house early morning. Angel asked which people had used his house? And where he was last night? Prince answered that People asked his house to celebrate the birthday of one of their friends, and that probably those people came with the cats, and that it was the reason why there was cat food in his living room. And that he did not have time to clean the mess, because he was outside as he had spent his whole night in the nightclub. Angel asked Prince if he knew people who had spent the night at his house. And Prince answered that no, that couple days ago, he met someone in front of his house when he was getting out to go to school, and that person asked him at his house to celebrate the birthday of one of their friends. Then, Prince asked Angel how she found his house? And Angel answered Prince that he had given her his address the day he had invited her to his house, and she had an accident on her way.

Then, Angel told Prince that they must clean the mess in the house, and she walked till close to the sofa, and she wanted to put her purse and the newspapers that she had in her hand in the sofa, and something attracted her intention, and she started to stare at the couch with a surprised face. Then, Angel turned her head and she looked at Prince, and Prince looked in her eyes by asking her if everything was all right? And Angel answered to Prince that there were the marks of the footprints in his couch. And Prince asked her what she was meaning. And Angel demanded Prince to come close, and Prince walked till close to Angel, and Angel showed the footprints that were in the sofa to Prince, and Prince looked at those footprints in the sofa, and he remembered that last night when he watched Hero on television, he became angry and he turned into the tiger and he started to run inside the house to calm down his anger. Then, Prince looked at Angel by asking what it was, by pretending to not know what it was. And Angel answered Prince that it was the footprints of the tigers. Prince asked Angel how she knew that it was the footprints of the tigers? Angel answered that she was doing research on tigers, and she learned a lot on the tigers. Prince demanded her why she was doing the research on the tigers, and Angel answered that it was a long story. And Prince did not try to insist because he knew well that Angel was doing research on tigers, because she doubted Hero's identity.

Then, Angel showed the newspapers to Prince, and there were the photos of Hero in front of those newspapers, and Angel asked Prince if the one who was in front of newspapers was at the party that happened at his house last night. Prince answered that he had no idea, because he did not know people who were inside his house for that party, and that he did not even have the contacts of the one who had approached him to ask him his house for the party. And Prince went on by telling Angel that the one who was in front of those newspapers was a friend of her named Hero, then Angel looked at Prince without saying a word.

Then, there was silence between both, and they were staring at each other's eyes. And Angel understood that she could not keep on with that conversation because Prince thought that she was in love with him. The only way to avoid talking about him, was to stop that conversation even if she wanted to have more information about people who had spent the night at Prince'sparty. And Prince knew well that he should be careful because Angel could start to have doubts about him too, as she had the doubts about Hero, knowing that he had the same attitude as Hero, as they were supernatural beings of the same family. And that through his behavior, she could find out that he had the same behaviour as Hero. Then, Prince turned his head through the window as he had heard the noises coming from the window of his house, and he saw three eagles that were flying around the window of his house, and he understood the message. Then, Prince turned his head towards Angel again, and he looked in her eyes by asking her if everything was all right. And Angel answered him that everything was fine. Prince asked her if she wanted to eat or drink something, and Angel answered that no, that she was okay. Then, Prince walked two steps face to Angel, and he looked in her eyes, then the light got out from his eyes, and he moved his mouth towards Angel's mouth, and he started to kiss her.

After a few minutes kissing, Prince held Angel's hand, and he started to walk with her through his bedroom, then they got inside the bedroom, and Prince took the purse, and the newspapers that Angel had in her hand, and he walked two steps through the table that was in his bedroom, and he put Angel's stuffs on that table, and he turned, and he walked again two steps face to Angel. Both Prince and Angel were looking at each other in the eyes with the silence, and Prince lifted his right hand, and he put on the right cheek of Angel, then he started to caress Angel's cheek and her hair too by looking in her eyes. Then, Prince moved his head towards Angel, and he started to kiss her, and there were three eagles that were flying around the window of the bedroom of Prince, and the window was closed.

Then, Prince stopped kissing Angel, and he looked in her eyes, and he grabbed the t-shirt of Angel, and she lifted her both hands, and he removed the t-shirt of Angel, and Angel put her hands around Prince's neck, and she started to kiss him. And there were still the eagles that were flying around the window, and Prince had noticed those eagles that were flying around the window, and he was understanding the message that those eagles were sending to him. Then, both Prince and Angel started to move through the bed by kissing, and Angel grabbed the t-shirt of Prince and Prince lifted his both hands and she removed his t-shirt. And Angel turned face to Prince still by kissing him, and she put her both hands on Prince's chest, and Prince was understanding that Angel wanted him to lie in the bed. And Prince asked Angel to hold down, and he walked till to the window, and he opened the window then he turned, and he started to walk through Angel while she was looking at the window that was opened, then she turned her head and she started to look at Prince. After a few steps, Prince was face to Angel, and she looked in his eyes by asking him why he opened the window, and he lied to her by answering that he opened the window because he wanted the fresh air to get inside the room.

Then, Prince held Angel's hand that had the rosary, and Angel grabbed the hand of Prince with her other hand as Prince wanted to remove her rosary. And she looked in his eyes by asking him to not remove the rosary on her wrist. Prince asked her for what? Angel answered that it was a long story. Prince asked her if she believed in God, and she answered that yes. And Prince said that he too he believed in God, and that he could not make love with her, when she had the rosary on her. And Angel said that she could not remove her rosaries. Prince told her that he was not asking her to remove her rosaries for forever, just to remove them for less than an hour. Angel asked him why he wanted her to remove them? Prince answered that he could not make love with a woman who wore the rosaries, because it would be as if he was insulting God. Angel asked him if it meant that they would never make love together, because she would always wear her rosaries. Prince looked in Angel's eyes, and he asked her if she loved him? Angel answered that she did. Prince told her to let him remove her rosaries. Angel told him that she was afraid. Prince asked her if she trusted him? She answered him that she did.

Then, Prince stared at her for three seconds without uttering a word, then he opened his mouth and he told her not to be afraid, that he was with her, and that nothing would happen to her. Then, he asked her to let him remove her rosaries and that if something happened, he would never ask her again to remove them. Angel asked him if it meant that if something happened, they would never make love again. Prince answered that if something happened today, next time she would not remove her rosaries when they would be making love. Angel asked him why to take the risk to remove her rosaries just to see if something was going to happen, if next time he could make love with her when she wore her rosaries. Prince answered that he wanted to say that if something happened today because she had removed her rosaries, next time they would be already married when they would be making love, and at that moment he would have no problem if she wore her rosaries. Angel smiled at him by asking if he was ready to marry her? Prince smiled back at her by answering that he knew that she was going to be his wife, since the first day she had saved his life in downtown.

Then, Prince stared in Angel's eyes by telling her to not worry, that everything would be fine, and he demanded Angel let him remove her rosaries, only for today. Then, Angel removed her hand who was on Prince's hand without saying a word, and Prince started to take off the rosary on Angel's wrist, and suddenly Prince lifted his head as he had felt that the light had got inside the bedroom through the window, and the expression of his face changed as he saw that that light had turned into the invisible phantom of Hero. Prince was staring at the invisible phantom of Hero who was face to him and behind Angel with a face full of anger, while the invisible ghost of Hero was staring at Prince too, and those three eagles were still flying around the window. And there was silence in the room, Prince knew well that he could not fight the invisible phantom of Hero, because by fighting, it would attract the attention of Angel, and she would find out that Prince was a tiger too, mostly that she knew a lot about the tigers. Angel looked at Prince by asking him if everything was all right. Prince answered that everything was fine, and he asked her to wear her t-shirt. Angel asked him why he had changed his mind? And Prince lied to her by answering that he had promised to God that he was going to make love only after the marriage, and when he had started to remove her rosary, he remembered about the promise that he had made to God, and he felt that he was breaking that promise.

Then, Prince told Angel that he was sorry. Angel looked in his eyes by telling him that he did not have to be sorry, that he was a wonderful man, and that she was lucky to have him, and that it was a good idea to wait till after the marriage. Then, Prince bent, and he took the t-shirt of Angel that he had thrown on the carpet, and he handed it to her, and Angel took her t-shirt in the hand of Prince. And Prince walked till his wardrobe, and he took a t-shirt and a pant, and he started to take off his pants, while Angel was turning the side of her t-shirt to wear. The invisible phantom of Hero was still in the room behind Angel, and he was staring at the bra that Angel had on her with an amazed face as if he was seeing something strange. Then, Angel wore her t-shirt, and she turned, and she looked at Prince and asked him why he had changed his clothes? Prince answered that they were going outside. Angel said that she thought that they should clean the house and spend the day at home. Prince told Angel to not worry about the mess in the house, that he had a housekeeper named Alexa who came to clean his house when he called her, and that he was going to call Alexa tonight, and Alexa would be there the next day to clean the house.

Then, both Prince and Angel walked outside, and there was sun shining. And Prince's face was full of anger, and the weather was increasing the anger that Hero had already provoked in him. Especially because it was hot, and Prince was usually nervous when it was hot. And the light got inside Prince's eyes when he was getting inside the car, and there was the silence in the car as Prince was driving. Then, Angel broke the silence by asking Prince where they were going? And Prince answered that they were going to an amazing place, and that they would get fun there.

After thirteen minutes of driving, Prince parked the car in the parking of a building, they got outside of the car and they walked till to the door of that building, and they got inside the building, and Angel noticed that they were in a mall. And they walked until to the side of the games, and Prince bought the tickets for the games, and they walked in the bowling's room, and they noticed that there was a crowd, and they started to walk through the crowd. And suddenly Angel stopped walking, and she started to breathe deeply as she was staring at Hero who was bowling, and she noticed that the crowd was staring at Hero, as he was playing. Prince turned his head and looked at Angel and he asked her if everything was all right. And Angel looked into Prince's eyes and answered that everything was fine. Then, they kept walking, and the eyes of Angel were focused on Hero who was playing the bowling, and there were people who were watching at Hero as he was playing, and those people were amazed by the way that Hero was playing, and those people knew that Hero was the one that they had watched on their televisions last night, and that they had seen in the newspapers this morning, and there was Bella close to Hero.

Then, both Prince and Angel reached the place where Hero was playing, and Bella ran, and she gave a hug to Angel, and Hero had stopped playing. And both Hero and Prince were looking at each other in the eyes. And Hero knew well that Prince had used his magic to find where he was, and that Prince was there with Angel just to bother him, and to take his revenge as he had prevented Prince to remove the rosaries of Angel for that William, Sol and Matt killed Angel. Then, Prince walked till close to Hero, and he demanded to play, and Hero agreed. Then, Prince started to play, and people were staring at Prince with smiles on their faces, as he was playing as well as Hero, even Angel was very surprised by the way that Prince was playing. Then, people asked for a challenge between both Prince and Hero, and Prince agreed first for that challenge, then Hero accepted too. Then, both Prince and Hero started playing a game called bowling. And people were looking at them, and some people were filming them with the phones as they were playing. After fifteen minutes of play, there was no winner between them, and some people were saying that they wanted to see a winner, while most people were saying that there would never be a winner between both Prince and Hero. Hero threw the ball, and the light got out from Prince's eyes and went through the ball, and that light deviated the ball that Hero had thrown, and it made Hero lose, and People were amazed to see Hero lose, and only Hero who knew that it was Prince who had made him lose through his magic, then Prince turned his head towards Hero and he smiled at Hero. Then, Prince grabbed the ball and he threw the ball, and the light got out from Hero's eyes, and when through the ball that Prince had thrown, but unfortunately for Hero the light that had got out from his eyes did not have the effects on the ball that Prince had thrown.

Suddenly, there were the screams, and People were clapping their hands as Prince had won, even Bella was clapping her hands, except Angel who was not clapping her hands, and she was staring at Hero, and by looking at Angel, we could see that she was sad as Hero had lost. Then, the smile appeared on Angel's face, as she had seen Prince who was walking towards her by smiling at her, and after a few steps Prince was face to Angel and Angel looked into his eyes and said, "Congratulations." Prince said, "The victory is for my lover who is you." And he added, "I won for you, because I love you." Angel smiled and said, "Thank you." Then, the light got out from Prince's eyes and he started to kiss Angel. While people were looking at them by smiling and some were even clapping their hands, and except Hero who was looking at them with the anger on his face, then Bella walked till close to Hero, and she looked in Hero's eyes by telling him that even if he had lost, he was the best player for her. And Hero thanked Bella for her words, and Hero demanded Bella that they should leave, and Bella agreed, then Hero Held Bella's hand, and they started to walk through the door.

Prince and Angel were staring at Hero and Bella who were walking away, then Prince screamed at Hero by saying, "Do not run away." Hero and Bella turned, and they stared at Prince, then Bella said, "Prince, we are not running away, just that we are tired, and we want to go somewhere else." Prince said, "I am giving another chance to that loser close to you, to get his revenge on me." Bella said, "Hero is not a loser." Prince looked in Bella's eyes by saying, "The name of people who lose are the losers. So, like the man who held your hand lost, he is a loser." People started to laugh, and Angel was embarrassed by what was going on and she was asking Prince to stop it, and that they should leave, but Prince was not paying attention to Angel. Bella looked at Prince by saying, "It's not because you got a chance to win, that you would call Hero a loser." Prince cried out, "A chance?" And he added, "I won because I am a better player than that loser who grabbed your hand." And People started to scream, by laughing while Hero was still staring at Prince without saying a word, and by looking at Hero, we could see a rage inside him. Bella said, "Prince, you won today, and may be tomorrow or after tomorrow you would lose, so do not treat Hero as a loser just because he lost." Prince said, "I won today, and I would win tomorrow, and after tomorrow I would win again, then I would win everyday forever, because I am a winner, and I was born to win, so I am not like the loser who held your hand." And he added, "That loser is not even a man, because he is unable to defend himself and he let a woman to defend him." And people started to scream loudly by laughing, and Angel was telling Prince that it was enough to stop it, and both Prince and Hero were looking at each other in the eyes, and the face of Hero was full of rage, while the face of Prince was full of smiles.

Then, Hero opened his mouth and he asked, "Are you ready?" Prince answered, "A real man like me is always ready." Then, Hero turned his head towards Bella, and he looked in her eyes by saying, "Let's go." Then, Hero and Bella started to walk through a door, still by holding their hands, and Prince held the hand of Angel and they started to walk by following Hero and Bella, and there were people who were walking behind them. Hero was walking by thinking, Hero knew that his magic was different from the magic of Prince, that there were things that his magic could do and that the magic of Prince could not do, like there were things that the magic of Prince could do and that his magic could not do. And Hero knew that his magic could not change the direction of a ball, as he had failed to change the direction of the ball of Prince a couple minutes ago, and that the magic of Prince could change the direction of the ball. Then, Hero started to think how he was going to take his revenge on Prince, and he started to think about a game where Prince could not use his magic to change the direction of the ball.

Then, they got inside a huge room, and there were a lot of games in that room, and Hero started staring at the games that were inside the room, and he noticed a game that did not need the ball to be played, and he started to walk through that game, and Prince and other people were following Hero. Then, Hero stopped close to a video game, and he looked at Prince by saying, "Let's play." And Prince looked at that video game that Hero had chosen, and he looked at Hero without saying a word, but Prince understood the reason why Hero had chosen that game, and Prince knew that even if he did not expect that game, he was going to play, because people were going to yell at him like a loser, if he refused to play. Then, both Prince and Hero sat in the chairs, and each of them grabbed his joysticks in his hands, and they started to play, and the eyes of everyone were focused on the screen, they were all watching on the screen how the game was hard.

After twenty-one minutes, there was still no winner between both Prince and Hero, and people were still watching, then the light started to get out from Prince's eyes and went through the screen, but Prince noticed that the light that was getting out from his eyes had no effect on the game. Then, the light started to get out from Hero's eyes and went through the screen, and Hero noticed that the light that was getting out from his eyes had no effect on the game, then both Prince and Hero kept playing without using their magic. And after nine minutes, people started to scream by clapping their hands, and Angel was staring at Hero with her face full of happiness and even if Angel was the only one who was not clapping her hands, by looking at her, we could see that she was very happy that Hero won. Then, the smile that was on Angel's face went when she saw Bella kiss the cheek of Hero to congratulate him for his victory, and the face of Prince was full of anger as people were looking at him by laughing.

Then, Prince saw Hero and Bella who were walking away, and he got up from his chair, and he screamed at Hero that the game was not yet over, that they have to play the last game to see the real winner. Hero and Bella turned, and they started to stare at Prince, while people were cheering at Hero to accept the last challenge. Angel walked until close to Prince and she grabbed the hand of Prince by telling him that they should leave, but Prince was not paying attention to what Angel was telling him, and he was just focused on staring at Hero. Then, Hero accepted Prince's proposal for another game, and Prince started walking through a game, and Hero other people were following Prince. Then, Prince stopped close to the billiards and he smiled at Hero by telling Hero to grab his stick, and Hero looked at Prince and he understood why Prince had chosen the billiard. Hero grabbed his stick in his hand, and Prince grabbed his stick in his hand, then they started playing, and people were watching them play, and none between Hero and Prince was using the magic. After a few minutes, both Prince and Hero had the same numbers of the mark, and both had put all their balls inside holes, but it was lacking two balls on the billiard for each of them, and if each of them was putting his ball inside the hole, it should be a draw. Then, Prince put his stick on the ball, and he pushed his ball with his stick, and the eyes of everyone were focused on the ball that Prince had pushed with his stick, and that ball was going through the hole. Then, the light got out from Hero's eyes and went through the ball that was going through the hole, and Prince smiled at Hero as he noticed that Hero had sent the light on his ball.

Then, that light that had got out from Hero's eyes, had an impact on the ball once when that light touched the ball, and everyone noticed that the ball was going faster through the hole, and suddenly they all pushed a scream of despair, and except Hero who had

## SUPERNATURAL BEINGS

not pushed a scream, as they had all noticed that the ball had missed the hole. Prince turned his head and he looked at Hero angrily, and Prince understood that Hero had used his magic to make his ball go faster, that even if the magic of Hero did not change the direction of his ball, Hero's magic had had an impact on his ball by making his ball go faster, and that was the reason why his ball had missed the hole. And Prince was not very worried because in his mind he thought that he was going to win that game, like his magic had the ability to change the direction of the ball, and that even if Hero had taken an advantage on him, he was going to win. The first idea of Prince was to put his last ball in the hole and use his magic to prevent the last ball of Hero to go in the hole by changing the direction of the ball of Hero through his magic, then become the winner of the game. But unfortunately, Hero had changed Prince's plan, and now the plan of Prince was to use his magic to make Hero lose, by changing the direction of the ball of Hero, and there would be no winner, no loser and they would retake the game like it would be a draw. And for the next turn of the game, he would make Hero lose, by using his magic to change the direction of the balls of Hero. Everyone was looking at Hero, and they were all waiting for him to play, and Hero was staring at the billiard by thinking, and he knew well that Prince was going to use his magic to prevent his ball from getting inside the hole.

Then, Hero Put his stick on the ball, and he pushed the ball with his stick, and he immediately he saw the light that was getting out from Prince's eyes and going through the ball that he had pushed with his stick, and Hero made the light get out from his eyes and go through the ball that he had pushed with the stick, as he had understood that Prince had sent the light on his ball to change the direction of his ball. And everyone had their eyes focused on the billiard, and except Prince and Hero, the rest of people were looking at the ball that Hero had pushed with the amazed faces as that ball was turning on the billiard. Except Angel who had an idea of what was going on, the rest of people were completely lost, and they were wondering why the ball was turning, and why the ball was not moving to go through the hole. And Angel knew that it was Hero who was making the ball turn, but she did not know that even Prince was responsible for the fact that the ball was turning. Prince, Hero and the rest of people were watching at the ball that was turning on the billiard, and both Prince and Hero knew that the ball was turning because they were fighting to control the ball through their magic that had been sent on the ball. And Prince was fighting through his magic to prevent the ball from getting inside the hole, while Hero was fighting through his magic to prevent the magic of Prince to change the direction of the ball. After eleven minutes, the ball had not moved, and the ball had not changed direction, so the ball was still turning on the same place.

And both Prince and Hero started to feel the impact of the fight of their magic on the ball inside them, and Prince was feeling that he was sweating, and he knew that he could not let Angel see the sweat on him, because if Angel saw the sweat on him, she should start having the doubts about him. And Prince knew that the only solution he had was to give up the game and let Hero win to prevent Angel from having doubts about him, then Prince got another idea, and he told Angel that he would be back, that he was going to washroom, then he turned, and he left.

Then, people started feeling how someone was breathing deeply, and they lifted their heads, and they turned their heads and they all noticed how Hero was breathing deeply by sweating, and they also noticed that Hero was looking tired. And people started wondering what was going on with Hero, and Bella started to ask Hero if he was doing well. But Hero was not paying attention to the words of Bella, and he was still focused on looking at the ball that was still turning, and people were wondering how Hero was sweating in a cold room, with the air conditioner. Angel was looking at Hero how he was sweating, and she was not really surprised, because Hero was a mystery to her, and she could expect everything weird coming from Hero, then Angel turned, and she started to run away by saying that she was going to find Prince, then Angel stopped running and she turned her head from behind as she had heard the screams coming from behind, and she was staring at people who were clapping their hands, and Bella who was congratulating Hero. And she understood that Hero had won, then she turned, and she kept running through the washroom. Prince was in the toilet and he was cleaning himself, as he was sweating too and he was also very tired, and he knew that Hero had won the game. And if Hero had won the game, it was because Prince had given up the fight on the ball when Prince found out through his magic that Angel was coming to the bathroom to look for him, and he did not want Angel to see him sweating, breathing deeply and looking tired, because it was important for him that Angel still thinks that he was a natural human being. Angel reached the door of the toilet, and she opened the door and she saw Prince face to her who was trying to get out, and she looked in his eyes, then she rushed in his arms, and Prince had taken Angel in his arms.

Then, Angel turned her head, and she looked in Prince's eyes, and she told him that she was afraid that something had happened to him. Prince answered that he ran away from the game room, because he was afraid of Hero, that Hero was scaring him, and he was not feeling good about himself. And Angel told Prince that she was not surprised, that Hero was a strange man. Then, Prince asked Angel what she knew about Hero, and Angel looked in Prince's eyes and she opened her mouth ready to talk, but she remembered that she had promised to Hero that she should be silent about him. Then, Angel lied to Prince by saying that she knew nothing about Hero, because Hero was so mysterious, and Prince knew well that Angel was lying to him, then Angel told Prince that Hero had won the game, and that they should leave, then Prince and Angel left. Hero and Bella spent the rest of day to Bella's home to talk, and to watch movie, and Bella had tried to convince Hero to come with her to the birthday party of one her friends that would be held the next day without succeed. Prince and Angel spent their rest of the day to Angel's home to talk and to watch movie, and Angel had demanded to Prince to go with her to the birthday party of her friend the next day, and Prince agreed.

# CHAPTER VI

# THE DEATH OF THE GHOST OF MATT

It was evening Prince, William, Sol and Matt were in the living room of Prince's house, and they were all making the plan for the next day, and they spent the rest of the night talking about their plan. The following day, it was 6 pm, Angel was walking inside her bedroom with the towel tied on her coming from the washroom, then Angel started to get dress, and after a few minutes she had already got dressed, and she was walking through her wardrobe when a sheet of paper that was leaned on her teddy bear, that was on her bed attracted her attention. Then, Angel stopped walking and she turned face to her bed, and she was staring at that paper that was folded on her teddy bear with a surprised face, by wondering who had put that sheet of paper on her bed. Then, she walked till close to her bed, and she bent, and she handed her hand, and she took that sheet of paper on the teddy bear, then she opened that sheet of paper and she cried out "Hero?" With an astonished face, as she had recognized the handwriting of Hero on that sheet of paper, then she read, "Do not go to the birthday party of your friend, because it's dangerous, and if you went there, maybe you would not come back alive." Suddenly, the fear appeared on the face of Angel, and she was staring at that sheet of paper in her hands with her heart that was beating faster as if she was going to have a heart attack, then the phone of Angel started to ring, and she was not paying attention to the phone that was ringing.

After three seconds, the door opened, and Angel was hearing the footsteps behind her, but she did not turn to see who it was, then she felt a hand on her shoulder coming from behind her, and a voice who was asking her if everything was all right. And she understood that it was Prince as she had recognized his voice, then she turned face to him, and she handed him the sheet of paper that she had in her hand. Prince took that sheet paper, and he read what was written on it, and he once understood that it was Hero, and he looked in Angel's eyes by asking her if she knew who it was, and Prince was pretending to not know that it was Hero who had written that letter. And Angel wanted to say that it was Hero, but again she remembered that she had promised Hero to keep the silence about him, and she told Prince that she did not know who it was. And Prince told her that it would be someone who wrote it to make a joke to her, and Angel told Prince that she was very afraid, that she was not going anymore to the party. And Prince replied to her that it was okay, if she did not want to go to that birthday party, and that he was going to stay with her.

Then, Prince turned his head through the window, as he had heard the noises coming from the window, and he saw three eagles that were flying around the window, and he understood the reasons why those eagles were flying, then he turned his head towards Angel by telling her that he would be back that he had forgotten something in his car, and that he was going to take it. Then, Prince turned, and he left. After a few minutes, Prince was in the yard of Angel's house, with William, Sol and Matt. And Prince told them that Angel did not want to go anymore to that birthday, because she had found a letter that was warning her of a danger in her bedroom coming from Hero. And Sol told Prince to convince Angel to go to that birthday party, because they could not change their plan, and that it would be their chance to kill Angel.

Then, Prince turned, and he walked till the bedroom of Angel, and he succeeded to change the mind of Angel, and Angel finally agreed to go to the party. Bella was at the birthday party and she was talking with her friends, then she removed her phone from her purse, as she had heard her phone ringing, and she noticed that she had got a message. Then, the smile appeared on her face, as she was reading the message, and she started to walk towards the door, and after three minutes, Bella was outside facing the Hero, and both were talking. Bella told Hero that she was not expecting him, but that she was very happy as he had changed his mind and he came to the party. Then, Bella asked Hero how he found the party house? Hero answered Bella that in their conversation yesterday, she told him the address of the house where the party was going to take place, when she invited him to come with her. And Bella told Hero that she did not remember at the moment she told him about the address, but that what mattered was the fact that he came to the party. But Hero had lied to Bella, because he had used his magic to find the party house.

Then, Hero and Bella walked till into the party hall, and the eyes of everyone were focused on Hero, and Bella was introducing Hero to her friends, but everyone in the room already knew who Hero was, because they had recognized him as they had watched him on television, and they had seen his pictures in front of newspapers. And some people were afraid of Hero, and they did not want to approach him, while other people were very happy to see him, and they were going to talk with him. And most people had noticed that Hero was not comfortable. Hero was standing up in a corner of the room, and he was staring at people, then he saw Angel and Prince who were walking in the room by holding their hands. And Hero started staring at Angel who was greeting people, then his eyes met with Angel's eyes, and both were staring at each other eyes in eyes, then Hero turned, and he walked away, and Angel turned her head through him, and she was still staring at him as he was walking away. While, Prince was staring at William, Sol, and Matt who were in the room talking with some men, and Prince was understanding what was going on, then William looked at Prince, and William made the signs to Prince with his eyes, and Prince understood the message of William.

Then, Prince turned, and he walked away, and William started to follow Prince. Prince got inside the washroom, and William followed him in the toilet, and both started talking in the washroom, then William told Prince that the plan had changed, because Hero was at the party as they did not expect Hero to come, but that he had a new plan and that new plan was to distract Hero to have the chance to kill Angel.

After four minutes, Prince and William left the washroom. Angel was looking for Prince in the room with fear inside her, then she saw Prince who was walking towards her, and she ran, and she hugged him. Then, they started to walk to find a place to sit, and a man walked and stopped face to face, then that man looked at Angel, and that man told Angel that she had the good rosaries, and that he was interested in buying them. Angel replied to that man that she was not selling them, then she walked away with Prince. Hero sat in the chair around a table, and he was staring at William, Sol and Matt who were sitting in their chairs too, and William, Sol and Matt were looking at Hero too. And Hero knew that Sol had used her magic to get inside the party house with her two brothers and other people. And it was exactly what Sol had done, when Sol reached the door, she looked in the eyes of security men who were responsible to take the invitation tickets to the guests, and her green eyes became blue, and security men forgot to ask her invitation ticket, and she told security men that she was with William, Matt and other people, and that's how they all got inside the party house.

Angel and Prince were sitting around a table, and the eyes of Angel were focused on Hero, then a waiter came, and he gave a sheet of paper to Angel, and Angel opened that sheet of paper, and suddenly the panic appeared on her face, as she was reading what was written on that sheet of paper. Then, Angel tried to get up from her chair, and Prince held her hand, and he asked her what was going on? And Angel gave that sheet of paper to Prince, and Prince looked at it, and he read, "I want those rosaries, and I would get them now. So, if you care about your life, you can sell me those rosaries now, or I would kill you before taking them." Then, Prince turned his head and he looked in Angel's eyes by telling her to not worry, that he was with her. Angel told Prince that she was very afraid, that she wanted to return to her house, and Prince told her that everything would be fine.

Then, another waiter came, and he handed another sheet of paper to Angel, and Angel stared at the waiter with her face full of fear without taking the sheet of paper, then Prince handed his hand and he took the sheet of paper in the waiter's hand, and Prince opened that sheet of paper. Then, Angel turned her head through the sheet of paper that was in Prince's hand, and she read, "You can not run away from me, because I have my men outside waiting for you, as I also have my men inside watching at you. So, the better idea it's to take off your rosaries and sell them to me, or my men would kill both your boyfriend and you." Angel looked in the eyes of Prince with his mouth opened, but she was shaking of fear that she could not even pronounce a word. And Prince told her that she should remove her rosaries and keep them, and Angel replied to Prince that she could not remove her rosaries, because if she removed them, she would die. But Prince succeeded in convincing Angel to remove her rosaries, and keep them in her purse, that it was the only solution to prevent people who wanted her rosaries from getting them.

And Angel told Prince that she would remove her rosaries, but that he was the one who was going to keep them, because she was afraid to lose them, then Prince agreed to keep them. Then, Angel handed her hand that her wrist had the rosary to Prince by asking Prince to remove the rosary, but Prince refused by telling her that they should go to the washroom, and there he would remove them, and keep them. Because, he did not want someone to see how he was keeping them, mostly that people who wanted those rosaries were in the room, and they did not know who those people were. Then, both Angel and Prince got up from their chairs, and they started to walk through the bathroom, and the eyes of Hero, William, Sol and Matt were focussed on Angel and Prince, because they knew exactly what was going on. Then, William, Sol and Matt got up and they started to walk through the washroom too. And Hero knew what was going on because he had read all the messages that Angel had received through his magic. Angel and Prince were still walking through the washroom, then a man stopped face to them, and that man opened a sheet of paper that he had in his hand by showing it to Angel, and Angel looked at that sheet of paper, and she read, "Please, do not remove your rosaries, do not get inside the bathroom and do not get out. Stay in your place, and nothing would happen to you, and I am in the room with you. I promise you that everything would be okay, and that you would be safe."

Then, Angel turned her head and she stared at Hero who was staring at her too, as she had recognized the handwriting of Hero on that sheet of paper. And William, Sol and Matt had stopped walking, and they were staring at Prince and Angel, then Prince looked at William, Sol and Matt and he made them a sign with his left eye, and they understood what was going on. Then, Angel turned, and walked till in her place without saying a word, and Prince turned and followed her, then William, Sol and Matt turned, and they walked to their places too. Prince looked at Angel and he asked her what was going on? Angel replied that she did not want to remove her rosaries. Prince asked her why she had changed her mind, and Angel answered that for no reason, just that she felt safe with the rosaries. But Prince knew that Angel was lying, that it was the letter of Hero who had made her change her mind, as he had read that letter too. Angel was more relaxed, and she was not anymore feeling the fear since she had read the letter of Hero, and her eyes were focused on Hero who was talking with Bella, and by looking at Angel, we could see that she was jealous to see Bella and Hero who were talking by laughing together.

There was anger in Prince, and that anger was not because Angel was not paying attention to him, but because Hero had prevented Angel to remove her rosaries, and there was also the rage in William, Sol and Matt as Hero had prevented Angel to remove her rosaries. Then, the food was served on the tables, and the light got out from the eyes of Hero, William, Sol, Matt and Prince before they started eating, and it was their ghosts that they had removed from their bodies. And Hero had turned his head towards the table of William, Sol and Matt, and Hero was watching them eat, and Hero was noticing that they were only eating the carrots, and he was very surprised to see that William, Sol and Matt loved the carrots as Angel. After an hour, there were some people who were dancing on the dance floor, and Prince invited Angel to dance but she refused by saying that she was not doing well, and Angel's eyes were still focused on Hero. Then, Angel saw Hero and Bella who were getting up from their chairs, and she watched them walk till to the dance floor, then she turned towards Prince, and she grabbed Prince's hand by telling him that she wanted to dance. Both Angel and Prince got up, and they started to walk through the dance floor, and Prince understood why Angel had changed her mind about the dance, once he had seen Hero who was dancing with Bella. Angel and Prince were dancing close to Hero and Bella, again Angel was not really focused on the dance, because her eyes were on Hero, but Prince did not care that Angel was always staring at Hero, because Prince was there for a plan.

After fifteen minutes, a security man came close to Hero and Bella, and that security man told Bella, then Bella demanded to Hero to wait for her, that her mom was outside, that she was going to see what her mom wanted, then she left.

After three minutes, Bella was not yet returned in the room, and Hero felt that something was going wrong, and he used his magic to find out what was happening, and he suddenly found out a car with Bella inside, and he understood that it was a trap. Then, Hero turned, and he tried to run through the door, but unfortunately, he was grabbed by two women who wanted to take the pictures with him, by saying that they had watched him on television. And Hero agreed to take the pictures with those women just because he wanted to be polite, and he was trying to take the pictures with those women, when other women came by asking him pictures too, while some women were asking him for a dance. William, Sol and Matt were staring at Hero who was surrounded by women with the smiles on their faces, and they were very happy that those women were preventing Hero to get out, even if it was not them who had sent those women, they were happy because it was making their plan more better, and there people who had kidnapped Bella could go so far with Bella. Angel had stopped dancing, and her face was full of jealousy as she was staring at those women who had surrounded Hero, and who were telling Hero that he was handsome.

Then, a man came with a phone in his hand, and that man started to push women who had surrounded Hero, then that man handed the phone he had in his hand to Hero, and Hero took the phone and he put the phone on his ear, and he heard the voice of Bella who was crying on the phone. And Hero used his magic, and he found where Bella was, and he saw a man who had put the gun on Bella's head through his magic, then Hero threw the phone away angrily, and he pushed people who were close to him, and he started to run through the door. And the magic of Hero was warning him that Angel was in danger, but Hero was not paying attention to his magic. And people had turned their heads looking at Hero who was getting out with the amazed faces, by wondering what was going on with him, and Angel wanted to follow Hero, but Prince grabbed her hand by saying that it was dangerous to get out. Hero was in the car driving faster, and his magic was still warning him that Angel was in danger, but for the first time Hero was not obeying to his magic. And Angel was asking Prince to let her hand, that she wanted to go out, that may be someone was in danger outside, and that that person might need help, and Prince was seeing the fear on Angel's face, and he knew that Angel was worried about Hero, as Hero had left the room by running, and he was trying to calm her.

Suddenly, everyone screamed in the room, as they had heard bullet shots on the ceiling of the house, they turned their heads and they saw three men who had the guns, and who were asking them to be quiet and to sit on the floor, and there was the fear on the face of everyone in the room, except Prince, William, Sol and Matt who did not feel fear. And Angel was staring at Sol, William and other men who were walking through her with her heart that was beating with fear, and it was now that Angel was noticing that William, Sol and Matt were in the room, because she had not seen them since she was in the room. Then, Angel started to turn her head in the room by looking for Hero, by wondering where Hero was. Then, Angel turned her head in front of her, and she saw Sol face to her who was staring in her eyes, and a man handed a gun on Prince by asking Prince to get up, then Prince got up, and Angel screamed as she had seen Prince faint close to her, because that man had hit Prince with the gun. Then, that man asked Angel to get up, and Angel got up and that man grabbed Angel's wrist that had the rosary, and another man bent, and he held Angel's ankle that had the rosary, and those men were trying to remove the rosaries that Angel had.

Suddenly, everyone turned their head through the window by yelling, as they had heard the loud noises coming from the window, and they all noticed that the window's glass was broken. William and Sol turned their heads through the window, and they saw the invisible phantom of Hero who was running through them, and Sol shouted at men who were removing Angel's rosaries to remove them quickly. Matt was running through the invisible phantom of Hero, and that invisible phantom ran, and he carried Matt, and he threw Matt on the man who had held Angel's wrist, and people started screaming by running away. Even Angel had moved away, because men who had grabbed her wrist and her ankle had lost the balance as Matt had fallen on the man who had held her wrist, and even the one who had held her ankle had lost the balance, and those men had not succeeded to remove the rosaries of Angel. William and Sol were fighting against the invisible phantom of Hero, and people were watching the fight in the room with the panic on their faces, without understanding what was going on, and they were wondering who Sol and William were fighting. And some people were trying to get out, but the doors were locked, and all doors had been locked when Hero had got out, and it was to prevent Hero from getting inside the room.

Hero was still on the street driving faster, and the light got out from his eyes and that light got out through the car's window. Bella was standing up in a darkness a place with her face wet of tears, and she was surrounded by three men, and one of those men had put the gun on her head, she was crying by begging them to not kill her, and there was a light in the space that was coming through them and they were not seeing that light. Then, light turned into the tiger, and before they saw the tiger, the tiger had already bitten the hand of the one who had put the gun on Bella's head, then they all ran away by shouting once they had seen the tiger. And each of them was running in his own way, and the one that the tiger had bitten had the difficulties to run, because he was bleeding from his hand as the tiger had bitten that hand, and he was feeling pains too.

Bella was running without even knowing where she was going, and a car stopped close to her, but she did not turn her head to look at that car, and she was still running, then she turned her head from behind as she had heard a voice who was calling her name. And Bella saw Hero who was close to a car, and she ran till where Hero was, and they got inside the car, and Bella turned her head and she looked at Hero and she noticed that there was the blood on Hero's mouth, and she asked him why he had the blood on his mouth, and Hero answered Bella that he fought with someone and he had been hit in his mouth by that person. But Hero had lied to Bella by saying that the blood that he had on his mouth was coming from the fight, because the blood that Hero had on his mouth was coming from his ghost, as his ghost had bitten the hand of the one who had put the gun on Bella's head. So, the blood that was on Hero's mouth was the blood of that person that his ghost had bitten as the blood of that person had stayed on the mouth of Hero's ghost, then Hero wiped the blood that was on his mouth, and he drove away. There was still the fight in the party house, and Matt had joined the fight, and people were screaming with terror on their faces, some of them were bleeding as Matt was throwing the chairs, the tables and other stuff on them. Prince was watching the fight with anger on his face, and he wanted to go fight Hero's phantom, but he was afraid that Angel would start having the doubts about him, then he turned his head and he looked at Angel and he noticed that she was little bit far from where he was, and he was thinking how he could remove her rosaries.

Then, Matt walked till face to Angel and he yelled at her to remove her rosaries by looking in her eyes, and Angel looked at Matt by trembling with panic, and he screamed at her again by telling her that he would kill her if she did not remove those rosaries. Then, Angel bent her head, and she was trying to remove the rosary that was on her wrist with her other hand. Then, Angel heard a voice that was yelling by calling her name to not remove her rosaries, and she screamed out, "Hero?" By looking in the room, she had recognized that the voice who had yelled her name was the voice of Hero. Then, the invisible phantom of Hero jumped on Matt, and he threw Matt on the floor, and Angel and other people ran away, as Matt and Hero's phantom were fighting where they were, and Angel was still turning her head in the room by looking for Hero, and she could not imagined that it was Hero's phantom who had called her name. Sol came to where Angel was, and Sol yelled at people who were around Angel to remove the rosaries that Angel wore, and they were just staring at Sol with their faces full of fear, and Sol screamed again at them by telling her that she would kill them if they did not obey. Then, some people turned their heads towards Angel, and they put their hand on Angel by trying to remove the rosaries, but their whole bodies were shaking of fear that it was hard for them to hold the rosaries. And Sol was shouting at them to hurry up, and suddenly Sol pushed a scream as the tiger had bitten her behind the neck, then she turned, and she started to fight with the tiger, then Angel and other people ran away without them succeeding to remove the rosaries of Angel.

Prince was watching the fight with his eyes full of anger, as he was seeing the two phantoms of Hero that were fighting, and the invisible phantom was fighting against Matt and William, while the tiger was fighting against Sol. Then, Prince understood that he should take part in the fight as Hero had his two ghosts in the room, and Prince turned his head through Angel, and he looked at her by saying in his mind that it was their last chance to kill Angel, then the light got out from his eyes and went through where Sol was fighting with the tiger, and that light turned into the tiger and started to fight. Then, Sol stopped fighting, and she let the two tigers fight together, and Sol was turning her head in the room looking for where Angel was, and she suddenly opened her mouth widely by screaming the name of Matt, with the tears that were flowing down her cheeks, and with the rage on her face, as she was seeing the invisible phantom of Hero who was killing Matt by electrifying him. The invisible ghost of Hero had held Matt's neck with one of his hands, and he had his other hand on Matt's face, and there were the blue lights that were getting out from the fingers of Hero's ghost, and those blue lights were electrifying Matt. And Matt was dying by losing his strengths, and Matt was shaking and there was the blood that was coming out from Matt's mouth, and Matt had already given up the fight because Matt could no longer fight as Matt was being electrified by Hero's ghost.

Then, Sol started running through Matt who was falling down the floor, with the tears and anger on her face, then Sol knelt close to Matt and she looked at him by crying as she was seeing the blood that was getting out from Matt's mouth, and Matt was looking in her eyes too, then she asked Matt to remove his phantom from his body as she was noticing that Matt was dying. Then, the light got out from Matt's eyes, and that light turned into the eagle and that eagle laid on the floor, and Sol turned her head to her to her left and she saw that eagle that was dying, and she also noticed the wounds on that eagle that were coming from the blue lights. And Sol understood that Matt had his ghost inside his body when Matt was electrified by Hero's ghost, and she started to breath deeply, as she was seeing that eagle that was closing his eyes, then she turned her head towards Matt and she noticed that he had closed his eyes, and she understood that Matt's ghost was dead. Then, Sol lifted her head and she saw Hero's phantom who was beating William, and then got up and she ran through Hero's phantom, and she started to fight Hero's phantom with rage and with all her strength. People were in the room shaking of fear, with their hearts that were beating faster than the normal, as they were seeing two tigers that were fighting, also an eagle that was dead, and a dead body lying on the floor, and except Angel, it was the first time for all people to see that kind of fight. Suddenly, people turned their heads through the front door as they had heard a noise coming from there, and Angel cried out, "Hero?" As she had seen Hero who had forced the door and got inside the house.

Then, Hero turned his head looking for Angel, then he saw her and he started to run towards her, and suddenly Angel screamed Hero's name with a face full of fear, as she had seen one of the two tigers that was jumping on Hero, and Hero grabbed that tiger, and he threw that tiger away, and some people saw Prince who was moving from where he was as if he was flying, and they screamed with fear on their faces as they had seen Prince hit himself against the wall, as Hero had thrown Prince's phantom against the wall. And the eyes of Angel were focused on Hero that she did not see how Prince went and hit himself against the wall. Then, Hero ran till Angel and he grabbed Angel's hand, and he started to run through the door with her while his two phantoms were still fighting, and Hero shouted at everyone to get out of the room, and people started to run towards the door by screaming, and some people were falling on others. Then, Hero and Angel reached out, and they got inside the car, and two lights got inside Hero's eyes and he drove away. Angel turned her head towards Hero, and she looked at him how he was looking tired, then she opened her mouth and asked, "Are you in love with her?"

Hero turned his head through Angel by asking, "Are you talking to me?"

Angel asked, "I am here with someone else?"

Hero asked, "In love with who?"

Angel replied, "Of course with Bella."

Hero answered, "No."

Angel said, "You are not in love with her, but you spent your whole weekend with her."

Hero said, "She invited me, and I accepted."

Angel said, "I invited you first, but you refused, then Bella invited you after me and you accepted."

Hero said, "I had asked you, if you still wanted to hang out with me, and you said no, then you left."

Angel asked, "Where is Bella?"

Hero replied, "She is at her home."

Angel asked, "What time did she leave?"

Hero answered, "I drove her to her home a half hour ago."

Angel said, "It means when I was worried about you, you were with Bella."

Hero replied, "I came with Bella, so I was responsible for her security."

Angel said, "You sent me a letter, and in your letter, you told me that everything would be fine, to not worry that you were with me. But you abandoned me when I was in danger."

Hero said, "I did not abandon you."

Angel said, "Of course that you did, because you were not even there when the fight started, and when that mysterious woman and man scared me by asking me to remove my rosaries."

Hero turned his head and he looked in Angel's eyes by saying, "I was in the room."

Angel cried out, "You were in the room?" And she added, "Do not forget that you told me yourself, that you were with Bella, and that you got in the room a couple minutes ago, and you got my hand to get out with me."

Hero looked in front of him still by driving and said that the fight started by the bullet shots on the ceiling of the house, and some people walked till face to you, and a man handed the gun on your boyfriend by asking both your boyfriend and you to get up, and you screamed when you saw your boyfriend fainted on the floor, because he was hit with a gun. Then, two men tried to remove your rosaries and suddenly a violent noise came from the window, and the window's glass was broken, and a man named Matt fell on the man who had held your wrist to remove your rosary, then you and some people moved away. Then, Hero turned his head and he looked at Angel and he noticed that she was looking at him with an amazed face, and he asked, "Do you want me to continue?"

Angel asked, "How did you know that?"

Hero said, "Matt died during the fight because he was electrified, and there was also an eagle that was lying dead on the floor when Matt died."

Angel started to remember how Sol had run through Matt as Matt was dying by screaming the name of Matt, and that Matt was acting as if he was being killed by someone, but just that she was not seeing the one who was killing Matt. And Angel understood that Hero was telling the truth, then she looked at Hero by asking, "How did you know that because you were not in the room when it happened?"

Hero said, "When people who were around you wanted to remove your rosaries, because they had received the orders coming from the mysterious woman, that mysterious woman screamed because she was bitten by the tiger, and she turned, and she started to fight with the tiger, and that how you ran away with other people. Also, you called my name in the room when you heard my voice, and you started to look for me in the room."

Angel asked, "It was really you?"

Hero looked in her eyes and answered, "Yes, it was me."

Angel asked, "Where were you?" And she added, "Because, I looked for you all the time that the fight was going on, and I did not see you."

Hero said, "I was in the room watching you, I was fighting to protect you, and to make sure that everything was all right, and that you were safe, as I had promised you. Just that you could not see me." Then, Hero turned his head through Angel by looking in her eyes, and he asked, "Did you believe me now?"

Angel replied, "I believe you, and I have no doubt that you were in the room, although the fact that I did not see you."

Hero said, "I have a favor to ask you."

Angel said, "I listen to you."

Hero said, "I want you to promise me that you would never take off your rosaries, no matter who would ask you to remove them, even if it's your parents or your boyfriend, you would not remove them."

Angel said, "I want you to make me a promise first, before I make you that promise."

Hero asked, "What did you want me to promise you?"

Angel said, "You must promise me that you would not fall in love with Bella."

Hero looked in her eyes by saying, "I Promise you."

Angel said, "I promise you too."

Hero said, "Thank you."

Angel asked, "Who killed Matt?"

Hero stopped the car's engine, and he looked at Angel and said, "We are at your home."

Angel said, "You did not answer my question."

Hero said, "You can not understand, even if I explained to you."

Angel said, "I want you to tell me who killed Matt, because I saw Matt die, but I did not see the one who killed him."

Hero said, "And if I told you that I am the one who killed Matt."

Angel cried out, "You?" By looking into his eyes with a surprised face.

Hero asked, "Are you afraid?"

Angel asked, "Afraid of what?"

Hero answered, "Afraid of me."

Angel looked into his eyes and answered, "No, I am not afraid of you." And she added, "Even if I have no idea about who you are, I am not afraid of you."

Hero said, "I can explain to you what happened to Matt."

Angel looked at Hero and she saw two scars on his neck, and she noticed that those scars were made through the claws of the tiger, and she remembered about the two tigers that were fighting in the party house, then she opened her mouth and said, "No, I do not want to hear how you killed Matt, if you are really the one who killed him." Then, she turned her head and she opened the car's door, and she got out, then she started to walk through her house. Hero watched Angel get inside her house without even turning her head to look behind, and he started the engine of his car, then he drove away.

Angel was walking in her bedroom, by thinking about everything that happened at the party house, she was thinking about the tigers, the eagle, the death of Matt and she was trying to understand the mystery that was happening. And there were the questions that were going on in her mind like, who killed Matt? It's really Hero who killed Matt? Why did she not see Hero in the room? And why was she not seeing the one who was fighting against Sol, William and Matt? And after more than an hour of thinking, Angel did not succeed to answer even one of her questions. Then, Angel started to think about Hero, and she was wondering about how Hero knew that people would try to kill her as he had put a letter in her bedroom, by telling her to not go to the party. And she started to wonder who was really Hero, and if Hero was really a tiger as she thought, because although the fact that he was acting like a tiger, Hero also had a lot of things that were not related to the tigers, like the fact that he was invisible in the party house, as he knew that she was going to the washroom to remove her rosaries in the party house, as he knew everything that was going to happen as if he was god, and as he was always on time to save her when she was in danger. Then, Angel remembered the day that Hero had saved her when George wanted to kill her, and she remembered that George had demanded Hero if Hero was taking himself for a Superhuman, then she remembered the story of Superhuman. Then, Angel rushed through her study's table and she sat in the chair, then she opened her computer, and she searched for the book called Superhuman 1 by Thierry Kouam, then she spent her whole night reading that book.

The next day, it was 1:00 p.m., William, Sol and Prince were in the living room of Prince's house, and they were all sad and tired, and they were also feeling pains in their whole bodies as they had fought last night. And there was anger inside them too, and Sol told Prince that it was not only Angel who was going to die, that she would also kill Hero to avenge Matt's death. And Prince removed his t-shirt and showed his body to Sol and William, and both William and Sol were looking at the body of Prince with the surprised faces, as they were seeing the scars on his body coming from the claws of the tiger. Then, William asked Prince why Prince had the scars on his body? Prince answered that he got those scars last night when his phantom was fighting against the phantom of Hero, that it was the ghost of Hero who had torn his ghost with the claws.

Then, Prince looked in Sol's eyes by telling her that she was not only the one who wanted to kill Hero, and that even if one of the rule of the tradition of the tiger world banned them to kill a member of their family knowingly, he was ready to break that rule and kill Hero, even if he was going to be killed after on the orders of the ancestors of the tiger world. Sol told Prince that she had been bitten behind the neck by the phantom of Hero, just that she was lucky that the wound was not deep enough to touch her ghost. And William said that he was feeling pains on his whole body, as he had fought against the invisible ghost of Hero.

Then, Sol said that she did not know that Hero was stronger like that, that if Hero had succeeded to save Angel last night, by beating all of them although the plans that they had organized to kill Angel, that meant that it would be not easy for them to kill both Angel and Hero. William told them that three of them should get inside the bedroom of Angel, when Angel would be asleep and Prince would cut the rosaries of Angel, and Sol and him would kill Angel. Prince looked at William by telling William to not forget that Hero had a magic that had an advance on the time, that before they would get inside Angel's bedroom, Hero would be already there to protect her, and that even before they would fix a plan, Hero would be already aware of that plan. And Sol said that she had never seen a supernatural being as Hero, that he was faster, and stronger than any supernatural being that she had met so far, and Sol went on by saying that the only way to kill Angel was to kill Hero first. Because, if they stayed focused on Angel, they would never kill Angel when Hero would be alive. Prince said that it would be almost impossible for them to kill Hero, because Hero had two phantoms, and Hero was protected by his two ghosts, so, to kill Hero, it meant to kill his two phantoms, and that it was not going to be easy, and it would be almost impossible to kill the two phantoms of Hero.

Sol looked at Prince by saying that it would be almost impossible to kill the two phantoms of Hero, but that it was not impossible, and that they did not have choice than to kill the two ghosts of Hero. It was the only solution they had if they wanted to succeed in their mission, because once they would kill the two phantoms of Hero, it would be easy for them to kill Angel, and once Angel would be buried, they would start to eradicate the race of the natural human beings. Prince looked at Sol by saying that if they succeeded one day to kill the two phantoms of Hero, it would take them years, that the better solution was to kill Angel by shooting at her with the bullets. Sol replied to Prince that they would not use the guns to kill Angel, and they would not let someone else kill Angel except a member of the family of eagles.

Prince asked Sol why she insisted on the fact that only a member of the eagle family would kill Angel, and Sol answered that Angel had something important inside her that the eagle family needed, that it was the reason why only a supernatural being from the eagle world would kill Angel. Because, if someone who was not from the family of eagle killed Angel, that person would kill that important thing that was inside Angel when that person would be killing Angel, and it would be a disaster for the eagle world. And Sol went on by saying that if Angel was killed by the bullets, accident, knife or something else, it would be a tragedy for the eagle family, because the eagle family would lose that important thing that was inside Angel forever, because that important thing would die with Angel. And Prince asked Sol how the eagle's family would kill Angel without killing that important thing inside her. And Sol answered Prince that it was the reason why it was important that only a supernatural being from the eagle world would kill Angel, because when a supernatural being of the eagle family would be killing Angel, that supernatural being would remove that important thing inside Angel, before Angel died. Prince asked Sol how a supernatural being from the eagle world would remove that important thing inside Angel before killing her? Sol answered Prince that he could not understand, even if she spent a year explaining to him it, because it was something mystical.

Prince asked Sol why she and her brothers could not kill Angel with the rosaries on Angel? Sol answered Prince that what Angel wore on her wrist, and on her ankle were not the rosaries, even if it looked like the rosaries. Prince asked what it was if it was not the rosaries? Sol answered that what Angel wore on her wrist and on her ankle were the poisons, and that those poisons were dangerous for the supernatural beings of the eagle world. And that the supernatural beings of the eagle world could not even touch those poisons, because if the supernatural beings of the eagle world touched those poisons, it would have the effects on their ghosts, and their phantoms would get very sick, and their phantoms would die. Because, the eagle world did not have the antidote for that kind of dangerous poison, and the doctors of eagle world could not cure a sickness caused by that poison.

Prince looked at Sol by saying that it meant that if Sol touched what Angel had on the wrist and ankle that looked like the rosaries, Sol's ghost would get sick, then Sol would die because her phantom would be dead. Sol answered that it was exactly what would happen if she dared to touch what Angel wore on the ankle and on

## SUPERNATURAL BEINGS

the wrist. Prince asked Sol why the supernatural beings of the eagle world could not remove their ghosts from their bodies and kill Angel, because there their ghosts would be not affected by those poisons that Angel had on her. And Sol answered Prince that it was necessary that the supernatural beings of the eagle world kill Angel when they had their ghosts inside them, because it would be useless and it would be a big loss if they killed Angel without using their ghosts, because they would take what they wanted from Angel through their ghosts. Prince asked Sol where Angel got those poisons? Sol answered that even Angel had no idea of what she was wearing on her ankle and on her wrist, that Angel thought that it was the rosaries that she was wearing.

Prince asked Sol who gave those poisons to Angel? Sol answered Prince that it was a long story that happened more than a century ago, that if they were going to talk about it, they would spend a year just to talk about it. Prince asked how Angel was related to a story that happened more than a century ago, if Angel was just sixteen years old now. Sol looked at Prince by saying that she knew well that Angel was sixteen, and that it was the reason why she told him that if they were going to talk about Angel's story, it would take them a year for him to understand what was going on with Angel. Prince asked if Angel knew all those mysteries about her? Sol answered that except the supernatural beings of the eagle world, nobody else even Angel herself, and Angel's parents had an idea about the mysteries that surrounded Angel.

Then, Prince took a deep breath and he lifted his head through the ceiling, and there was the silence in the room. After six minutes, Sol turned her head through Prince by saying that he should stop thinking about Angel and use that time that he was wasting to think about Angel to think about how to kill the two phantoms of Hero. Prince turned his head through Sol by looking in her eyes, and by asking her how she knew that he was thinking about Angel. Sol replied to Prince that she could even talk to him about what he was thinking about. And Prince replied to Sol that he wanted her to tell him what he was thinking about. And Sol told Prince that he was afraid that Angel found out that he was a tiger, as he had hit himself against the wall last night when Hero had thrown his phantom against the wall. Prince asked Sol how she knew that? Sol answered that she had the power to read in the mind of people, and she could even change the mind of people if she wanted.

Then Prince remembered the day he had fought with Hero in the house, and Sol came after that Hero had left, then they heard policemen get inside the house, and Sol told him to not worry that she was there to help him. And policemen looked at the mess inside the house without saying a word, then policemen left without even asking a question, then Prince understood that Sol had used her magic to change the mind of policemen. Then, Prince looked in Sol's eyes by asking her why she could not use her power to change the mind of Hero, by making Hero give up the fight when Hero would come to fight them to protect Angel or even use her power to change the mind of Angel by making Angel remove the poisons that Angel wore called the rosaries. Sol answered Prince that there were only two humans that she could not read in their minds, and that she had no idea about what those two humans thought, and one of those two humans was a natural human being and the other was a supernatural human being, and unfortunately for her those two humans were Angel and Hero. Prince asked Sol why she could not read in the minds of Hero and Angel? Sol answered that the destiny had made that among all the natural human beings as Angel, and the supernatural beings as Hero, there were only those two named Angel and Hero that she could not read in their minds. Prince said that it seemed that even the destiny was against them, and that he did not understand why among all the supernatural beings the destiny had chosen the best, the stronger, the powerful, the faster and the one who had an amazing magic to protect Angel. Sol replied that the destiny had chosen Hero to protect Angel, because Hero was the best, and because only Hero had the abilities to protect Angel.

Prince said that he would get rest only the day he would bury the two phantoms of Hero. Sol told Prince that she found out through her magic that the supernatural beings of the tiger world had ten senses, but that she did not know about the senses of Hero as her magic could not get inside Hero's body, and she wanted to know if

## SUPERNATURAL BEINGS

Hero had ten senses too. Prince answered that yes, even Hero had ten senses like all the rest of the supernatural beings of the tiger world, and that even their king had ten senses. Sol asked Prince if the magic of Hero was linked to his senses, or even to one of his senses? Prince answered that his magic and the magic of Hero were not linked to their senses, that even the magic of their king was not linked to his senses, that all their ten senses were free. Because, the ancestors of the tiger world controlled all the supernatural beings of the tiger world through their senses, so that the ancestors of the tiger world who were the gods of the tiger world knew what was going on with each kid of the tiger world, through the ten senses of each kid.

Then, Sol took a deep breath by saying that it would be harder than what she had imagined, to kill the two phantoms of Hero. Prince asked Sol why she wanted to know about the senses of Hero? Sol answered that the only chance to kill the phantoms of Hero was to know where the magic of Hero was located inside his body, because if they had the control on the magic of Hero, it would be easy for them to kill the phantoms of Hero. Prince replied that he had no idea about where the magic of Hero was located, and Prince went on by telling Sol that one of the parts of the magic of Hero like his own magic was blocked by their mysterious enemy. Sol replied to Prince that even one part of her magic was blocked each time when she put her feet in the land of natural human beings or when she flew in the space of the world of natural human beings by the same mysterious enemy, that they had that enemy in common, because that enemy was protecting the race of natural human beings. Prince said that they must set a plan before fighting Hero again, or Hero would kill all of them as Hero killed Matt, mostly that the invisible ghost of Hero was very dangerous, and that even if that invisible ghost did not have the magic, that invisible ghost had the strengths that were dangerous for them like the blue lights that that invisible ghost had used to kill Matt, because once that those blue lights had the control on the ghost of a supernatural being, it was impossible for that supernatural being to survive. Sol said that they had three days to set a plan.

Prince asked why three days? Sol answered that they were going to fight only after three days, because according to one of the rules of the tradition of the eagle world, when they lost a member of their family, they had three day of mourning, and during those three days, they would not fight, they would not kill someone, they would not even fight and kill their enemies. And that the eagle world was in mourning for three days like the eagle family buried Matt's phantom this morning. And suddenly, there was silence in the room, as they had heard the phone of Prince ring, and Prince took his phone that was close to him and he looked at the screen, and he noticed that it was Angel who was calling, and his heart started to beat with fear as he was staring at the phone that was ringing. And Sol asked Prince to pick up the phone, then Prince picked up the phone and he started talking with Angel. And after eleven seconds, William and Sol turned their heads through Prince looking at him with the amazed faces, as he was talking to Angel.

After three minutes, Prince hung up the phone, and he told Sol and William that Angel did not find out that he was a tiger. And Sol asked Prince why he told Angel that he should be absent for a week? Prince answered Sol that he was going to the tiger world the next day, for the traditional feast of tiger world that would happen in two days. Sol asked Prince if Hero would be at that traditional feast? Prince answered that all kids of the tiger family were obliged to attend that traditional feast, even Hero because their tradition forbade them to miss that important feast, no matter where you were, when you were a kid of the tiger world, you must attend that meeting.

Sol demanded if the tiger world was aware of the betraying of Hero. Prince replied that no, that it has been a long time he did not talk with the king of the tiger world. Sol asked Prince what would happen when the tiger world would find out that Hero betrayed them. Prince looked at Sol with a smile on his face, and he told her that Hero was no longer a problem for them, because Hero would be killed for his betrayal when he would talk about the treason of Hero. Then, the smile appeared on the face of Sol and William, when they heard Prince say that Hero would be killed, and both Sol and William demanded to Prince if they could participate in the traditional feast of the tiger world. And Prince agreed to go to the tiger world the next day with Sol and William, then three of them spent the whole night talking about Hero and Angel.

# CHAPTER VII

# THE TRADITION FESTIVAL OF SUPERNATURAL BEINGS

It was 6:00 a.m., Prince, Sol and William left for the tiger world. Hero was lying in his bed, and he was feeling pains in his whole body as he had fought through his invisible phantom and his identity phantom a day ago, and there were also some scars on his body that were made by the phantom of Prince during the fight. And Hero had not closed his eyes during the whole night, because he had spent his entire night following the conversation between Prince, Sol and William through his magic. And Hero was wondering what was the important thing that Angel had inside her that the eagle world needed, and Hero was remembering his conversation with Prince about Angel a few weeks ago. When Prince told him during that conversation that it was as if Angel had something inside her, and that he was attracted by that thing inside Angel, and that thing inside Angel was making her different from the rest of the race of natural human beings.

Hero understood that Prince was right, that Angel had really something inside her, and Hero did not know what that important thing was, but Hero started to understand why the supernatural beings of the eagle world wanted to kill Angel. And Hero understood too the reasons why the supernatural beings of the eagle world could not kill Angel by themselves, when Angel wore those poisons on her that looked like the rosaries. But the question that was going on in the mind of Hero was who gave those poisons that looked like the rosaries to Angel? But unfortunately, Hero could not answer that question, but Hero knew that the one who had given those poisons that looked like the rosaries to Angel knew the mysteries that were on Angel, and that one had given those rosaries to Angel to protect her from the supernatural beings of the eagle world.

And Hero was wondering why that important thing that the eagle world needed was in the body of Angel who was a natural human being? How was Angel who was a natural human being linked to the eagle world? And how did Angel who was just sixteen was linked to a history that happened more than a century ago? But unfortunately, Hero could not answer those questions, but there were two other questions that were going on in the mind of Hero, and those questions were, why when Angel would be alive it would be impossible for the race of supernatural natural beings to destroy the race of natural human beings? And how was Angel who was a natural human being without any power preventing supernatural beings from eradicating the race of natural human beings? Then, Hero remembered that he had heard Sol tell Prince that all supernatural beings had the same mysterious enemy, and that one part of her own magic was blocked by that mysterious enemy. And that it was that mysterious enemy who was preventing the supernatural beings from destroying the race of natural human beings, and that that enemy was not Angel. Even, if Hero knew that there was a mystery on the life of Angel, and he knew well that Angel could not be the one who was preventing the supernatural beings to destroy the race of natural human beings, and that even the death of Angel would not allow the supernatural beings to destroy the race of natural human beings. Also, when the supernatural human beings would not find out who was their mysterious enemy, they would never succeed to eradicate the race of natural human beings even if they succeeded to kill Angel.

Then, Hero started to think that the supernatural beings of the eagle world had lied to Prince by saying that when Angel would be alive, they would never succeed in destroying the race of natural human beings. And that Sol and William were using Prince to get their important thing that Angel had inside her, as Prince was in a relationship with Angel, then Sol and William thought that by approaching Prince, it would be easier for them to get what they wanted from Angel. And for that they lied to Prince by saying that the only way to destroy the race of natural human beings, it was to kill Angel first, knowing that Prince was in the world of natural human beings to eradicate that race of natural human beings.

Then, Hero started to think about another thing he heard from the mouth of Prince, when Sol had demanded to Prince if the magic of the supernatural beings of the tiger world was linked to their senses, or to one of their senses. And Prince had answered Sol that no, that all their ten senses were free, that magic of supernatural beings of the tiger world was not linked to their senses, or to one of their senses because their ancestors were controlling them through their senses. And Hero remembered that Prince was right that it was impossible that the magic of a magician kid of the tiger world be linked to his senses, because their ancestors were aware of everything that they were doing through their senses, and for that all their ten senses should be free, for that their ancestors controlled them.

And Hero understood that he was mistaken when he thought that the part of his magic that was always warning him when Angel was in danger was linked to his last sense that was his tenth sense. And Hero started to wonder where in his body was located the part of his magic that was always warning him when Angel was in danger, because he knew where the rest of his magic was located in his body. And Hero thought that that part of his magic that was warning him when Angel was in danger was located in his last sense, but he was wrong, and he started to think where could be located that part of his magic. And after three hours of thinking without finding where was located the part of his magic that was warning him when Angel was in danger, Hero decided to follow what was happening in the tiger world through his magic. Prince, Sol and William were in the car, and Prince was driving in the land of the tiger world, and Sol was feeling something strange inside her, as she was staring at the landscape through the car's window, and she was remembering that the first time that she had come in the tiger world, it was the day she came to fight the supernatural beings of the tiger world, and she had felt that strange thing that day.

After forty-five minutes of driving, Prince parked the car in the large family yard of the tiger world, and there were the supernatural beings who were playing in that yard. Then, Prince, Sol and William got outside from the car, and supernatural beings who were playing had the smile on their faces as they had seen Prince get out of the car, but that smile turned into the anger when they saw William and Sol, as they had noticed that William and Sol were with the enemies who had attacked them couple months ago. And those supernatural beings turned into the tigers by looking in the eyes of William and Sol. Then, Prince started talking to the tigers in their traditional language that was the Latin, by trying to calm them, and by telling them that William and Sol were not the enemies but instead the friends. And Sol started to look in the eyes of the tigers, and her green eyes became blue, then those tigers turned into their bodies of supernatural beings, and Prince introduced William and Sol to them. And they asked Prince where was Hero? Prince answered that Hero would come later, then Prince, Sol and William started to walk through the palace, by greeting the supernatural beings that they were meeting on the road, and each time when the supernatural beings were approaching them, Sol used her magic by looking in the eyes of supernatural beings to change their minds. And almost all the supernatural beings were outside, because they were preparing their traditional feast that was going to happen the next day. Sol and William were amazed by seeing how the tiger world was preparing their traditional feast, and they were seeing how the supernatural beings of the tiger world were preparing the activities.

Then, Prince, Sol and William reached the palace, and they were welcomed by King Philip, and Philip took them to a room, and they started to talk. And Philip was amazed to hear that Hero had betrayed the tiger world, and Philip told Prince that the ancestors did not talk him about the betraying of Hero, but that the ancestors told him about the fight that had happened between Hero and Prince, and the ancestors told him too about some mistakes that Hero had done as Hero had saved a kid, and the game of the basket-

## SUPERNATURAL BEINGS

ball that Hero had played. Prince asked Philip if the ancestors told him about the young woman named Angel, that Hero was fighting to protect. Philip replied that the ancestors did not talk about that young woman, and Philip also told Prince that it had been three days that he did not talk with the ancestors, because he was busy with the preparation of the activities of the traditional feast. Then, Philip told Prince to not say a word about the betraying of Hero to someone, that they have to keep the silence about that betrayal to not destroy the traditional feast, and they would wait for Hero, then after the traditional feast, he would talk with the ancestors, and the ancestors would decide. After three hours of conversation, Philip told Prince, Sol and William that they would continue with that conversation later, because he was going to meet his advisors to talk about the activities of the feast.

Then, Prince, Sol and William got up and they walked till outside, and they were climbing down the stairs of the palace, and there were supernatural beings who were staring at them. And one of the supernatural beings named Brad ran till the stairs, and Brad greeted Prince, and Prince introduced Brad to Sol and William, then Brad looked in the eyes of Sol, and he started to remember about the attack that had happened in the tiger world few months ago, and he remembered that he had fought against Sol that day where the tiger world was attacked by Sol and her family. Then, Brad turned his head through Prince, and he asked where Hero was? And Prince answered that Hero would come later. Then, Brad told Prince that he would like to talk with Sol, and they all looked at Brad with amazed faces, and there was silence. And after eleven seconds, Prince broke the silence by telling Brad to ask Sol if she would like to talk with him. And Brad turned his head through Sol, and he looked in her eyes by asking her, if she would like to talk with him, and Sol was looking in Brad's eyes by reading his mind without saying a word. Then, Sol opened her mouth, and she told Brad that she had no problem listening to him, but Sol already knew what Brad was going to talk to her about.

Then, Brad tried to hold Sol's hand, and she told Brad that she could follow him without holding his hand, then both Brad and Sol walked till the yard of the palace. And they were standing up under a tree, and they were face to face looking at each other in the eyes, and Sol told Brad that she was listening to him. And Brad told Sol that he wanted to thank her as she did not kill him during the fight when the tiger world was attacked by her family. Sol told Brad that he did not need to thank her, because if she did not kill him that day, it was because she did not have the opportunity to kill him, not because she wanted to let him alive. Brad told Sol that it was not true, because she had an opportunity to kill him that day, and she looked in his eyes then she chose to let him alive. Sol told Brad that she was not remembering, but Sol was lying, because she knew well that she could kill Brad that day, but she had decided to let him alive. Then, Brad told Sol that he would like to take her for a walk and show her the tiger world.

Sol demanded to Brad why he was so nice with her, knowing that she and her family had attacked the tiger world a couple months ago. And Brad answered Sol that the ancestors of tiger world had told them through their king that the supernatural beings who had attacked the tiger world were not the enemies of the tiger world, but instead the friends of the tiger world, and that it was a mistake if the tiger world was attacked by the eagle world. Sol replied to Brad that she understood why most of inhabitants of the tiger world were nice to her and William, then she demanded to Brad how he should behave if the ancestors of the tiger world had told them that she and her family were the enemies of the tiger world. Brad looked in Sol's eyes and he opened his mouth to talk, but no word was coming out from his mouth, while Sol was looking in his eyes too by reading his mind, then Brad told Sol that he would always protect his family against the enemies. But Sol knew that Brad had lied to her, that what Brad said it was not what he was thinking.

Then, Sol told Brad that she was ready to follow him, and Brad wanted to grab Sol's hand, but she refused, and she told him that he did not need to hold her hand to show her the tiger world. Then, Brad took Sol to the museum of the tiger world, and Sol had the smile on her face as she was walking inside the museum, and Brad was telling her the story of the tiger world, and by showing her the pictures of supernatural beings who had made the history of the tiger world. And walls of the museum were full of the pictures of the tigers, and those tiger's photos on the walls were the ghosts of the ancestors of the tiger world. Sol was looking the pictures of the former kings of the tiger world on the walls, and Brad showed the holy book to Sol and he told her the history of that holy book.

Then, Brad took Sol to the sacred place, and when Angel walked in the sacred place, she started to feel strange reaction inside her, and she was staring the big stones and the skulls of the ancestors of the tiger world, and the skeletons of the tigers that were the skeletons of the ghosts of the ancestors of the tiger world with her eyes wet of tears. Brad was looking at Sol with an astonished face, by wondering what was going wrong with her as he was seeing the tears that were flowing down her cheeks. Then, Brad demanded Sol if everything was all right, and she looked at him by making the gestures with her head by saying yes, then she started to walk in the sacred place by staring at the skulls that were on the stones. After more than three hours in the sacred place, both Brad and Angel spent the rest of the day visiting the statues of the ancestors of the tiger world and other places, while William and Prince were helping the supernatural beings to prepare the activities of the traditional feast.

The next day, it was the day of the feast, and everyone had worn the red clothes that were the traditional clothes of the tiger world, and even William and Sol had received their red clothes. They spent the whole day to make the feast, to eat and to dance their traditional dance, to do some activities, and they even organized the games and they played volleyball which is one of their sports. Brad spent his time to show Sol how to dance the traditional dance of the tiger world. They spent three days making the feast according to the rules of the culture and the tradition of the tiger world, and they were all surprised to see that Hero had not come, and they were wondering what had happened to Hero, even Prince was surprised to see that Hero had missed the traditional feast.

# Chapter VIII

# Hero Sentenced to Death for Treason

The next day of the feast, Philip called a meeting in the sacred house, and Philip announced to all inhabitants of the tiger world that the tiger world was going through a tragedy, that the tiger world had been betrayed by one of his kids, that one of the children of the tiger world had broken the rules of the tradition of the tiger world. Everyone in the room turned their heads looking at each other with the surprised faces, and some of them had the fear on their faces, and they were all wondering what was going on, and who Philip was talking about. Except Prince in the room, who knew that Philip was talking about Hero. Sol and William were waiting outside the room, because they were not allowed to get inside the sacred house at the meeting time as they were not kids of the tiger world. After a few minutes, Philip announced to everyone that he was going to the secret room to talk with the ancestors, and to hear the decision of the ancestors, about the traitor who had betrayed the tiger world. Then, he would call a meeting, when he would get out of the secret room to tell them the name of the traitor, and the decision of the ancestors about the traitor who had broken the rules of the tradition of the tiger world.

Then, everyone left the sacred house, by wondering who the traitor was, but no one could answer their question, and Prince did not tell anyone that it was Hero the traitor, despite the fact that his brothers and sisters asked him if he knew that traitor. And except Prince, the rest of the supernatural beings spent the entire day wondering who the traitor was, and they went to the bed with the fear inside them. It was evening, Angel sat in the chair of her study's table, and she was reading the book of Superhuman 1 by Thierry Kouam, and by reading that book, she was understanding that Superhuman was a magician boy who had the magic, and that his magic had an advance on the time, and Superhuman could see things that were going to happen through his magic, before it happened.

Then, Angel started to understand that Superhuman and Hero had something similar, both Superhuman and Hero had an advance on the time, and both were able to see a danger that was going to happen. And Angel started to wonder if Hero had the magic as Superhuman, but she had no doubt that Hero had an advance on the time, as Hero knew what was going to happen, before that happened, and as Hero also warned her about a lot of things that were going to happen, and those things happened. And Angel found out by reading that book that Superhuman was a magician boy, who was fighting against a wizard boy to save the planet where he was living, and to save the inhabitants of that planet to prevent that wizard boy from destroying that planet. But, also that Superhuman was a natural human being, despite the fact that he had the magic, and that Superhuman was almost immortal, because nobody knew how to kill him. And Angel was wondering too, if Hero was also almost immortal, and if Hero was fighting just to protect her, but Angel had the doubts that Hero was a natural human being.

Then, Angel lifted her head through the ceiling by taking a deep breath, then she bent her head, and suddenly her eyes opened widely as she had seen a sheet of paper in the book of Superhuman that was opened in front of her, and that she was reading. Then, she looked at that sheet of paper, and she remarked the handwriting of Hero, then she took that sheet of paper in her hand, and she read, "Please, do not forget that you had promised me to never remove your rosaries, and I want you to keep that promise forever. Because, I would lose most of my strengths soon." Angel started to panic, and she was not understanding very well the meaning of the message of Hero, when he said that he would lose most of his strengths soon, and she was afraid that Hero was in danger. Then, she got up from her chair, and she started to walk in her bedroom with that sheet of paper in her hand, by thinking and with her heart that was beating with fear. She wanted to go see Hero, but unfortunately, she had no idea about where he was living, and she did not have his phone number, so she spent all night thinking about Hero with the fear inside her.

It was early morning. There was fog outside and the whole inhabitants of the tiger world were still in their beds, and most of them had not closed their eyes during the whole night, because they had spent their whole night to think about who the traitor of the tiger world was. Then, they heard the bell that had begun ringing, and they were all surprised to hear the bell that was ringing, and they were all wondering what was going on in the tiger world. As they knew that the bell that was ringing was a message to tell them that Philip had got out of the secret room, because every time that their king was inside the secret room, the bell was ringing the day he was getting out to announce to everyone that he had got out of the secret room.

They were all wondering why Philip had spent less than twenty-four hours in the secret room, and it was the first time in the history of the tiger world that a king spent less than twenty-four hours in the secret room, because the minimum hours that a king had spent in the secret room in the secret room was seventy-two hours. Then, they started to get up from their beds, and they started to get ready with the fear inside them, and with the questions that were going on in their minds that they could not answer, even Prince was very surprised to hear the bell ring. After a half hour, the sacred house was full of the inhabitants of the tiger world, and they were all staring at Philip with fear on their faces while Philip was staring at them too, and there was silence in the room, but we could hear some of them breathing deeply. After three minutes, Philip broke the silence by saying that he had no word to talk about the tragedy that the tiger world was living, and that the ancestors had decided to show them who the traitor of the tiger world was, with the evidence through the magic wall. And Philip went on by saying that since he had been crowned king of the tiger world, he had never used the magic wall, and that even as a child of the tiger world, he had never seen his dad who was the former king used the magic wall. And that if the ancestors had demanded him to use the magic wall, it meant that something worse was going on, and the ancestors wanted to warn everyone, and to send a message to everyone.

Then, Philip walked to the left side, and he pulled the curtain that covered the wall, and the heart of everyone started to beat faster as if they were going to have a heart attack, and their eyes were focused on the magic white wall. And for most of them, it was their first time to see the magic wall, but they had already heard about the magic wall, because the magic wall was taught to them at school in the course of the culture, and the tradition of the tiger world. And they had all noticed that Philip had pulled the curtain to the left side of the wall, and that meant that the ancestors were very angry, and that something worse was going to happen. Because, they all knew that when the curtain was pulled from the left side, it meant that the ancestors had taken the worst decisions, and when the curtain was pulled from the right side, it meant that the ancestors had taken the good decisions. And their eyes were still focused on the magic wall, and they were all waiting for the ancestors to send them the message through that magic wall.

Suddenly, the expression on the face of everyone changed, as they were seeing a video of Hero and Prince on the magic wall, then they started watching the life of Hero and Prince in the world of natural human beings. After fifteen minutes, the expression of their faces changed as they were seeing Prince and Hero who were fighting in their house, then they watched Hero who was playing basketball, they watched Hero who was explaining the maths to students, Hero who had saved a kid by climbing a building. And they watched how Hero had saved a young woman named Bella who was surrounded by men and one of men had put a gun on her head. And they watched the relationship between Prince and Angel, how both Prince and Angel were spending their time together, kissing together, and also the friendship between Prince, Sol and William.

After more than three hours the video was over, and there was a silence in the room and they were all turning their heads looking at each other with amazed faces, and Prince was completely lost, he did not understand why the ancestors had not shown any picture of Hero and Angel. And Prince was wondering why the ancestors did not show the fight of Hero against him and against the supernatural beings of the eagle world to save Angel? And why did the ancestors not show how Hero killed Matt? And Prince had noticed that the ancestors had shown everything that Hero had done, except things that were related to Angel that the ancestors did not show, and that the ancestors had even shown how Hero had saved Bella as a man had put the gun on Bella's head, but the ancestors did not show anything about Angel. Prince was still not understanding why the ancestors showed his relationship with Angel, and the ancestors did not show the relationship between Angel and Hero, even if both Angel and Hero had never kissed together, but Prince knew that Angel and Hero were in love.

And Prince wanted to run to where Philip was, and to use his magic to show to everyone how Hero had betrayed the tiger world by saving Angel who was an enemy who was preventing them from destroying the race of natural human beings. But Prince knew well that he could not run through where Philip was, and use his magic to show to everyone the evidence of the betraying of Hero, because it was against one of the rules of tradition of the tiger world. Because, by doing that, he was not only breaking one of the rules of the tradition of the tiger world, but it was as if he was challenging his ancestors, and for that he would be killed as he had dared to oppose the ancestors. Then, there was silence in the room, and Philip had already closed the curtain, and everyone was looking at Philip by waiting for him to talk about the decision of the ancestors.

Then, Philip broke the silence, and he announced the decision of the ancestors by saying that the relationships between Prince and Angel was not condemned by the ancestors, although the fact that Angel was a natural human being, because Prince was not in love with Angel, and that Prince was using Angel as a guinea pig to know how the body of natural human functioned. So that Angel was just a plan for Prince to succeed his mission, and for that the ancestors had considered that Prince should be not punished, mostly that Prince had not made love with Angel, even if Prince had had broken one of the important rules of the tradition of the tiger world by kissing Angel who was a natural human being. Then, Philip took a deep breath, and he went on by saying that Hero had not only broken a lot of important rules of the tradition of the tiger world, but Hero had also betrayed the tiger world, and for that Hero had become a traitor and an enemy of the tiger world. And the eyes of everyone opened widely, and the hearts of most of them started to beat with fear, and some of them were even trembling with panic.

Then, Philip said that the ancestors had decided to destroy nine of the fourteen vampirism powers of Hero, as Hero had missed the traditional feast of the tiger world, and the ancestors had decided to sentence Hero to one hundred years in prison as he had played basketball to participate to that fundraising for natural human beings, and another one hundred years of imprisonment as Hero had explained the maths to natural human beings. And suddenly, there were the screams in the room, as they had heard Philip say that Hero had been sentenced to hang by the ancestors as Hero had saved the life of two natural human beings by climbing the building to save that kid named Raul, and as Hero had saved that young woman named Bella.

Suddenly, Sarah who was the mom Hero fainted on the floor, when she heard that Hero was going to be hanged according to the rules of the tradition of the tiger world the day where Hero would put his feet in the land of tiger. Then, Philip told everyone that Hero knew well that the natural human beings were the enemies of the supernatural beings, and Hero knew too that the rules of their traditions banned the supernatural beings to help, or to save a natural human being, and that Hero was sent in the world of natural human beings to eradicate the race of natural human beings not to save the race of natural human beings. Then, Philip added that Hero would never spend a night again in the tiger world, and whenever that Hero would come in the tiger world, Hero would be arrested and hanged according to the rules of the culture and tradition of the tiger world, also that Hero had lost his identity as a supernatural being of the tiger world, then Philip turned and left. Then, Sarah was carried by some supernatural beings, and they walked out with her.

William and Sol were outside, they were seeing some supernatural beings who were getting out of the sacred house with tears that were flowing down their cheeks, while others had faces full of sadness, and only few of them had the smile on their faces. And Sol was seeing Brad and Prince who were walking out, and she was noticing that Brad had a face full of sadness, while Prince had a face full of smile, and Sol understood the decision of the ancestors, as she knew that Brad was the best friend of Hero, and Prince was the worse enemy of Hero.

Then, Prince saw Sol and William who were staring at him, and Prince walked till them, and Prince told Sol and William about the decision of the ancestors, and both Sol and William were very happy to hear that Hero would no longer be a danger to them. It was a tragic day in the tiger world, and for most inhabitants it was the first time to hear the ancestors condemned a supernatural being to death. And most supernatural beings were very sad, till some were crying like the childhood friends of Hero, but there were few of them who were very happy to know that Hero should be hanged soon like the childhood friends of Prince. As Prince and Hero were the enemies when they were kids, and each of them had his friends. Some childhood friends of Hero were standing up under a tree, and they were talking about the situation of Hero with sadness, and the rage inside them, then some of childhood friends of Prince came and joined them. And suddenly, the fight started between them, once that Prince's childhood friends had said that they were happy to know that Hero was going to be hanged. And the police of the tiger world came, and arrested them, and they were all locked in the jail. And the day was getting worse and worse in the tiger world, there was a fight everywhere and anywhere that a friend of Hero and a friend of Prince were meeting, and the police were outside to arrest all those who were fighting.

The parents were worried about the arrest of young supernatural beings, and parents were afraid that a war was going to start between the friends of Hero and the friends of Prince, and that the young of the tiger world were going to be divided like seventeen years

## SUPERNATURAL BEINGS

ago. Because, seventeen years ago, the children of the tiger world were divided into two groups, and one group of Hero and his friends, and another group of Prince and his friends. Sol and William were very amazed to see how the young supernatural beings of the tiger world were fighting between them, Sol saw Brad who was arrested by the police, and Prince was trying to calm the situation by asking his friends to stop fighting, but his friends were not paying attention to him. And Prince was accused by the friends of Hero of being responsible for the death sentence of Hero. It was evening, and there were no young of seventeen years old in the streets, or in a house of the tiger world, because they were all in jail, and parents were very worried about their kids.

The inhabitants went to bed with fear inside them, and the sentence of death of Hero was still in their heads, and most of them were saying that Hero arrived in the world of natural human beings, and he forgot about his tradition and culture. And that Hero also forgot about the reasons why he was sent into that world of natural human beings, and he started to build a friendship with the race of natural human beings, by forgetting that natural human beings were the worst enemies of the tiger world. And that's how Hero started to break the rules of the tradition of the tiger world by playing with the natural human beings, as they had watched Hero play basketball and save the natural human beings named Raul and Bella through the magic wall.

It was morning. No one in the tiger world had closed their eyes during the night, the night had been horrible for the inhabitants of the tiger world, they had all spent their whole night thinking about the situation of Hero, and the situation of the tiger world with the young supernatural beings who were in prison. Prince, Sol and William were in the yard of the palace talking with Philip, and they were close to the car of Prince. And Prince, Sol and William were on their way to return to the world of natural human beings to continue their mission. After six minutes, Prince, Sol and William got inside the car, and Prince started the engine of the car, then Philip demanded to Prince to wait as Philip had seen a woman who was running through them by screaming the name of Prince. Then, Prince,

Sol and William got out of the car, and they turned their heads and they saw that woman who was running towards them, and William asked Prince who was that woman. And Prince answered that it was the mom of Brad, then Sol turned her head through Prince by saying that she hoped that Brad was all right.

Then, Brad's mom reached them, and she greeted them, and she removed a sheet of paper that was folded from her pocket, then she handed that sheet of paper to Sol by saying that it was a letter coming from Brad. And Sol looked at Brad's mom without knowing what to do, by wondering if she should take that sheet of paper, then after a couple of seconds of hesitation, Sol handed her hand and she took that sheet of paper in the hand of Brad's mom. Then, Sol thanked Brad's mom, and Brad's mom begged Sol to read the contents of that letter, that her son told that it was important that Sol read it, then Sol opened that sheet of paper and she looked at it, as she was reading, "I am so sorry for the way I behaved, I am not asking you to forgive me, because I know myself that I broke the promise that I had made to you, as I had told you that I would be with you during all your time in the tiger world, and that I should make you enjoy the tiger world. But please I am asking you this favor from deep in my heart to give me another chance to see you again, my heart is beating faster than the normal every time I am thinking of you, it is as if I am going to have a heart attack just by thinking of you. And I know well that it's a sin to think of you as we are not kids from the same family even if we belong to the same race, and I know that I am breaking some rules of the tradition of the tiger world by thinking of you, but for you, I am ready to break all the rules of the tradition of the tiger world, and I am even ready to accept the death by hanging for you. Because, I can not stop thinking of you, and I can not prevent myself from thinking of you, and I would voluntarily choose death if it happens that I am forbidden to think of you. I miss you."

Sol looked at Brad's mom and Sol asked her if Brad was still in jail, and Brad's mom answered that yes, that Brad was still in jail. And Philip asked Sol if she wanted to visit Brad, and Sol turned her head through Philip and she opened her mouth but no word was coming out, she did not know what to say, and after less than a minute of hesitation Sol said no, that she did not want to see Brad, then she said to Prince and William that they have to go. Then, Prince, Sol and William got inside the car and they left the tiger world.

## CHAPTER IX

# THE GHOST OF HERO PRISONER

Angel and Hero were in the class sitting in their places, and they had not told each other since the night of the fight where Angel had got out of the car of Hero in the yard of her house, they were looking at the instructor who was explaining them the course. But Hero was not really paying attention to the instructor, because he was thinking about the nine of his fourteen vampirism powers that would be destroyed, and he did not know when those nine vampirism powers were going to be destroyed.

And Hero was very afraid that after the destruction of most of his vampirism powers, he would not be able to protect Angel, and he was thinking what to do, but he knew himself that there was no solution. Because he could not prevent those nine vampirism powers from being destroyed, mostly that those nine vampirism powers were going to be destroyed mystically, so he did not need to be in the tiger world for those nine vampirism powers to be destroyed. Hero had followed everything that had happened in the tiger world through his magic, and he knew that he was sentenced to death by hanging. But, Hero was not worried about the fact that he was going to be hanged the day he would put his feet in the tiger world, and he was not surprised at all about the decision of the ancestors, because he knew himself that he was already a dead man, since the first day that he had broken one of the rules the tradition of the tiger world by saving Angel in the lake. But what had attracted the attention of Hero, it was the fact that the ancestors did not show how he had saved Angel, and Hero was not understanding why the ancestors did not show anything about him and Angel. And mostly that the ancestors had shown how he had saved Raul and Bella, even how he had explained maths to the natural human beings, and the ancestors had also shown the relationship between Prince and Angel.

And Hero was trying to understand the reasons why his ancestors did not show how he saved Angel, because the real reason why he had broken the rules of the tradition of the tiger world, it was to save Angel, and he had started to break the rules of the tradition by saving Angel. And the worst for Hero was that he had not even been sentenced to death because he had saved Angel, but he had been sentenced to death because he had saved Raul and Bella that his own magic did not ask him to save. And Hero remembered that he had disobeyed his magic to save Bella, and Hero was wondering if he had not saved Raul and Bella, his ancestors should show the evidence of his fight to save Angel to sentence him to death? But Hero could not answer that question, and the main question was still why the ancestors did not show how he saved Angel, mostly that Angel was the dangerous enemy that the supernatural beings were trying to kill. Again, Hero could not answer that question, and for Hero only the ancestors knew the reasons why they did not show how he had saved Angel.

Suddenly, Hero started to not feel good, and he was feeling pains inside his joints, and he was wondering what was going on, then the light got out from his eyes and he felt that those pains were becoming worse and worse. Then, he noticed that those pains were not coming from his body, but instead from his identity phantom, and he was still feeling pains although the fact that he had removed his identity phantom from his body. And Hero started to be afraid that his phantom was sick, and he tried to get up from his chair, but it was impossible because he was feelings pains in his legs, and he was becoming very weak, then Hero understood that nine of his vampirism powers were being destroyed as he was losing his strengths.

Then, Hero understood that he could not stay in class, because he did not know what was going to happen, and what would be his reaction mostly that he was losing the control of his ghost. But the problem was that Hero did not know how he should reach his hotel, or how to get out of the classroom as he could not walk, and he could not ask for help from his classmates, because they were going to call the emergencies. Then, Hero got an idea, and he tore a sheet of paper from his notebook, and he wrote on that sheet of paper, then the light got out from his eyes and turned into his invisible phantom, and that invisible phantom took that sheet of paper and walked away with it.

Angel had bent her head in her book, and she was writing in her book, then she noticed a sheet of paper on her book, and she looked at it and she noticed the writing of Hero on that sheet of paper. And she turned her head from behind, and she stared at Hero who was getting up from his chair with the difficulties, then she turned her head towards her book, and she took that sheet of paper that was on her book, then read, "Please, do not let someone call the emergencies." Then, she turned her head from behind, and she saw Hero who was holding the tables, by dragging his both legs to walk, and the students had turned their heads looking at Hero by wondering what he had, and by looking at Hero, they could see that he was feeling the pains.

Then, the instructor demanded to Hero to sit down, that she would call the emergencies, and suddenly Angel replied to the instructor that Hero was fine, that Hero had eaten a food that he was allergic to it, that they did not need to call the emergencies. Then, Angel got up from her chair, and she ran till where Hero was, and she put one the arms of Hero around her shoulder, and she asked Hero to lean on her. The students were looking at Hero and Angel who were walking through the door of the classroom with the amazed faces, and the students were wondering since when both Angel and Hero were close, till Angel knew of what Hero was suffering from. And the students could understand if It was Bella who had helped Hero to get out of the classroom, because they all knew that Bella was the only one who was close to Hero, and for most of students it was their first time to see Hero and Angel together.

Angel and Hero were walking in the yard of the campus, and the pains of Hero was becoming worse and worse, till he had the difficulties to drag his legs, then Angel told Hero that they have to find a place where he would sit down, and she would run to parking and she would take the car, then she would come take him. And Hero replied to Angel that the car was already close to them, then a car parked close to them, and Angel looked inside the car and she did not see someone, but the invisible phantom of Hero was inside the car, and it was that invisible phantom who had parked the car. And Angel heard as if someone opened the car's doors, and she looked at the car, but she did not see someone, and she noticed that the car's doors were opened, then she turned her head through Hero and she asked him who parked the car, and who opened the car's door. And Hero looked in her eyes, by asking her if she was afraid, and she answered that no, that was not afraid, then Hero asked her to help him get inside the car, and Angel helped him to get in the car, and Hero wanted to sit in the seat of the driver, but Angel refused by saying that she would drive. Then, both Angel and Hero were in the car, and Angel started the engine, then she drove till to her house without saying a word to Hero.

Then, Angel helped Hero to walk to her bedroom, and she laid Hero in her bed. And Hero asked Angel why she took him to her house, and she answered him that she wanted to look after him as he was sick, she also told him to not worry about his stuff in class, because she had already texted Bella to come with their stuff. And Hero wanted to go, but Angel prevented him from getting up from the bed, and they both spent the rest of the day together, Angel spent her day to stare at Hero who was suffering in her bed with her face full of sadness.

It was the next day, Prince, Sol and William were standing up in the living room of Prince's house, and they were all face to the wall, by staring at the photos of Hero and Angel that Prince had made appear on the wall through his magic. And they had all the smiles on their faces, as they were seeing Hero who was suffering in Angel's bed, and they knew that Hero was sick, because he had lost most of his strengths, and they were thinking about a strategy to kill Angel. And for them it was already a victory, because they knew that Hero could not anymore protect Angel, as Hero already had lost most part of his strengths, then Sol told Prince and William that they could not wait, and that it was the good moment to kill Angel mostly that Hero was sick. Then, they spent two days talking about a plan. It was midnight, Hero was still in Angel's house, and Angel had not put her feet in school since the day she had left school with Hero, and her parents did not know that Angel had stopped going to school, and that there was a man in Angel's bedroom.

Hero was still lying in the bed of Angel and he was still suffering from pain, and Angel sat in the chair face to the bed, and she was staring at Hero who was suffering without knowing what to do to help him, and since that Hero was in her bedroom, he had not put something in his mouth, and he had refused everything that Angel had proposed him like food. Angel had proposed to Hero to take him to the hospital, but Hero had refused by saying that the doctors could not help him, and Angel had asked him how she could help him, and Hero had answered that nobody could help him. Angel was staring at Hero who was lying in bed and suddenly she noticed that the expression of the face of Hero had changed, that he was looking at her anxiously, and she opened her mouth to talk, but Hero interrupted her by telling her to not remove her rosaries no matter what would happen. And Angel demanded Hero what was going on?

Suddenly, Angel screamed as she had heard the noise coming from the window, then she turned her head through the window, and she noticed that the window's glass was broken. Then, Angel saw two eagles flying inside her bedroom through the window, and those two eagles turned into the supernatural beings who were Sol and William, and the light got out of the eyes of Hero, and that light turned into the invisible phantom of Hero. Then, the invisible phantom of Hero started to fight Sol and William, and Angel was in a corner of the room watching the fight, and the stuff was falling from everywhere, then Angel turned her head and she saw Hero who was shaking on the bed by suffering. Then, Angel ran till close to the bed, and she bent close to Hero, and she held the arm of Hero by telling him that they should get out of the room, and Hero replied to her that he was fine. Angel told him that he could get killed by people who were fighting, that they must leave the bedroom, and Hero replied that nothing would happen to him, that she just needed to stay with the rosaries on her wrist and on her ankle. But, Angel was not paying attention to Hero, and she was trying to lift Hero from the bed, and suddenly she screamed the name of Hero as she had felt a hand around her, and she also felt that someone had grabbed her foot, and that the one who had grabbed her foot was trying to remove the rosary that was on her ankle. Then, the light got out from Hero's eyes, as Hero had seen that Angel was in danger, and that light turned into the tiger, and suddenly the two men who had grabbed Angel ran through the door once they had seen the tiger.

And Angel turned, and she started to run through the door too, and the tiger was following Angel. Angel reached the living room, and she saw her parents who were tied in the chairs, and there were three men in the living room, and those three men screamed when they saw the tiger behind Angel, and those three men turned, and they ran through the door. Rebecca started to scream as she was seeing the tiger, and Angel ran till to her mom and she untied her mom, then Angel and Rebecca untied Angel's dad, and there was still the tiger that was looking at them.

Then, Rebecca grabbed Angel's hand by telling Angel that they should run away, but Angel refused by telling her parents that Hero was in her bedroom, that they have to save Hero first. And Rebecca shouted at Angel that there was no time to save whoever that they must run away before the tiger that was staring at them killed them, and Angel turned her head and she looked in the eyes of the tiger, and the tiger was staring at her too. Then, Angel started to remember the expression of Hero's face, every time when Hero stared at her, and she noticed that the tiger that was staring at her had the same look as Hero, that the eyes of the tiger were turning like the eyes of Hero, and that tiger had the same color eyes as Hero, and that she was feeling the same feeling by staring at that tiger as if she was staring at Hero, and that Hero and that tiger had the same reaction in her body, then she started to feel that that tiger was Hero. Then, Angel started to walk towards the tiger while her parents were shouting at her to not approach the tiger, that the tiger would kill her, and suddenly they turned their heads through the door, as they had seen that tiger that Angel was staring at was running through the door. And Angel's parents started to yell as they were seeing another tiger that was running inside the house coming from outside, then the two tigers started to fight, and Angel's parents were screaming at Angel that they should get out of the house. Angel was watching the fight between the two tigers, and she noticed that the tiger that she was feeling was Hero was very weak, and that the other tiger was beating the tiger, that she was feeling that it was Hero, and that that tiger that she was feeling was Hero was losing the fight.

Then, Angel remembered the letter of Hero that had appeared on the book of Superhuman 1 when she was reading that book, and that Hero had told her in that letter that he would lose most part of his strengths soon, and Angel started to understand what going on, then Angel turned, and she started to run towards the kitchen. While Angel's parents were still yelling at her to get out of the house, Rebecca demanded her husband to call the police, that she was going to see if Angel was doing well, then Rebecca saw Angel who was getting inside the living room by running with a long knife in her hand. Then, Angel ran till where the tigers were fighting, and she bent close to the tigers, and those two tigers were concentrated in their fight that they did not notice that Angel was bent close to them, then Angel stabbed the tiger that was beating the other tiger with that long knife that she had in her hand. And they suddenly heard a loud scream coming from outside, and that scream was coming from Prince as his ghost had been stabbed by Angel, and the tiger that Angel had stabbed started running through the door by bleeding.

Then, Angel knelt face to the tiger that was in the room, and she looked in the eyes of that tiger, then she asked, "Are you okay?" And the tiger made the gestures with his head, and Angel understood that the tiger was saying yes, then Angel opened her arms through the tiger, and the tiger walked in her arms, then she started to caress the tiger. Angel's parents were looking at her with amazed faces, with their hearts beating with fear without understanding what was going on, and they were wondering how Angel was taking that tiger in her arms, and Rebecca was shaking of fear with her mouth opened, but no word was coming out from her mouth. After a minute, the tiger that was in the arms of Angel turned into the light, and Angel and her parents noticed that the tiger had disappeared, and Angel got up and she started to run through her bedroom by calling the name of Hero. Angel's parents started to run after Angel, then Angel got inside her bedroom and she noticed that Hero had left, and she started to walk in her bedroom by staring at the mess that was in her room, with her heart that was beating faster than the normal, with the fear that may be something had happened to Hero.

Then, a sheet of paper that was on the teddy bear on the floor attracted the attention of Angel, and she bent in front of her teddy bear, and she took that sheet of paper and looked at it, then she read, "You are a real angel, you saved my life couple minutes ago. And the words would be not enough to say thank you to you." And she understood that it was Hero, as she had noticed his handwriting, and Angel looked at her teddy bear, and she noticed that her teddy bear had been torn during the fight.

Then, Angel turned her head from behind, as she had heard the footsteps, and she saw her parents who were looking at the mess in her bedroom with the terror on their faces, and there were the tears that were down the cheeks of Rebecca. And Angel's parents were understanding what had happened, because they knew that Angel was persecuted by the monsters, since she was born. After a few minutes, Rebecca told Angel that Angel would come sleep with them, but Angel refused by saying to her parents that she would stay in her bedroom to wait for Hero, that Hero would may come. And her parents demanded her who was Hero? And after a half hour of hesitation, Angel demanded her parents to sit down, and her parents sat on the bed, and Angel sat in the chair facing her parents, then Angel told her parents about Hero. But Angel did not talk about all the mysteries and the doubts that she had about Hero, and her parents asked her why she took the tiger in her arms, and Angel answered that she had no idea, that she could not answer that question, because she just felt that she wanted to take that tiger in her arms. Then, Angel's parents started to ask the questions about Hero, but unfortunately for them, Angel could not answer those questions, because she did not know herself who Hero was, where he was really coming from, and where he was living. Then, Angel and her parents spent their whole night talking about Hero.

It was 6:00 a.m., Prince was lying in his bedroom, and he was in the coma, because his ghost was in the coma in the hospital of the tiger world, and the doctors were taking care of his phantom, as Angel had stabbed his phantom early this morning with the knife. And there were Sol and William in the bedroom of Prince, and they were staring at Prince who was lying in his bed like a dead man with the terror on their faces, and they were just praying the ancestors of the eagle world to help Prince, to save the life of Prince and to not let Prince die.

It was afternoon, Angel was lying in the bed of her parents deeply asleep, then she opened her eyes and she got up from the bed, then she turned her head through the clock that was on the wall, and she read 3:00 p.m. Then, Angel walked till the door of her bedroom, and she put her hand on the handle of the door, then she opened the door, and suddenly the expression of her face changed as she was looking inside her bedroom. Angel started to walk inside her bedroom, then she stopped in the middle of her bedroom, and she turned her head by staring inside her bedroom, and she was noticing that her bedroom was tidy. And Angel was remembering that her bedroom was messy, when she left her bedroom early this morning at 7:00 a.m., with her parents, and she was wondering if it was her parents who had tidied in her bedroom. But, at the same time, she was wondering what time her parents had tidied up in her bedroom, because her parents went to work at 9:00 a.m., when she was still awake, because she went to bed at 10:00 a.m., and mostly that she did not see her parents tidying her bedroom.

After less than a minute, Angel understood that it could not be her parents who had tidied up her bedroom, because everything was arranged in its place, as if it was herself who had tidied her bedroom. Then, Angel turned her head her through the bed, and the smile appeared on her face, and she started to walk through the bed by smiling and by looking at the teddy bear, then she bent through the bed and she carried the teddy bear, and she started to look at that teddy bear with the joy on her face, and she was understanding that it was Hero who had tidied her bedroom. Because the teddy bear that she had in her hands was a new teddy bear, and she understood that Hero had bought her a teddy bear like the teddy bear she had had been torn during the fight, then Angel started to look on the bed looking for the letter. And after eleven seconds she cried out, "He did not write me a letter."

A voice said, "Sorry, I did not write you a letter." Then, Angel turned from behind as she had heard that voice coming from behind her, and there was the invisible phantom of Hero face to her, but she was not seeing that invisible ghost that was staring at her, then she cried out, "Hero?"

The invisible phantom replied, "Yes."

Angel asked, "Why can I not see you?"

The invisible phantom asked, "Are you afraid?"

Angel said, "Yes, I am afraid."

The phantom replied, "I thought that you were not afraid."

Angel said, "I am not afraid of you. But I am afraid that I would lose you."

The phantom asked, "Why did you say that?"

Angel replied, "I do not know why I am saying that, just that I have that feeling."

The phantom said, "I am not afraid."

Angel asked, "Can you promise me?" There was a silence, and after a minute.

Angel asked, "Are you there?"

The phantom answered, "Yes, I am here."

Angel asked, "Why can you not promise me that you would still be there?"

The phantom asked, "How did you find your teddy bear?"

Angel replied, "Thank you for the teddy bear, I liked it. But your question was not the answer to my question."

The phantom said, "I have to go."

Angel said, "Please, promise me that you would always be there."

The phantom said, "I am sorry, I can not."

Angel asked, "Why can you not?"

The phantom answered, "The only thing I can tell you it's that I would do everything in my power to be always with you."

Angel said, "If you would do everything in your power to be always with me. Why can you not promise me that you would always be with me?"

The phantom said, "The only thing that is matter, it's that you are fine and safe."

Angel said, "As you can not answer that question, at least let me see you."

The phantom said, "Your parents are coming, and I have to go."

Angel said, "I am worried about you."

The phantom said, "I am fine."

Angel said, "Please, I want you to come back to this room, and let me take care of you, as you are sick."

The phantom replied, "Do not worry about me. I am doing well."

Angel said, "I miss you."

The phantom said, "We would see soon."

Angel asked, "Are you coming tonight?"

The phantom said, "I always watch you when you sleep."

Angel said, "I mean that I want to see you as a human. Because, I can not see you as a ghost as you are now."

The phantom asked, "Why did you call me a ghost?"

Angel said, "When you talk with someone who is invisible, that means that that person is a phantom."

The phantom asked, "Did you think that I am a phantom?"

Angel said, "It doesn't matter who you are, I do not care if you are a tiger, an immortal, a vampire, a phantom, a superhuman, a superhero, or a supernatural, because the only thing that matters is that I want to be with you." Then, they heard Rebecca who was knocking at the door by calling the name of Angel.

The phantom said, "I have to go."

Angel said, "I hope that you are not angry, as I broke my promise by talking about you to my parents."

The phantom said, "No, I am not angry."

Angel said, "Thank you for tidying up my bedroom." And she added, "Thank you so much for the teddy bear, I really appreciated that teddy bear, I would name that teddy bear Superhero as you, because you are my Superhero, I would call him Hero sometime as you, and I would sleep in his arms when you would not be there."

The phantom said, "I am glad that you like the teddy bear." And the phantom added, "See you soon." Then, Angel continued to talk but the phantom did not reply, and she understood that the ghost had left, and she walked till the door, then she opened the door to her mom who was knocking since, three minutes then Angel and her mom started talking.

The days were passing, and Sol and William were happy to see that Prince was recovering well, Prince was out of danger, but his phantom was still in the hospital of the tiger world, and Prince could not make his phantom return in his body, because his phantom was still on the treatment in the tiger world. And Prince had been very surprised when Sol and William told him that during their fight in the bedroom of Angel, they had noticed that the invisible phantom of Hero had still his same strengths, that nothing had changed on the strengths of the invisible phantom of Hero. And Prince was wondering how the invisible phantom of Hero had still his same strengths, if Philip had destroyed most of the strengths of Hero on the orders of the ancestors. And Prince had told William and Sol that during his fight against the identity phantom of Hero in Angel's house, he had noticed that the identity phantom of Hero was very weak, and that he had no doubt that most of the strengths of Hero had been destroyed.

Then, Prince, Sol, and William were wondering how it could be possible that the invisible phantom of Hero had still his same strengths, and the identity phantom of Hero that was the tiger had lost most of his strengths. And William had suggested that they should keep fighting Hero, till they kill the identity phantom of Hero who had lost most of his strengths, and after that they would focus on the invisible phantom of Hero, then they would kill Angel, and then they would start their mission that was the destroying of the race of natural human beings. And Prince had replied to William that he was not ready to fight Hero for the moment, because his phantom was still sick to the hospital, and that all his strengths were located inside his phantom, so that it was impossible for him to fight now. And Sol had said that they must think about another strategy to kill the phantoms of Hero, that the fight was not the solution, that they had already lost Matt, and that couple days ago Angel had stabbed the phantom of Prince with the knife. And they were lucky that the doctors of the tiger world had succeeded to save Prince's ghost on time, and that when the invisible phantom of Hero would have all his strengths, it would be not easy to burn the dead body of Hero. And that all the time that they had hired people to remove the rosaries of Angel, it did not work, because once when those people had seen the phantom of Hero that was the tiger, those people just ran away, because those people were scared of the tiger.

And Prince had asked Sol what was the solution? And Sol had replied to Prince that they should know the weakness of Hero. And William had asked if Hero had weaknesses? And Sol had answered William that it was not only the natural human beings who had the weaknesses, and that even the supernatural beings had the weaknesses, and that each supernatural being had his weaknesses like each natural human being. Then, Sol had demanded to Prince what he had noticed about Hero when both Hero and Prince were growing up in the tiger world, like what Hero hated? What Hero was afraid of? And what Hero liked? And Prince had answered Sol that he had grown up in the tiger world with Hero, but that he was not close to Hero, because he and Hero were the enemies, so that he had no idea about what Hero hated and what Hero liked. And that the person who knew Hero was Brad, because Brad and Hero had grown up together, by playing together, and that Brad and Hero were the best friends. And Sol had told Prince and William that she would try to use Brad to get the information from him about Hero.

Hero was in his hotel bedroom, lying in his bed, and he was very sick, and he was feeling pains on his whole body, and there were

## SUPERNATURAL BEINGS

the scars and the wounds on his body coming from the claws of the tiger, and it was the phantom of Prince that had made those scars on the body of Hero during their fight in Angel's house, as Prince's ghost had torn the skin of Hero's ghost. Hero had stopped going to school, not only because he did not want people to see all those scars and wounds that were on his body, but because he was very sick, and that sickness was coming from his identity ghost. Because, during that fight in Angel's house, the phantom of Prince had succeeded to injure the identity phantom of Hero, like most of the strengths of that Hero's phantom had been destroyed, and that identity phantom of Hero was not strong enough to fight Prince's phantom. And Hero could not send his identity phantom to the hospital of the tiger world, because he was no longer an inhabitant of the tiger world, as he was sentenced to death in the tiger world, and his identity phantom would be killed if he dared to send his identity phantom in the tiger world.

And Hero could not go to the hospital of natural human beings, because the doctors who were natural human beings could not cure his identity ghost, because those doctors had no idea about the functioning of the body of supernatural beings, so the only solution for Hero was to bear the pain. And Hero was very grateful to Angel, he knew that he was still alive thanks to Angel, because if Angel had not stabbed the phantom of Prince during that fight, the phantom of Prince could kill his identity phantom that day. And Hero was very surprised by the courage that Angel had had that day, and mostly when Angel had taken his identity phantom in her arms, and Hero was very surprised too by the way that Angel had recognized his identity ghost that day. But there was a question that was going on in the mind of Hero, and that question was why his invisible phantom had not lost his strengths, while most of his strengths had been destroyed. Hero was not understanding why his invisible phantom still had the same strength, because normally his invisible ghost would lose most of his strengths like his identity phantom. But unfortunately, Hero could not answer that question.

It was 3:00 a.m., there was the moon shining in the sky of the tiger world forest, and Sol and Brad sat on the top of a tree branch in the forest of the tiger world, and they were talking, and it had been more than three hours that they were talking, and the conversation was only based on Hero. And Sol was trying to get the information about Hero from Brad, and Brad did not know that Sol was there because she wanted to get the information about Hero. And Sol had told Brad that she had come to visit him, as he had asked her in his letter, and Sol was not completely lying to Brad even if the information about Hero was her goal, she had visited Brad because she wanted to see him too. And Sol was noticing that Brad was very sad, as Hero was sentenced to death, and that Brad was also surprised that Hero had betrayed the tiger world. But Sol was noticing that although the fact that Brad knew Hero very well, Brad had no idea about the weaknesses of Hero, and she understood that she could not get the information that she wanted on Hero from Brad.

Then, Sol told Brad that she had to leave, and she turned into the eagle and she flew away before Brad opened his mouth to say a word, then Brad lifted his head through the sky, and suddenly his blue eyes became dark blue, and he turned into the tiger, then the tiger jumped on the ground and the tiger started running by following the eagle that was flying in the sky. After fifteen minutes running, the tiger stopped under a tree, and the tiger was staring at Sol who was under that tree, and she was staring at the tiger too. Then, Sol asked, "Are you going to keep staring at me like that?" Then, the tiger turned into the shape of a supernatural being who was Brad, and Brad asked, "Why did you run away?"

Sol replied, "I told you that I was leaving."

Brad said, "You flew away before I opened my mouth to say a word."

Sol said, "Sorry for my behavior."

Brad said, "It seems that you are running away from me."

Sol asked, "Why did you say that?"

Brad replied, "Since you came here, you avoid looking in my eyes."

Sol said, "I do not understand."

Brad said, "Even right now as we are talking, you avoid looking in my eyes."

Sol looked in the eyes of Brad without saying a word, and she started to shake as Brad was walking face to her, then Brad stopped face to Sol, and he looked in Sol's eyes, then he lifted his right hand and he put that hand on Sol's hair, and Sol started breathing deeply as Brad was caressing her hair and her cheek with his fingers. Then, Brad put his hands on the hips of Sol, and Sol opened her mouth to talk, but her mouth was shaking that she could not pronounce a word, then Brad moved his head towards Sol, and he started to kiss her. But both Brad and Sol had difficulties kissing each other, because their bodies were trying to reject each other, so the body of Brad was rejecting the body of Sol, while the body of Sol was rejecting the body of Brad. Then, Sol put her palm's hands on Brad's chest, and she pushed him, then Brad took a step back, and he looked in Sol's eyes by asking, "Everything is alright?"

Sol asked, "Did you have your phantom inside you?"

Brad answered, "Yes, I have my ghost inside me."

Sol took a deep breath, and she looked into Brad's eyes, without saying a word.

Brad asked, "Everything is okay?"

Sol looked at Brad with a surprised face and asked, "Are you asking me if everything is alright?"

Brad said, "I want to know what is going wrong."

Sol asked, "You did not notice something?"

Brad said, "No."

Sol said, "We kissed together."

Brad took a deep breath and said, "I imagine that you broke one of the rules of the tradition of the eagle world, by kissing a supernatural being from the tiger world."

Sol said, "Yes, I broke one the rules of the tradition of my family by kissing you, but that's not the problem."

Brad said, "Me too, I broke one of the rules of the tradition of my family by kissing you. But I do not regret, even if the ancestors of the tiger world are going to sentence me to death to punish me as I broke one of the rules of the tradition by kissing you."

Sol said, "Me too, I do not care to be killed by the king of the eagle world on the demand of the ancestors of the eagle world as I kissed you. But, that's still not the problem."

Brad asked, "What is the problem, if both of us do not regret what happened?"

Sol looked in Brad's eyes by answering, "The real problem is that we kissed each other with our ghosts inside us." Brad said, "Yes, we should not be able to kiss each other with our phantoms inside us, as we are not from the same family."

Sol said, "Even if we had had the difficulties to kiss each other, our bodies should reject each other, once that my lips had touched your lips. So, there is something unclear happening."

Brad said, "Me too, I am surprised that our lips succeeded to make some move, even if our bodies were trying to reject each other."

Sol said, "It means that there is a mystery."

Brad said, "Yes, there is something going wrong that we can not explain."

Sol said, "The only explanation of that it's that one of us has the same destiny or the same story as Angel."

Brad asked, "What do you mean by one of us having the same destiny or the same story as Angel?"

Sol answered, "Do not pay attention to what I said."

Brad asked, "Who is Angel?" But Brad noticed that Sol was not paying attention to him, that she had her head lifted through the sky, and that she was breathing deeply as if she was feeling something, and Brad was asking her if everything was fine, then Sol looked at Brad and she told Brad to run away. Brad asked her why he should run away? Sol answered that she was feeling that a member of her family was around, that he should run away, because she did not want a member of her family to see them together. Then, Brad turned into a tiger, and he ran away. And Sol lifted her head through the sky, and she saw an eagle that was flying towards her, then that eagle landed face to her, and that eagle turned into a supernatural being of the eagle world. And Sol cried out, "Collin?" By looking at that supernatural being face to her with an astonished face.

Collin replied, "Are you surprised to see me here?"

# SUPERNATURAL BEINGS

Sol answered, "Yes, I am very amazed to see you here."

Collin said, "You are outside of the eagle world for a mission, and that mission is to kill Angel, and to destroy the race of natural human beings."

Sol said, "I am working hard every second to succeed in my mission."

Collin asked, "By kissing an enemy?"

Sol said, "Brad is not an enemy."

Collin said, "Brad is not from the eagle world."

Sol said, "I know it well."

Collin said, "You would be replaced by another supernatural being for this mission."

Sol said, "I would go till the end of this mission. Because, I would kill Hero to avenge Matt's death." Collin said, "Your mission is over, since you kissed Brad."

Sol said, "You have no right, and no power to end my mission."

Collin said, "I would talk to the king that you broke one of the rules of the eagle family by kissing Brad, and even if you are the granddaughter of king, the king would consult the ancestors, and the ancestors would punish you, and maybe you would be killed on the demand of the ancestors."

Sol said, "I know a lot of secrets about you too, so if you betray me, I would betray you too. And both of us are going to be in the same situation."

Collin said, "Do not even dare to threaten me."

Sol said, "I do not threaten you, but I am telling you what would happen if you betray me."

Collin said, "I do not even need to betray you, because the ancestors are already aware that you broke one of the important rules of eagle family by kissing Brad, and the ancestors would talk about it to the king, when the king would be in the secret room to talk with the ancestors."

Sol said, "You would stay quiet till the day that the ancestors would decide to punish me by talking to the king."

Collin said, "I want you to stop seeing Brad."

Sol said, "You are not the one who give me the orders." Suddenly, the expression of the face of Collin changed, and he was staring at Sol with a face full of rage, then he handed his both hands and he grabbed Sol's neck and he started to press the neck of Sol with all his strengths, and Sol was fighting by trying remove Collin's hands from her neck. Suddenly, a tiger jumped from the top of a tree, and that tiger landed on Collin, and Collin started to scream while the tiger was tearing the skin of Collin with his claws, then the tiger threw Collin on the ground, and Sol was yelling by calling the name of Brad to stop. Then, Sol bent, and she grabbed the tiger, and she succeeded to remove the tiger on Collin, then Collin got up from the ground and his body was full of blood and the wounds coming from the claws of the tiger. Then, Collin stared in Sol's eyes, and his green eyes became dark green, then he turned into the eagle and he flew away. Then, Sol bent, and she looked in the eyes of the tiger, and she asked the tiger if he was doing well, and the tiger made the gestures with his head, and Sol understood that the tiger was saying that everything was fine. Then, Sol opened her arms by smiling at the tiger, and the tiger walked till in her arms, and she started to caress the tiger. After a couple of minutes, Sol looked in the tiger's eyes by saying that she was leaving, and she got up, then the tiger turned into the supernatural being who was Brad, then both Brad and Sol were looking at each other. And Brad started to kiss Sol, but they had the difficulties to kiss each other, because their bodies were trying to reject each other, and Sol told Brad that they should remove their phantoms from their bodies, to be able to kiss each other very well without a problem.

Then, both Sol and Brad looked at each other, and the light got out from their eyes, and they started to kiss without a problem, and Sol removed the t-shirt of Brad, and Brad removed the t-shirt of Sol. And both looked at each other, and Sol lifted her head through the sky, and she told Brad that the stars were watching at them, and Brad lifted his head through the sky, and he stared at the stars that were shining, and he said that those stars that were shining in the sky were the witnesses of their love. And Sol replied that only those stars that were shining in the sky could understand what they were feeling for each other. And Brad said that they should prove to those stars in the sky that they really love each other, and that no rule of their traditions could stop that true and pure love, and Sol asked Brad how they were going to prove their love to those stars. Brad demanded to Sol to look in his eyes, then they turned their heads towards each other by staring at each other in the eyes, and Brad walked a step face to Sol and he started to caress her chin and her lips with his hand, then they started to kiss each other, and they spent the rest of the night to make love on the ground in that forest.

It was 12:00 p.m., Angel was walking downtown looking for Hero, and it was a few days now that Angel had not set foot in school, and she was spending her time looking for Hero. Angel was very worried about Hero, and she had not seen Hero since the day that Hero had left her bedroom, and Hero had not put his feet in school since the day that he had left the classroom by asking for help from Angel. Angel had taken the number of Hero to Bella, and she had called Hero but unfortunately the phone of Hero was off, and she was very afraid mostly that she knew that Hero was not doing well. And Hero was still lying in his hotel bedroom, and his health status was going worse and worse, and he was very sick, and he knew that Angel was looking for him, but he could not go to class or go to see Angel, because he was not doing well. And the wounds and the claw marks of the tiger that were on the body of Hero were not yet healed, because he had not received the treatment for the wounds that were on his ghost, as he could not send his identity ghost that was sick to tiger world to get cured, because he was not any more a citizen of the tiger world, as he was sentenced to death.

The magic of Hero was warning him of a danger, but he did not know where that danger was coming from, and Hero was very surprised because the danger that his magic was warning him was not about Angel, but instead about himself, but he was not really paying attention to that danger that he was feeling. And Hero was spending his time to watch what was going on through his magic, and he had watched the conversation between Sol and Brad, and he was very worried about Brad as Brad had broken one of the rules of the tradition of the tiger family by making love with Sol. Hero was afraid that the ancestors of the tiger world could sentence Brad to death, as Brad had made love with Sol, and Hero was thinking how he could save Brad. But something strange had attracted the intention of Hero during the time that Sol and Brad had spent in the forest, Hero had noticed that Brad and Sol had kissed together with their phantoms inside them, even if they had the difficulties to kiss each other, because their bodies were trying to reject each other.

Hero was wondering how it could be possible that both Sol and Brad who were not coming from the same family had succeeded to kiss each other, and that was really uncomprehending for Hero. Because, nobody could explain how Brad and Sol had succeeded to kiss each other with their ghosts inside them, and Hero knew that there was something going wrong, and that there was a mystery that he could not explain or understand, because it was not normal that Brad and Sol kissed had each other with their ghosts inside their bodies. Then, Hero remembered that both Brad and Sol were very surprised too, that they had succeeded to kiss each other with their phantoms inside them, and that they could not explain how they had succeeded to kiss each other with their ghosts inside their bodies. And Hero remembered that Sol had told Brad that the only explanation for the reason why they had succeeded to kiss each other was that one of them had the same story or the same destiny as Angel.

And Hero was wondering what Sol was meaning by saying that she or Brad had the same destiny or the same story as Angel, and at the same time, Hero was wondering what the story, or the destiny of Angel was. And Hero was completely lost with all the mysteries that were happening, and that none could explain those mysteries, and Hero was understanding that the life of the race of supernatural beings was full of secrets and the mysteries. And Hero started to think of all the questions that were going on in his mind, that could not find the answers, like how the race of natural human beings were responsible for the destruction of the race of supernatural beings more than a century ago? Because, Hero was remembering that the day that Prince had used his magic to make the pictures appear on the wall of what had happened more than a century ago, there was not a natural human being on those pictures on the wall.

## SUPERNATURAL BEINGS

And in those pictures on the wall, there were only the race of supernatural beings who were fighting each other, and who were killing each other, so Hero was wondering how it could be possible that the natural human beings be responsible for the destruction of the race of supernatural human beings. Not only because there were not the natural human beings on the photos that Prince had made appear on the wall through his magic, but also because natural human beings could not beat the supernatural beings, because the supernatural beings were stronger than the natural human beings.

And Hero knew well that it was impossible that the race of natural human beings won a war against the race of supernatural human beings, because it should be easier for supernatural beings to kill the natural human beings, and harder for natural human beings to kill the supernatural beings. Because, the only way to kill a supernatural being, it was to kill his phantom first, and it should be almost impossible for the natural human beings to kill the phantoms of the supernatural beings, because the supernatural beings could remove their ghosts from their bodies before fighting, and the supernatural beings could also remove their ghosts from their bodies anytime when they were in danger. And Hero knew that there were the secrets that were hidden from supernatural beings about what had happened more than a century year ago, that all the truth had not been told in the holy book, that the ancestors did not explain exactly how the race of the natural human beings was responsible of the destroying of the race of the supernatural human beings.

And other questions that Hero could not answer were about the secrets and the mysteries who were on Angel, about the reasons why the ancestors did not show the pictures of his fight to save Angel, about the reasons why most of the strengths of his invisible phantom were not destroyed, about the secrets and the mysteries on Sol and Brad as both had succeeded to kiss each other, and other questions again full of secrets and mysteries that Hero could not answer. And Hero was remembering the day that he had used his magic to make appear on the wall the pictures of the future of the tiger world, and he was seeing on those pictures that the tiger world had become a desert in the future. And he was very afraid and worried about the future of the tiger world, and he was wondering what would happen for that the tiger world would become a desert in the future, and he was wondering too if the race of supernatural beings would disappear in the future, or if all inhabitants of the tiger world would be killed in the future. And although the fact that Hero knew that he did not have much time to live as he was sentenced to death, he was thinking how to save the race of supernatural beings by preventing the tiger world from becoming a desert in the future.

It was midnight. Prince, Sol and William were standing up face to the wall in the living room of Prince's house, and they were all staring at the pictures that Prince had used his magic to make appear on the wall. And the pictures that were on the wall, were the pictures of Hero lying in the bed of his hotel bedroom, and there were also the pictures of Brad, and Brad's parents on the wall, and it was Sol who had asked Prince to make the pictures of Brad appear on the wall. And Sol had demanded Prince to make the pictures of Brad appear on the wall, because she wanted to make sure that Brad was fine. But Sol had lied to Prince and William by answering that she wanted to see the pictures of Brad and Brad's family on the wall to check through her magic, if Brad had lied to her during their conversation, and that by looking Brad's pictures on the wall, she would remember of their conversation, when Prince and William had demanded Sol why she wanted to see the pictures of Brad and Brad's family on the wall. But Prince and William knew that there was something going wrong, that Sol was hiding something from them, because since Sol had come back from her mission to the tiger world, as she had gone to the tiger world to get information from Brad about Hero, her attitude had changed.

Prince and William had noticed that Sol was always absent when they were talking, and that when Sol was opening her mouth, it was to ask questions about Brad and Brad's family, also about the ancestors of Brad. And Sol had just told Prince and William that she did not get any information from Brad about Hero that could help them to kill the phantoms of Hero. William, Sol and Prince were thinking about how to kill the phantoms of Hero, but Sol was not really focused on the conversation, and she was pensive because she could not stop thinking about what had happened in the tiger world between her and Brad. And she was very worried about Brad that he could be sentenced to death on the demand of the ancestors of the tiger world as she had made love with Brad, and she was still not understanding how she and Brad had succeeded in kissing each other with their ghosts inside them. Prince, Sol and William had not found the solution to how to kill the phantoms of Hero, but they knew that one of the phantoms of Hero was very sick, because they could see the wounds on the body of Hero through the pictures of Hero that were on the wall. And they knew that Hero could not heal his identity phantom that was sick, because Hero could not go to the hospital in the tiger world, and they also knew that if Hero dared to send his identity phantom to the tiger world, that identity ghost would be hanged, and if Hero put his feet in the land of the tiger world he would be hanged too.

Then, Prince told William and Sol that the only solution that they had, it was to wait the day that Hero would be dead in the world of the natural human beings, or the day that Hero would decide to return to the tiger world for his sentence, and that after the death of Hero they would kill Angel and they would start to eradicate the race of natural human beings. And Sol told Prince that they could not stay and wait until the day that Hero would die, or the day that Hero would decide to go to the tiger world for his sentence, because by waiting for the death of Hero, they could all die before Hero. Prince replied to Sol that Hero would die soon, because Hero could not survive without eating, because the phantoms of Hero would get sick and tired if those ghosts stayed a long time without eating. And that the only place where the phantoms of Hero could get food it was in the tiger world, and Hero could not send his phantoms in the tiger world, and the phantoms of Hero could not stay without seeing the doctors mostly that one of the phantoms of Hero was already sick. And William said that the better solution to kill the phantoms of Hero, it was to keep fighting Hero, and to keep hurting the ghosts of Hero and there, Hero would have no choice than to give up the fight by stopping to protect Angel, or Hero would choose himself to go to the tiger world for his sentence. And Sol agreed with the idea of William by saying that it would be helpful to make Hero weak and tired by fighting Hero everyday, and by hurting his phantoms till Hero did not have the energy and the strength to keep protecting Angel. But Prince told Sol and William that he was not ready yet for the fight, because his phantom was still in the hospital in the tiger world for treatment, as Angel had stabbed his phantom with the knife.

Then, Sol told Prince that Prince should contact Angel, and Prince would try to get the information from Angel about Hero, that may be Angel knew some weaknesses of Hero that could help them to kill the ghosts of Hero, as Angel spent time with Hero. And Prince told Sol that it was a waste time to try to get the information from Angel about Hero, not only because Angel did not know exactly who Hero was, but because even if Angel knew the weaknesses of Hero, she would not talk him, and that although the fact that he was the boyfriend of Angel, Angel never told him about Hero. And Sol demanded to Prince to invite Angel, and to use his brain and try to make Angel talk about Hero, and that may be during the conversation Angel would talk him something about Hero that Angel had noticed about the behavior of Hero, and that could help them to get rid of the phantoms of Hero.

And Prince told Sol to not forget that Hero had the magic, that Hero would be probably watching at them, and that Hero was probably already aware of their plan, and that when he would be talking with Angel, Hero could appear at anytime to prevent Angel to talk, if Hero felt that Angel was going to say something that Hero did not want them to know. And Sol told Prince to not worry about that, that they would plan to prevent Hero to appear during his conversation with Angel, and they would also try to find something that would make Angel hate Hero, and that would make Angel talk about everything she knew about Hero. Then, Prince, Sol and William spent the rest of the night to think about their plan, of how to prevent Hero from appearing during the meeting between Angel and Prince.

It was evening. Angel sat in a restaurant, and the restaurant was almost full, and there was music playing at very low volume, and some people were eating while others were waiting for their food.

## SUPERNATURAL BEINGS

Angel was waiting for Prince, who had called her in the afternoon to tell her that he had just arrived in the world of natural human beings, and that he wanted to see her, as Prince had lied to her by telling her that he was travelling for a week in the United States. And Angel had given him an appointment in that restaurant where she was sitting. And Angel was a little nervous because she had invited Prince because she wanted to break up with him, because she had realized that she was in love with Hero, and she was very worried about the reaction of Prince.

Then, Angel turned her head through the door, and she saw Prince who was walking inside the room by looking at her with a smile on his face, and she was seeing the flower and the small bag in the hand of Prince. Then, Angel noticed that Prince was already close to her, and she got up from her chair with the smile on her face, and she went, and she hugged Prince, and both Prince and Angel were very proud to see each other. Then, Prince gave the flower and the small bag that he had in his hand to Angel, and Angel looked in Prince's eyes by thanking him for the flower and for the gift, and Prince wanted to kiss Angel on her lips, but Angel turned her head to the left side to avoid that Prince kiss her lips, and she kissed Prince on his cheek.

Then, Both Prince and Angel sat in the chairs around a table, and they were face to face and their eyes were focused on each other, then they started to talk, and Angel was asking questions to Prince like how was his stay in the United States? How was his family? How were his friends? and why did he travel to the United States during the class period? And Prince was answering the questions of Angel by lying to her. Then, the waiter came, and the waiter took the command of both Prince and Angel, and Angel opened the small bag that Prince had given her, and she removed a box from that bag, then she opened the box, and immediately she put her right palm's hand on her nose as she had smelt the content that was in the box, and she closed the box with her other hand and she pushed the box away. And Prince looked at Angel by asking her what was going wrong? And Angel replied to Prince that he knew well that she was allergic to the meat, but he kept her the meat. And Prince remembered the reasons why Angel could not eat meat, and he apologised to her, and Prince had really forgotten that Angel could not eat meat for the reasons that were related to her identity, not because Angel was allergic to the meat as she thought.

Then, they continued the conversation, and Prince told Angel that he had something important to talk to her, then he looked in Angel's eyes and he told Angel that he was in danger, and that he needed her help, that there were mysterious people who wanted to kill him. Angel looked at Prince with a worried face, by asking Prince who wanted to kill him? Prince answered that he did not really know about those People, but that he had noticed that those people were not behaving like the natural human beings, but they were behaving instead like the eagles. And Angel stared at Prince with an amazed face by asking him if he knew who those people were, and Prince answered that not really, and that he did not want to know who those people were because he was so scared of them, and that the only thing he wanted, it was to avoid them. Angel told Prince to return to the United States, because those people were too dangerous, but Prince refused the proposition of Angel returning to the United States.

Then, Prince told Angel that he knew that she was close to the friend of Bella named Hero, and that he wanted to know how Hero behaved, or that he wanted her to introduce him to Hero. Angel demanded Prince why he wanted to know how Hero behaved, and Prince answered Angel that he watched a video, where Hero was fighting against those mysterious people, and at the end of the video Hero said that it was easy to fight those mysterious people, and that if someone studied his behavior that person could fight those mysterious people too. Angel asked Prince if she could see that video? And Prince removed his phone from his pocket, and he went to the gallery of his phone, and he selected a video, then he handed his phone to Angel, and Angel took the phone in Prince's hand. And Angel looked at the screen of the phone, and suddenly the expression of her face changed, and she was looking at the phone's screen with an astonished face, as she was seeing Hero who was fighting against Sol and William. And Angel knew that Sol and William were those who were trying to kill her, and she understood that Prince was really in danger, then she lifted her head and she looked at Prince by asking him how he got that video. Prince answered that he got that video from his classmate, and that his classmate who had sent him that video told him that Hero had made that video to help all people who were in danger. But Prince was lying because that video was fake, and Prince had made that video editing himself through his magic.

Then, Angel started to think, she did not know what to do, but she knew that she could not introduce Prince to Hero not only because Prince was her boyfriend, and that she was in love with Hero. But, because she knew herself that Hero was not a natural human being, and that it was a risk to introduce Prince to Hero, because Prince could find out that even Hero was not a natural human being. Then, Angel was wondering if it was really Hero who had made that video, or if it was someone who had filmed Hero when Hero was fighting, because she knew that Hero was very reserved, and she was not understanding the reasons why Hero had made that video. And she did not know if she was going to break the promise that she had made to Hero by talking about Hero to Prince, but Angel knew that she should help Prince who was in danger, but she did not know how to help him. Then, Angel tried to convince Prince to return to the United States, but Prince refused by saying that even in the United States, he would not be safe, because those mysterious people pursued him in the United States during the week that he was there.

Then, Angel asked Prince what he knew about Hero? And Prince answered that he knew nothing about Hero, just that Hero was a brave man. Then, Angel started to ask again some questions to Prince about Hero to know if Prince had doubts about the identity of Hero, and Prince was answering the questions of Angel, then Angel noticed that Prince thought that Hero was a real natural human being. Then, Angel decided to talk a little bit about Hero to Prince, but she decided to not talk about all the doubts and the mysteries she had about Hero, even not to talk about how Hero saved her. Then, Angel told Prince that she did not know much about Hero, and she started to talk about how Hero behaved in class, as all her classmates knew that behavior from Hero. And Prince was asking the questions to Angel about Hero, as Angel was talking about Hero and she was trying to avoid answering most of the questions of Prince, by saying that she did not know too much about Hero.

Hero was lying in his bed, and he was watching what was going on in the tiger world through his magic, and Hero was watching the tiger world to know if Brad was doing well, and it had been more than six minutes that one part of his magic was warning him that he was in danger, but Hero was not paying attention to his magic. Suddenly, Hero noticed that his magic was attracting his attention about Angel, and he used his magic to find out where Angel was, and immediately the expression of his face changed as he had seen through his magic Angel and Prince who were talking about him, and he understood why his magic was warning him for two days that he was in danger.

Then, Hero turned his head through the window, as he had heard a noise coming from the window, and he saw two eagles that were flying around the window by watching at him, and he understood that Sol and William were there to prevent him from interrupting the conversation between Prince and Angel. Then, Hero jumped from the bed, and he grabbed the t-shirt that was on the sofa in his bedroom, and he wore that t-shirt on him, then he turned his head through the window as he had heard the noises coming from the window. And he noticed that the window's glass was broken, and he saw William and Sol who were in his bedroom looking at him, then the light got out from Hero's eyes, and that light turned into his invisible phantom, and Hero ran through the door. And the invisible phantom of Hero started fighting against Sol. And William rushed through the door by following Hero. Hero was running in the veranda of the hotel and William was following him, but Hero had the difficulties to run faster because he was losing the balance like his invisible phantom was fighting against Sol. And people were looking at Hero and William who were running with surprised faces, wondering what was going on, and William was pushing people who were on his way.

Hero was running through the veranda and he was trying to reach the hallway that was showing to the parking, and there were three kids who were running face to Hero by playing, and Hero stopped face to those kids by waiting for those children to cross him, as he did not want to push those kids to cross. Then, Hero turned his head from behind and he noticed that William was right behind him, and that there were the security men who were running behind William too, then Hero turned his head through his right side, and he saw a car that was parked at the entrance of the hotel. Then, Hero climbed on the balcony, then he jumped from the twenty-one floors where he was, and the light got out from his eyes when he was falling on the ground, then Hero fell on the ground and he got up from the ground and he ran till the car that was parked at the entrance of the hotel. Hero wanted to open the car's door, but he felt a hand around his neck, and Hero tried to remove the hand that was around his neck, but he was too weak to remove that hand, and that hand was pressing his neck. And Hero was too weak to remove that hand around his neck, because his two phantoms were outside of his body, then the light got inside Hero's eyes, and he removed the hand that was around his neck, and he turned, and he noticed that it was William.

Then, both Hero and William started to fight, and Hero saw security men who were running through them, and Hero turned into the tiger, and he started to run away, and William turned into the eagle and he flew through the space. And security men stopped running, and they lifted their heads through the space looking at the eagle that was flying, with the amazed faces. Hero had turned into his body of supernatural being who he was, and he was running through the parking, then he reached a car, and he opened the door of that car, and he got inside that car, then he drove away. And an eagle landed in the parking lot close to a car, and that eagle turned into his body of a supernatural being who was William, and William turned, and he opened the car's door, and he got inside the car, then he drove through the direction of Hero by following Hero.

Hero was driving faster through the restaurant where were Prince and Angel, then an eagle landed on the hood of the car of Hero, and that eagle turned into the body of supernatural being who was Sol, and Sol turned on the car's hood, and she broke the windshield of the car by hitting that windshield with her feet, then Sol got inside the car through the windshield that she had broken, and she started to fight Hero. And people who were walking on the sidewalk were screaming as they were seeing Sol and Hero who were fighting in the car, and the car that Sol and Hero were fighting inside was losing the direction of the road, and suddenly the car that Hero and Sol were inside hit a car that was in front of them from behind, and another car hit Hero's car from behind too, and the car stopped.

Then, William parked his car, and he got out of the car and he started to run through the car that Sol and Hero were fighting inside, and Hero saw William who was running through him, and the light got out from Hero's eyes and went towards William, and that light turned into his invisible phantom, and his invisible ghost started to fight William. Sol and Hero were still fighting in the car, and the fight was very hard between them, while people were looking at William who was fighting with the amazed faces by wondering what was going on with him. And most people who were watching William thought that he was crazy as they thought that William was fighting alone, as they were not seeing the opponent of William. And even policemen who had arrived were staring at William with the surprised faces by wondering what was going on with him, mostly that they were all noticing that William was acting exactly as if he was fighting against someone. Then, the expression of their faces changed, and the fear appeared on the faces of some of them, while the hearts of others were beating faster than the normal as they were all seeing that William was bleeding from his mouth and his nose, and that William was acting as if he was beating someone.

Then, some policemen started to walk towards William, while other policemen men were walking through the car that Hero and Sol were fighting inside with the guns in their hands. Policemen reached where William was fighting, and they held William, and suddenly one of the policemen fainted on the ground, and other policemen looked at that policeman who had fainted on the ground, and they noticed that that policeman was unconscious and that that policeman was bleeding from his nose. Then, policemen lifted their heads and they looked at each other without understanding what was going on, they were all wondering why their colleague had fainted, and it was that invisible ghost who had knocked their colleague unknowingly, and only William knew that that policeman on the ground had been knocked by the invisible phantom of Hero.

Then, policemen turned their heads and they looked at William, and they noticed that William was breathing deeply, and that he was very tired, also that William's forehead had swollen, also that there were the wounds on William's body as on his mouth, his forehead, and his shoulder. And by looking at William, they were seeing that William had been punched by someone, but they did not know who had punched William, and they started to ask questions to William, but William was not responding. Sol and Hero were outside of the car facing policemen, who were asking them the questions, and both Sol and Hero were silent, they were not saying a word, then a policeman asked them to walk through the car's police. Sol noticed that the ambulance men were trying to take William to the hospital, and she understood that she should do something to prevent the ambulance men from taking William, then she looked in the eyes of policemen who were facing her, and her green eyes became blue, and she started to walk away. And those policemen turned their heads looking at Sol as she was walking away, then Hero turned, and he walked away too.

Sol reached the ambulance car, and she looked how ambulance men were taking care of the policeman who was unconscious on the ground, then Sol looked in the eyes of policemen who had held William, and her green eyes became blue, then she looked at William by saying in Latin, "Abeamus." That meant in English, "Let's go." And William walked till near to Sol. Then, both William and Sol turned, and they started to walk away while people and policemen were watching them, and some people were wondering why policemen did not take William to the hospital and arrest Sol.

Hero was in the car driving faster through the restaurant, and his heart was beating faster than normal, and Angel and Prince were still in the restaurant talking about Hero, and Prince had not still got information that could help him. And Angel was still trying to not talk too much about Hero, and she was even trying to change the conversation, but Prince was still asking questions about Hero, then Angel started talking about the day where she had demanded to Hero to make the sandwiches for them, and how Hero was behaving when she had asked Hero to open the fridge.

Suddenly, both Angel and Prince turned their heads through the door, as they had heard the voice of Hero who was calling the name of Angel, and they looked at Hero who was walking in the room, then Angel got up from her chair and she started to run towards Hero, then two eagles flew inside the room through the window that was opened. And people started to scream in the room with terror on their faces, as they had noticed that the two eagles that had landed inside the room had turned into a woman and a man, and people were running through the door, and Prince already had left the room. Then, William and Sol were staring at Hero and Angel who were staring at them too, then William looked in Angel's eyes by telling her to run away from Hero, that Hero was not a natural human being, but instead a supernatural being. And Angel cried out, "A supernatural being?" By looking at William with an astonished face.

Then, Angel turned her head towards Hero, and she looked at him with an amazed face, then the light got out from Hero's eyes, and that light turned into the invisible phantom of Hero, and that invisible phantom started to walk through Sol, and Sol was walking through that invisible ghost too. Then, Hero grabbed Angel's hand, and they ran until outside, then they got inside a car, and Hero started to drive, but Hero was not really focused on the wheel, because his invisible phantom was fighting against Sol and William in the restaurant.

Then, Angel shouted at Hero to drive slowly and to focus on the wheel, and Hero replied to her that he could not be concentrated, because he was fighting. Angel asked him how he was fighting? Hero answered her that she could not understand. And Angel started to scream at Hero by asking him to park the car, like the car was shaking by going in all directions, then Hero parked the car, and Angel looked at Hero by asking him if it was like that that the supernatural beings drove.

Then, Angel took the wheel, and she drove till to her house, and both Hero and Angel got out of the car, and they walked till Angel's bedroom, and Hero wanted to open the window, but Angel refused,

## SUPERNATURAL BEINGS

and she asked him to lie on the bed, that she wanted to talk with him. Hero was lying in the bed with his back and Angel sat on him and they were looking each other in the eyes, and Angel noticed that Hero was feeling cold, and she also noticed the scars on his hands, and she noticed that those scars were coming from the claws of the tiger.

Then, Angel wanted to rub the ointment on the scars that were on Hero's body, but Hero refused by saying that he was fine, and Angel asked him why he was feeling cold? And Hero answered that he was outside, and that he was feeling cold because the wind was blowing on him outside. And Angel looked at Hero with an astonished face by asking him how he could say that he was outside, while they were both in her bedroom in the bed. And Hero looked at her by telling her that she could not understand, and Angel wanted to cover Hero with the blanket, but Hero refused by telling her that the blanket could not help him. And Angel told him that he was shaking, that he had to cover himself, and Hero replied to Angel that even if he covered his body, he would still feel cold, because he was outside, and that the only way for that he stopped trembling of cold, it was that she opens the window for that he gets inside. And Angel refused to open the window by saying that if she opened the window, he would run away, and that she did not want him to run away again, as he did last time when he was in her bedroom. Angel was still sitting on Hero who was lying in the bed with his back, and she was looking at him as he was shaking of cold, without understanding what was going on with him. And Hero was trembling in the cold because his invisible phantom was outside, and the wind was blowing on his invisible phantom.

Then, Angel pulled the blanket and she covered Hero with, but she noticed that nothing had changed that he was still shaking of cold, and Hero was still asking her to open the window, that he would not run away, to open the window just for a second, that he would get inside then she would close the window. But Angel was still refusing to open the window, by saying that he was already inside, that she did not understand why he was saying that he was outside. Then, Hero told Angel that he would break the window's glass if she did not open the window, and she replied to him that he could not break the window's glass, because he was lying in the bed and she was sitting on him, and that she would not let him get up from the bed. Hero told Angel that he did not need to get up from the bed or to be close to the window to break the window's glass, and she replied to him that he could not break the window's glass if he was not close to the window.

Then, Both Angel and Hero were looking at each other in the eyes, and suddenly Angel turned her head through the window as she had heard a violent noise coming from the window, and she was staring at the window with an amazed face, as she was seeing the parts of the window's glass on the floor that were broken. And Angel was completely lost, then she turned her head through Hero, and she looked at him and she noticed that he had stopped shaking of cold, and she opened her mouth to talk, but her mouth was trembling that a word was not getting out. Then, Hero asked Angel to get up on him, that he was going to fix the window, and Angel got up on Hero, still without saying a word, and Hero got up from the bed, and he walked till close the window, and he bent close to the parts of the window's glass that were on the floor. And Hero picked up all the parts of the window's glass that were on the floor, and he put them together, by the way that it was broken, and Angel was standing up near to him by looking at him, and there was also the invisible phantom of Hero in the room.

Then, the light got out from Hero's eyes and shone on that parts of window's glass that were on the floor, and all those parts of window's glass stuck together, then Hero carried that part of window's glass, and he fixed it on the window with the part that had stayed on the window, and the light got out from his eyes and shone on the window, and everything fixed. Angel was looking at Hero with an amazed face, and she was not realizing what was going on, and she was staring at the window without understanding how Hero did to fix that window, and by looking at the window it was like if someone had not broken it.

Then, Hero wanted to leave, but Angel begged him to stay, that it was already midnight and that she was afraid to stay alone, and Hero accepted to stay with her. Both were in the bed, and Hero was lying with his back and Angel was sitting on him, and they were looking at each other eyes in eyes without talking. Then, Angel bent her head and she tried to kiss Hero, but she was not succeeding to kiss him because the lips of Hero were not making any move. And Angel was not succeeding to kiss Hero, because the body of Hero was rejecting her body. Then, Angel looked in Hero's eyes by asking him why his body was reacting like that? Hero looked in her eyes without saying a word, then the light got out from Hero's eyes, and he grabbed Angel and he started to kiss her. After a few minutes kissing, they took off their clothes, and they kept kissing by turning in the bed with the blanket on them, then Hero was on Angel and he looked in her eyes by asking, "Are you virgin?" And Angel looked in Hero's eyes by answering, "It's the first time that I am making love." Hero asked, "Do you want to make love?" Angel answered, "I want to make love with a supernatural being." Then, they continued to kiss, and they spent the whole night making love.

It was early morning. Prince, Sol and William were standing up face to the wall in the living room of Prince's house, and they were looking at the pictures of Hero and Angel that Prince had used his magic to make appear on the wall. Prince, Sol and William were very tired, they had spent all their night without closing their eyes, because they had spent the entire night thinking about the weaknesses of Hero, by using all the information that Prince had got from Angel about Hero. And Prince had used his magic to make appear on the wall everything that Angel had told him about Hero, and most of the pictures of Hero that were on the wall were the pictures of Hero in class. And some pictures were showing how Hero was behaving in class, and they were all looking at the pictures of Hero that were on the wall by thinking of what the weaknesses of Hero could be. But, unfortunately for them, among all those pictures that were on the wall, there was no picture that was showing them a weakness of Hero, and the behavior of Hero that they were seeing through the pictures that were on the wall was familiar to them. Because, all the race of supernatural beings had that behavior that they were seeing through the pictures on the wall, so there was nothing new for them.

They were completely lost; they did not know how they were going to kill the invisible phantom of Hero. Then, Sol told Prince and William that the only way to kill the phantoms of Hero, it was to keep fighting Hero. Because, they had an advantage that Hero was very weak and sick as Hero had lost most of his strengths, then Sol went on by saying that she had noticed that most of the strengths of Hero had been destroyed when she fought Hero yesterday, except the invisible phantom of Hero who had still his same strengths, but that that invisible phantom was very tired. William told Angel that himself he had noticed that Hero was weak during the fight of yesterday, but that he was not ready to fight Hero for the moment, because the invisible phantom of Hero had almost killed him in the fight of yesterday, that he was obliged to send his phantom to the hospital in the eagle world for that the doctors to heal his phantom that had been injured by the invisible ghost of Hero. And Prince looked at Sol by saying that they should give up the idea to fight Hero, because if they kept fighting Hero, Hero would kill all them, that his phantom was still to the hospital, and the phantom of William was to the hospital too, and Matt's ghost was already buried. And Sol replied to Prince that they could not stay like that and wait until the day that Hero would die, that they had to ask for more supernatural beings to confront Hero.

Prince told Sol that in the tradition of the tiger family, only the ancestors and the king had the right to send the supernatural beings for a mission outside of the tiger world, so that if they needed more supernatural beings to confront Hero, the decision would come from the ancestors or the king. And Sol replied to Prince that even in the tradition of the eagle world, only the ancestors and the king had the right to send the supernatural beings outside of the eagle world for a mission. William looked at Prince by saying that the only way to know the weaknesses of Hero was to consult the ancestors of the tiger world, and there the ancestors of the tiger world would help them to kill the phantoms of Hero, mostly that those ancestors had already sentenced Hero to death. And Prince replied to William that the ancestors of the tiger world could not help them to kill Hero, because although the fact that the ancestors had all the powers on the supernatural beings of the tiger world, there was only one thing that the ancestors could not control on the inhabitants of the tiger world, and that thing was the weaknesses of the supernatural beings of the tiger world. Because the ancestors had no idea about the weaknesses of supernatural beings. And Sol replied to Prince that even the ancestors of the eagle world had no idea about the weaknesses of the supernatural beings of the eagle world, because everyone was born with his weaknesses. And William said that it seemed impossible to kill the phantoms of Hero, that when they would not know the weaknesses of Hero, they would never kill the ghosts of Hero, even if the ancestors sent them more supernatural beings.

Suddenly, there was the silence in the room, and they were all very tired, and they did not know what to do, and for them they had already failed their mission, they could not kill the phantoms of Hero, and if they could not kill the ghosts of Hero, it meant they could not kill Angel, and if they could not kill Angel, that meant they could not destroy the race of natural human beings. After the hours of thinking without finding the solution, Prince started to remember about the last words that Angel had told him during their conversation, before Hero got inside the restaurant and screamed her name. Then, Prince started to walk face to the wall by thinking, and the light started to get out from his eyes and went through the wall, then Sol and William started to walk through the wall, by looking at the pictures that were appearing on the wall through the magic of Prince. And the pictures that were appearing on the wall were the pictures of Hero and Angel in the kitchen of Angel's house, and some pictures were showing Hero in front of the fridge, while other pictures were showing Hero who was trying to remove things from the fridge. And Prince was looking at those pictures on the wall by understanding the conversation that Angel and Hero had had that day through his magic.

Then, Prince opened his mouth, and he told William and Sol that he had found out one of the weaknesses of Hero, and immediately, Sol and William turned their heads through Prince by looking at him with surprised faces. Then, Sol asked Prince what was the weakness of Hero? And Prince answered Sol that the body of Hero was allergic to cold, then Prince walked till close to the wall and he started to explain through the pictures that were on the wall, the reaction of Hero in front of the fridge, and why Hero could not remove the things from the fridge. Suddenly, Sol and William started to breathe deeply, and they were feeling that a member of their family was around, then an eagle flew inside the house through the window that was opened, and that eagle landed on the floor, then that eagle turned into a supernatural being. Sol looked at that supernatural being and she cried out, "Solis?"

Then, Solis told William and Sol that she was sent by King Hector on the demand of the ancestors to help them for the mission, as William could not anymore fight as William's phantom was sick to the hospital. Then, Sol introduced Prince to Solis. And Solis looked at the pictures that were on the wall, then she asked who was the supernatural being on those pictures on the wall? And William answered to Solis that that supernatural being on the wall was their worst enemy named Hero, and Solis started to stare at the pictures of Hero. And Prince, Sol and William were looking at Solis with surprised faces by the way that Solis was looking at the pictures of Hero. And Solis started to ask the questions about Hero, and William told Solis that Hero would die soon, because Angel had made a big mistake by telling Prince one of the weaknesses of Hero, without knowing that she was killing Hero. Then, all of them started to talk about a plan to kill the phantoms of Hero.

The days were passing, and Hero was very sick, and he was in the bedroom of a small hotel and he had changed the hotel after the fight that had happened in his former hotel between him, Sol and William. Hero knew that he could no longer defend Angel, because he had found out through his magic that Angel had unknowingly betrayed him by telling one of his weaknesses to Prince. And Hero knew that everything was over as Prince, Sol and William had found out one of his weaknesses, and that Prince was going to use his magic to kill his invisible phantom. Hero was very worried about Angel, and he was spending his time thinking how he could keep protecting Angel after his death by preventing Prince, Sol and William from killing her. Angel was spending her time looking for Hero, and she had not seen Hero since the night they had spent together to make love in her bedroom, and Angel had received a lot of calls and messages coming from Prince, but she did not take the calls of Prince or answer to his messages. And Prince was trying to be in touch with Angel, because he wanted to invite her to a safe place for William, Sol and Solis to kill her, but unfortunately for Prince, Angel was not picking up his calls, and they did not want to kill Angel in school. And Prince had stopped going to school.

It was an evening. Angel and her mom were inside a drugstore, and they were walking through the counter, then they saw Prince who was walking face to face with a small bag of drugs in his hand, and Prince stopped and they started to talk. Suddenly, they all turned their heads from behind as they had heard the screams coming from behind, and they saw people who were running away with the dread on their faces, and suddenly the fear appeared on Angel's face as Angel had seen Sol and William in the drugstore. And Angel understood that People were running away because Sol and William had landed in the drugstore like the eagles before turning into the shape of supernatural beings.

Then, Angel turned her head through her mom, as she had heard Rebecca screamed, and Angel noticed that Rebecca had fainted because someone had knocked Rebecca, then Angel tried to bend to help her mom, but Angel felt that she was grabbed by two men, and Angel was yelling as there was another man who was trying to remove the rosary that was on her wrist. Then, a light shone close to Angel, and that light turned into the invisible phantom of Hero, and suddenly the man who was trying to remove the rosary on the wrist of Angel fainted on the floor, because that man had been knocked by the invisible phantom of Hero. And the invisible phantom of Hero started to fight people who had held Angel, then Solis joined the fight, and Solis started to fight the invisible phantom of Hero. And Prince was staring at the fight between Solis and the invisible ghost of Hero with the red lights that were getting out from his eyes and going though the invisible phantom of Hero. Sol was in the room, and she was staring at people in their eyes and her green eyes were becoming blue as she was looking in the eyes of people. And except

Angel, the rest of people who were in the drugstore had no idea of what was going on, they did not even know that Solis was fighting close to them, and they did not even know where they were, because the effects of the magic of Sol were reacting inside them, and Sol's magic was preventing them to think and to see what was going on.

Then, Sol noticed that Angel was turning her head in the room looking around, and she understood that Angel was looking for Hero, and Sol looked at William by asking in Latin, "ET clausit ostimun est?" That meant in English, "The door was closed?" And William answered in Latin, "Etiam." That meant in English, "Yes." Sol said in Latin, "Angelus autem tempus illud occidit." That meant in English "It was time to kill Angel." Then, both Sol and William rushed towards where Angel was, and Sol looked in the eyes of two men who were close to Angel and her green eyes became blue, then Sol asked those two men that she had looked in their eyes to remove the rosaries that were on the ankle and wrist of Angel. And those two men turned through Angel, and they grabbed Angel, and Angel was fighting by screaming as those two men were trying to remove her rosaries, and people were looking at Angel who was defending herself against those two men without saying a word, even Rebecca was staring at Angel without saying a word. And the invisible phantom of Hero could not defend Angel, because that invisible phantom was losing the fight against Solis, and that invisible phantom was becoming more and more weak. Because the red light that was getting out from Prince's eyes was still shining on that invisible phantom, and that red light was freezing that invisible phantom of Hero, and that was the reason why that invisible phantom was becoming more and more weak.

Then, people turned their heads through the door, as they had heard a violent noise coming from the door, and they noticed that the door was broken, and they saw Hero who was walking inside the room shaking from the cold. And they could see the cold water that was flowing down of Hero's body as if he was coming out from the freezer, then the light got out from Hero's eyes and went through Angel, and that light turned into the tiger, and that tiger jumped on people who were trying to remove Angel's rosaries. And the anger appeared on Sol's face, as she had noticed that the tiger had prevented those two men to remove the rosaries of Angel, and Sol looked at William by telling him to fight the tiger, while she would go fight against Hero, and William replied to Sol that he could not fight the tiger, because he did not have his phantom inside him, like his strengths were located inside his ghost. Then, Sol told William to make sure that Hero would not get out with Angel, then Sol rushed through the tiger that was close to Angel, and Sol started to fight the tiger.

Angel was still turning her head in the room by looking for Hero, then Angel saw Hero and she screamed his name, then Angel ran until Hero, and she was standing up face to Hero, by looking at him with a worried face, and she noticed that he was freezing, and that he was breathing with difficulties, then she asked him if he was doing well? And Hero opened his mouth to talk, but he had the difficulties to talk that he could not pronounce a word, then Angel grabbed the hand of Hero by telling him that they should leave. But, Angel noticed that Hero's hand was freezing, and she asked him what was going on, and why he was freezing, and Hero was trying to talk but a word was not getting out from his mouth, and Angel's face was full of fear, as she was noticing that Hero was breathing as if someone was choking him to stop him from breathing. And she was still asking Hero to tell her what was going on, but she noticed that Hero was trying to send her a message as Hero was putting his hand through his neck, and she was begging Hero to try to say a word, as she was not understanding the message that he was sending to her through his hand on his neck.

Then, Angel started to have an idea about the message that Hero was trying to send her by putting his hand on his neck, then she turned her head through where the tiger was fighting, and Angel saw Sol who had grabbed the neck of the tiger, and Sol was trying to kill the tiger by pressing tiger's neck. And Angel understood the message of Hero, and why Hero had the difficulties to talk, then Angel turned her head through the door, and she saw a small red gas bottle that was on the wall close to the door. And Angel rushed towards the door, and she removed that gas bottle, and she started to run through where the tiger was fighting with her face full of anger, and with that gas bottle in her hand.

Suddenly, Sol pushed a scream and she fainted on the floor, as Angel had knocked Sol's head from behind with the gas bottle that Angel had in her hand, then Angel bent, and Angel took the tiger in her arms. Then, Angel turned her head through Hero, as she had noticed that the tiger had disappeared in her arms, then Angel got up and she ran till Hero, and she grabbed his hand by saying, "Let's go." And both Angel and Hero ran till outside, and Hero opened the door of the car that he had come with, and he demanded Angel to get inside the car and to drive until her home, and mostly to remember to not remove her rosaries. And Angel asked Hero if they were not going together, and Hero replied to Angel that they could not go together because he had something to do. And Angel did not want to go without Hero, but Hero succeeded to convince her to go without him, that they were going to meet soon, then Angel kissed Hero and she got inside the car and she drove away.

Then, Hero stole a car that was parked in front of the drugstore, and he drove away, Hero was driving faster, and he wanted to reach his hotel bedroom, before Prince killed his invisible phantom. William was shaking Sol who was still unconscious on the floor, and people were still in the drugstore watching what was going on, but the new customers who were getting inside the drugstore were very surprised by what was going on, and some of those new customers had already called the police. After eleven minutes, Sol opened her eyes, and William helped her to get up, and Sol asked William where Angel was, and William answered her that he had no idea, and Sol looked in the room, and she did not see Angel and Hero, and she understood that both Hero and Angel had left.

Then, Sol turned her head through Prince, and she noticed that Prince was still sending the red light on the invisible phantom of Hero, and she also remarked that invisible phantom of Hero had already given up the fight, then Sol understood that that invisible phantom had already lost all his strengths. Prince had moved face to the invisible phantom of Hero, as Prince had noticed that Angel had left, so Prince was no longer hiding to send the red light on the invisible phantom of Hero, and that invisible phantom wanted to turn into light to disappear, but that invisible phantom could not disappear because the red light that was getting out from Prince's eyes, and that was shining on that invisible phantom was preventing that invisible phantom to turn into the light and to run away.

Then, Sol and William joined Prince and Solis with a long black bag, and William opened that black bag, then Sol and Solis carried the invisible phantom of Hero, and they put that invisible ghost inside that bag, and there were the ices inside that bag, and they closed the closure of that bag. And Sol told them that it was time to kill the invisible phantom of Hero, and they carried that bag and they started to walk through the door with them, then they met the police at the door, but Sol used her magic to prevent policemen from asking them questions by looking in the eyes of policemen. Then, they walked till the parking, and they got inside of the car with the invisible phantom of Hero in the bag, and they drove away.

After an hour, Prince, Sol, William and Solis were in the living room of Prince's house, and it was been more than half an hour that they were trying to kill the invisible phantom of Hero that was still in the bag on the floor in front of them, and they were all wondering why they were not succeeding to kill that invisible phantom. Then, Sol started to remember the conversation she had had with Brad in the forest of the tiger world, and Sol told them that they could not kill the invisible phantom of Hero, because Angel succeeded to save that invisible phantom of Hero that they were trying to kill. William, Solis and Prince turned their heads through Sol by looking at her with surprised faces, and Prince demanded to Sol how Angel succeeded to save the invisible phantom of Hero? Sol answered that they could not kill the invisible phantom of Hero, because Angel prevented her from killing the identity phantom of Hero. And William told Sol that they were still not understanding why they could not kill the invisible phantom of Hero, and how Angel was preventing them from killing that invisible phantom? Sol told them that Hero was a supernatural being of the tiger world, and like all the supernatural beings of the tiger world, Hero was a tiger, but Hero was born with a small difference from the rest of the supernatural beings of the tiger world. And that difference was that Hero was born with an invisible phantom, and that invisible phantom of Hero was making Hero special and different from the rest of supernatural beings, and that the only way to kill the invisible phantom of Hero, it was to kill his phantom that was the tiger first. Because, the real phantom of Hero was the tiger, because Hero was a tiger, and his invisible phantom was just a support for his phantom that was the tiger, and that the invisible phantom of Hero was linked to his identity phantom that was the tiger, and the only way to kill that invisible phantom, it was to kill his phantom that was the tiger first.

Everyone looked at Sol with the amazed faces, and William asked Sol how she knew that? Sol answered that during her conversation with Brad in the tiger world about Hero, Brad told her that when Hero was fourteen, the invisible phantom of Hero had been stabbed by Prince in the forest during a fight, and they were all afraid, and they thought that Hero should die, and Hero had spent more than six months in the coma that time. And Sol went on by saying that Brad told her that one of the doctors who was taking care of the invisible phantom of Hero, had noticed that Brad was very sad that his best friend who was Hero was in the coma, and that doctor told Brad a secret and that secret was that Hero could not die, because the real phantom of Hero that was the tiger and that was the identity ghost of Hero was doing well. And that they should be worried if it was the tiger that had been stabbed by Prince, and that the only way for that the invisible phantom of Hero would die, it was that the phantom of Hero that was his identity would die first.

Then, Prince took a deep breath with his face full of disappointment, as he had understood that they could not kill the invisible phantom of Hero, then Prince opened his mouth by saying that he remembered well that day where he had stabbed the invisible phantom of Hero in the forest during a fight between his friends and Hero's friends. And they had all thought that Hero should die, that him and his friends had even celebrated the death of Hero, as Hero was their worst enemy, and after six months everyone was surprised to see that Hero had got out of the coma, and when they had demanded to the doctors how Hero had succeeded to get out of the coma alive. The doctors had answered them that Hero had survived because Hero had two phantoms, and that the only way to kill Hero it was to kill his two phantoms, but the doctors did not talk them that the only way to kill Hero it was to kill his identity ghost first before killing his invisible phantom. And Prince went on by saying that even Hero did not know that the only way to kill him was to kill his identity phantom first, before killing his invisible ghost. Because, the few moments he had spent with Hero as the brothers, when him and Hero had planned the idea to destroy the race of natural human beings, they had talked about the invisible phantom of Hero, and Hero told him that his both phantoms were not linked, that someone could kill his both phantoms at the same time, or even kill the invisible phantom before killing his identity phantom. And Sol said that Angel had succeeded to save the identity phantom of Hero, because she was hit from behind her head by Angel with the gas bottle, when she was killing the identity ghost of Hero, and that without Angel, Hero should be burned now.

And there was the anger on their faces, and they were all thinking what to do, they were all hating Angel not only because Angel was their enemy, but mostly because Angel had succeeded to save the identity phantom of Hero, and that was preventing them to kill the invisible phantom of Hero that they had in front of them. And Prince said that he wanted to kill Angel for what Angel did to his phantom, that his phantom was still in the hospital, because Angel had stabbed his phantom. And Sol told Prince that maybe she would send her phantom to the hospital too, because she was feeling the pains in her head, because her phantom had been touched as Angel had knocked her with the gas bottle, and that her phantom was not doing well. Solis told Sol that Sol could not send her phantom to the hospital, because they were close to victory, mostly that Prince and William could not fight because their phantoms were in the hospital. And Sol said that she was going to support pains for some days again, before sending her phantom to the hospital, as they were close to killing Angel, and as Hero was no longer a threat for them, because Hero could not anymore defend Angel, as Hero had only his identity phantom that was very weak and sick. And Sol went on by saying that there was no doubt that they were going to kill Angel and start the destroying of the race of natural human beings, and that even if Hero appeared to protect Angel when they would try to kill her, it would be a good thing because they would kill their both enemies at the same time who were Hero and Angel.

And William asked them what they would do with the invisible phantom of Hero? Prince answered that they would kill the invisible phantom of Hero, after that they had killed the identity phantom of Hero. And Sol told Prince that Hero was an enemy who betrayed his family, who fought against his family and who killed a supernatural being to protect an enemy who was Angel, that they should use the death of Hero to send a message to the supernatural beings that it was a sin to betray his family. And Sol added that she would like to take the invisible phantom of Hero in the world of eagle, to send a message to the inhabitants of the world of eagle that anyone who would betray his family would end as Hero, also to show to the inhabitants of the eagle world the result of their mission, and to avenge the death of Matt by giving the dead body of the enemy who had killed Matt to the world of eagle. And Prince said that it was a good idea, that he was not breaking any rule of the tradition of the tiger world by accepting Sol's proposal, because Hero had stopped to be a kid of the tiger world since the day he had been sentenced to death by the ancestors. And Prince went on by saying that he would take the identity phantom of Hero in the tiger world, when they would kill that identity ghost of Hero to show the result of his mission to the tiger world. And William told Sol that he would like that the invisible phantom of Hero be killed in the land of eagle world, because it would be a good thing not only for the inhabitants of the eagle world, but also for the memory of Matt, and that Matt and the ancestors would be happy to see that the one who had killed Matt, has been killed in the land of Matt.

And Solis agreed with the proposal of William to kill the invisible phantom of Hero in the eagle world not only for Matt and the inhabitants, but also for the ancestors, to show the result of their mission to the ancestors.

Then, they all agreed to take the invisible phantom of Hero in the eagle world, mostly that it was that invisible phantom who had killed Matt, but Sol told them that they should plan how to kill Angel first before taking the invisible phantom of Hero in the eagle world. Then, they started to think about where to kill Angel, and Sol told them that the night club would be a good place to kill Angel, and that Prince should invite Angel to the nightclub the next day, as the next day was Saturday. And Prince replied to Sol that Angel would not accept his invitation, because it had been a while that Angel was not taking his calls. Sol told Prince to use his magic and to send the messages to Angel as if he was Hero. Then, Prince took his phone, and he used his magic to change his number by using the number of Hero and he started to send the message to Angel as if he was Hero.

After an hour, Prince smiled at Sol by telling her that Angel had agreed to meet him in the nightclub the next day at 9 pm. Then, Solis looked at the clock that was the wall, and she told them that it was midnight, that they had better take the invisible ghost of Hero in the eagle world now and come back in the world of natural human beings before 9 pm to kill Angel. Then, they all left for the eagle world with the invisible phantom of Hero. Hero was lying in the bed of his hotel bedroom, and he was feeling very cold, and he was suffering, and his body was freezing as if he was in the freezer. And Hero was breathing with difficulties, and his sight was reduced that he was not seeing well, and even his magic was blocked, and Hero was unable to use his magic because all the parts of his body where was located his magic were blocked by the ices, as he was freezing. So, Hero had no idea about what was going on outside, and he was in those conditions because his invisible phantom was kept prisoner in a huge cold box like a coffin in the world of eagles. And that box was freezing his invisible phantom, because that box was working as the freezer, but although the fact that Hero was living a torture, he was very worried about Angel, and although the fact that Hero's magic was not working, Hero was trying to concentrate to find out where Angel was through his magic.

## CHAPTER X

# THE MYSTERIOUS GHOST ENEMY AND THE TORTURE OF HERO

It was 8:00 p.m., William, Sol, Prince and Solis were in the nightclub. And the club was full of people, and some were dancing on the dance floor. Prince was sitting alone at his table, with the glass of wine in front of him, but he was not drinking, while Sol, William and Solis were sitting in the chairs around a huge table, and there were three other men who were sitting at their table, and it was William who had invited those three other men. And they were all talking, except Sol who was not paying attention to the conversation, and William, Solis and those three men were planning their plan.

And Sol was not focused on the conversation, because she could not stop thinking about what had happened in the eagle world, when they went to the eagle world with the invisible phantom of Hero. And Sol had noticed how the eagle world was very happy to welcome Prince, and she was not surprised by the way that Prince was welcomed in the eagle world. But Sol was instead surprised about something that had happened, Sol had remarked that Matt's sister was very proud to see that the ghost who had killed her brother was prisoner in the eagle world. And that Matt's sister had taken Prince in her arms by thanking him for his support, as Prince had come in the eagle world with the phantom who had killed her brother, and by mistake, Matt's sister had tried to kiss Prince, but their bodies had rejected each other, once when the lips of Matt's sister had touched Prince's lips. And Sol was remembering the day she had made love with Brad in the forest of the tiger world, and Sol was remembering that she and Brad had kissed together with their ghosts inside their bodies even if their bodies were trying to reject each other. And Sol was wondering why Matt's sister and Prince did not succeed in kissing each other, while she and Brad had succeeded in kissing each other? But unfortunately, Sol could not answer that question, but Sol knew that there was a secret between the history of the tiger world and the history of the eagle world, also that there was a mystery about her life or about the life of Brad.

Because, it was inexplicable that she and Brad who were not from the same family had succeeded to kiss each other with their phantoms inside them, while Matt's sister and Prince who were not from the same family too had not succeeded to kiss each other with their phantoms inside them. And mostly that she and Matt's sister were from the same family, and Prince and Brad were from the same family, and Sol knew that normally if she and Brad had kissed together, that meant Matt's sister and Prince should succeed to kiss together too. And Sol was trying to understand the secret and the mystery that there was between the tiger world and the eagle world.

Then, Sol felt a hand on her hand, and she turned her head through Solis as she had noticed that it was Solis who had touched her hand, and Sol noticed that Solis was looking through the door, and Sol turned her head through the door, and Sol saw Angel who was walking in the nightclub. Angel was walking in the club, and she was turning her head by looking for Hero, then Angel wanted to walk through her left side, and she noticed that there was a man face to her, and that man looked in her eyes by asking her for a dance, but Angel refused by saying that she was looking for her boyfriend. And that man told Angel that he wanted her rosaries, and Angel looked at him with the fear on her face, and she wanted to walk away, but Angel felt the hands around her hips, and Angel understood that someone had grabbed her from behind through her hips. And Angel opened her mouth to scream, but the man who was face to her put his palm's hand on Angel's mouth to prevent her to yell, and another man grabbed Angel's hand that her wrist had the rosary, and that man wanted to remove the rosary that was on Angel's wrist. And Angel was trying to fight against those men who had grabbed her.

And suddenly there was a loud scream in the club, and everyone in the room turned the head through the window of the club as they had heard a violent noise coming from that side, and they noticed that the window's glass was broken. Then, a light shone close to Angel, and that light turned into a young woman, that young woman knocked at the two men who had grabbed Angel, and those two men fainted on the floor, and that young woman grabbed Angel's hand, and she started to pull Angel's hand by running through the door with Angel. And Angel was not seeing the one who had grabbed her hand, but Angel was just following that woman by thinking that it was Hero. Sol, Prince, Solis and William were turning their heads in the club by trying to understand what was going on, as they had not yet seen that woman who had appeared in the club, then the expression of Sol's face changed as she was looking at the door with a face full of surprise, as she was seeing that woman who was getting outside the club by holding Angel's hand.

Then, Sol screamed by saying in Latin, "Habemus est inimicus." That meant in English, "We have an enemy." Then, Prince, Solis and William turned their heads through Sol, and they noticed that Sol already had turned into the eagle, and that she was flying through the window, and the green eyes of Solis became dark green, and Solis turned into the eagle, and she flew through the window too. And William wanted to turn into the eagle, but he remembered that he could not, because he did not have his phantom in his body, then William and Prince started to run through the door among the crowd that was in the club. And people in the club were screaming with their faces full of terror as they had seen the eagles fly in the club, and they were all running through the door trying to get out. That woman who had saved Angel in the club was running in the parking of the club still by holding Angel's hand, and they were running through a car, then they stopped running as they had seen an eagle landed face to them, and that eagle turned into a supernatural being who was Sol. And Sol was looking in the eyes of that woman who had grabbed Angel's hand, then another eagle landed close to them and that eagle turned into a supernatural being who was Solis, then Solis and Sol were noticing that the woman who had held Angel's hand was a phantom, and Solis turned her head through Sol by asking in Latin, "Quis est iste qui expiravit et tenuit manum Angelus?" That meant in English, "Who is that phantom who held Angel's hand?" Sol looked at Solis by answering in Latin, "Quia spiritus a facie maledictionis nullam quis est nobis." That meant in English "I have no idea about who is this cursed phantom face to us." Solis asked in Latin, "Quid facere?" That meant in English "What to do?" Sol answered in Latin, "Occidit ei lets" That meant in English "Let's kill her." Angel was calling the name of Hero by asking him what Sol and Solis were talking about, as Angel thought that it was Hero who had held her hand, and as she was not understanding Latin.

Then, the fear appeared on the face Angel, as she was seeing Sol and Solis who were walking face to them, then William joined them, and Sol and Solis noticed that that phantom and William were looking at each other in the eyes, and Sol asked William in Latin if he knew that phantom, and William answered that he did not know her. Then, Sol told William to kill Angel and that she and Solis were going to kill that ghost who came to save Angel, and William answered Sol that he could not kill Angel, not only because he did not have his phantom inside him, but also because Angel still had her rosaries on her. Then, that phantom let Angel's hand and that phantom started to walk through Sol, and Sol was walking through that ghost too, then they started to fight. William and Angel were watching the fight, but Angel was not seeing the phantom who was fighting against Sol and Solis, but Angel was understanding what was going on. And Angel could not see that phantom because it was an invisible ghost, and only the natural human beings who had the magic could see that ghost. And Prince was hidden behind a car and he was watching the fight, by wondering who that phantom was, but he could not come where the fight was happening, because he did not want Angel to see him.

After a few minutes of fighting that phantom was becoming weak, and Sol and Solis were beating that phantom, and Angel was not seeing how Sol and Solis were beating that phantom, but Angel had noticed that the fight had changed by the way that Sol and Solis were fighting. Because, Angel had remarked that at the beginning of the fight, Sol and Solis were acting as if someone was punching them, and now Sol and Solis were acting as if they were punching at someone, then Angel understood that Hero was in danger, and she started to turn her head by looking around her, then Angel started to run towards her car. William was watching how Sol and Solis were beating that phantom with fear on his face, and with his heart that was beating faster than the normal, and by looking at William, we could see that he was afraid that Sol and Solis would kill that phantom.

Suddenly, William screamed the name of Solis by telling her to run away, and Solis looked at William and he yelled at her again by telling her to look behind her, then Solis turned her head from behind, and she saw a car that was coming towards her at high speed. And Sol shouted the name of Solis with a frightened face, as Sol had seen that car that was getting in Solis, then the green eyes of Solis turned into dark green, and the light got out of Solis's eyes, then Solis fell on the ground as she was hit by that car. And the car was mounted on Solis, and Angel screamed the name of Hero in the car by asking him to get inside the car, then Angel noticed that the car's door where she sat was opened, and she thought that it was Hero, then Angel moved to another seat, and that phantom got inside the car, and that phantom drove away. Then, Sol and William started to walk through Solis with their hearts that were beating with fear, and their eyes were focused on Solis who was lying on the ground with her eyes closed like a corpse, then both Sol and William bent close to Solis, and they started to shake Solis by calling her name, and there was the fear in the voices of Sol and William as they were calling the name of Solis.

Then, Sol took a deep breath as she had remarked that Solis had opened her eyes, and Sol understood that Solis did not have her phantom inside her when Angel had hit Solis with the car, then Sol and William helped Solis to get up, and they looked at Solis and they saw a wound on Solis's forehead, and Solis was bleeding. And William asked Solis how she was feeling? And Solis answered that she was feeling well, and Solis added that she was lucky that she had removed her ghost from her body on time before Angel hit her with the car.

Then, Prince joined them, and he looked at Solis by telling Solis that her ancestors were with her, that she should be in her grave now if she had not removed her phantom from her body on time. Sol said that they should be careful with Angel, because Angel was dangerous like her lover named Hero. And Prince asked who the phantom who had saved Angel was? Sol answered that they had no idea about who that phantom was. Solis said that they should end the first part of their mission, by going to kill Angel. And Prince asked Solis what the second part of their mission was? Solis looked in Prince's eyes by answering, that the second part of the mission was the destruction of the race of natural human beings. And Sol told Solis that they had to make a new plan to kill Angel, not only because Angel was protected by a mysterious phantom, but because even if they had Angel face to them, they could not kill her, because Angel had still her rosaries on her and none of them except Prince could touch Angel with her rosaries on her. And Sol added that Prince could not take a risk that Angel saw him with them, because if Angel saw Prince with them, and that they did not succeed to kill Angel, Angel would understand that Prince was a supernatural being, and she would avoid Prince. Then, it would be harder for them to kill Angel again, because Prince pretended to be the boyfriend of Angel to be close to Angel, to get the information from Angel and to help them to kill Angel.

Then, they all walked till their car, and they got inside their car, and Sol drove away. The Phantom was driving through Angel's house, and Angel was talking to that ghost by thinking that it was Hero, but that phantom was not saying a word, and Angel had started to have the doubt that it was not Hero because she was feeling it inside her, and Angel asked that ghost if it was really Hero, but again that phantom remained silent. Then, that phantom parked the car in the yard of Angel's house, and that phantom opened the car's door, and Angel opened her car's door too, then they got out of the car, and

Angel started to look around and Angel asked. "Are you going to say a word." And no one replied to Angel, but Angel felt that her hand was held by someone, and that the one who had grabbed her hand was trying to walk through the house with her.

Then, that phantom and Angel walked till the door, then that phantom opened the door, and Angel got inside the house, and Angel noticed that the door was closed behind her, then that phantom turned into the light and she disappeared. Angel walked till inside her bedroom, and she looked at the clock that was on the wall and she noticed that it was midnight, then she started to look for the letter, then after an hour, she noticed that Hero had not let the letter, and she laid down in the bed, and she started to think about Hero, then she fell asleep.

Prince, Solis, William And Sol were all standing up face to wall in the living room of Prince's house, and they were all staring at the pictures that Prince had made appear on the wall through his magic. There were the pictures of the mysterious woman who had saved Angel in the club on the wall, and they were all looking at that woman on the wall by wondering who that woman was? And they were all noticing that that woman had the short yellow hair, and yellow eyes without the beauty mark on her face. And Solis said that that woman was an invisible phantom, and that may be that phantom belonged to a supernatural being. Prince told Solis that that phantom could not belong to a supernatural being, because that phantom had the yellow eyes, and that phantom had not the beauty marks on her face, the Prince went on by saying that the yellow color was the color of the devil, and that a supernatural being could not have the yellow eyes, and the yellow hair, also that all the supernatural beings born with a beauty mark on their faces. And Sol said that she remembered about a holy book that she had read in the museum of the eagle world, and that holy book was telling about the devil and the kids of the devil called again the zombies, and that holy book was telling that the devil and his kids had two colors of eyes the yellow eyes, and the red eyes, and that a supernatural being could not have the yellow and red eyes.

## SUPERNATURAL BEINGS

Suddenly, they turned their heads by looking at each other with silence, and they were wondering if they were attacked by a devil. And after three minutes, Prince walked two steps through the wall, and the light got out from his eyes and went through the wall, and they were all looking at the wall with the amazed faces as they were all seeing the supernatural beings who were fighting against the children of the devil called again the zombies. And they were all noticing that the devil's children had the yellow and red eyes, and the yellow and red hair, and that those kids of devil did not have the beauty marks on their faces. And they were all noticing that the supernatural beings were using their phantoms to fight, and that those kids of devil did not have the phantoms.

Then, William broke the silence by asking what was the reason for the fight between the supernatural beings and those kids of the devil? Prince answered to William that two centuries ago the world of supernatural beings was attacked by the devil and his kids called again the zombies. And the zombies had lost the fight against the supernatural beings. Solis asked what was the reason for that fight? Prince answered that the reason of that fight was the land, that the zombies did not have the land, and the zombies were looking for a territory where they should settle to build their world, and the zombies came in the world of supernatural beings to eradicate of race of the supernatural beings and to take the land of the supernatural beings. But unfortunately, the zombies lost the fight, and the supernatural beings killed almost all the zombies, but the few zombies who had succeeded to survive in the fight ran away, and during two centuries the supernatural beings had not seen a zombie again until last night when a zombie appeared in the club to save Angel. Solis asked Prince how he knew it? Prince answered Solis that his magic was linked to the past, and he could see and understand everything that had happened in the past through his magic. And Solis told Prince that she would like to know about the war that had happened more than a century ago between the race of supernatural beings and the race of natural human beings. And Prince told Solis that the war that had happened between the race of supernatural beings and the race of natural human beings was a long story, that they would talk about it after the destroying of the race of natural human beings.

And Sol asked Prince where those zombies were living now? Prince answered that he had no idea, that it was been almost an hour that he was trying to find the world of zombies through his magic, but his magic was unable to find the world of zombies, because he could not use all the abilities of his magic, like most part of his magic was blocked by their mysterious enemy. And that he would find the world of zombies, if he could use all his full magic, also that he would find who that mysterious phantom who had saved was, if he could use all the abilities of his magic. And Sol said that it seemed that the time for revenge had come. William asked Sol what she was meaning by that? Sol answered that it was obvious that the only reason why that zombie saved Angel in the club last night was to prevent them from killing Angel. And Sol added that she had no doubt that the zombies were watching them, and that those zombies knew well who Angel was and the reasons why the supernatural beings wanted to kill Angel.

Prince said that the zombies did not care about the race of natural human beings, and that the zombies hated the race of natural human beings. And that the only reason for which that zombie saved Angel, was to take their revenge on the race of supernatural beings about what had happened two centuries ago, by preventing the supernatural beings from killing Angel. Because, the zombies probably knew that the supernatural beings wanted to eradicate the race of natural human beings to take revenge on the race of natural human beings for what had happened more than a century ago. And that the zombies knew well that the only way for the supernatural beings to eradicate the race of natural human beings was to kill Angel first, and the zombies were protecting Angel to prevent the supernatural beings from killing Angel, not because the zombies cared about Angel or because the zombies loved the race of natural human beings. But, because the zombies wanted to take their revenge on the race of supernatural beings, about what had happened two centuries years ago by preventing the supernatural beings from destroying the race of natural human beings.

## SUPERNATURAL BEINGS

Then, William took a deep breath by saying that it was as if he was in front of television watching a movie about the story of supernatural beings. Sol looked at William by saying that herself it was as if she was watching a movie about the story of supernatural beings that was full of secrets, the mysteries, and that every time she thought that the movie would end, another secret and mystery appeared. Prince said that the history of the race of supernatural beings was full of secrets, and the mysteries. Solis said that now they had the new enemies who were the zombies, and that they should think about how to get rid of those zombies. Sol said that the first thing they should do now was to find out where the world of the zombies was.

Then, there was the silence in the room, and Solis was looking at the pictures that were on the wall with attention, then Solis started to walk through the wall still with her eyes focus on the pictures, and she was noticing that during the fight the zombies were fighting with their teeth and their venoms, while the supernatural beings were fighting with their phantoms, and that most of the corpses who were lying on the ground were the dead bodies of the zombies. Then, Solis stopped close to the wall, and she kept staring at the pictures of the fight that were on the wall, and she was also looking at the picture of the mysterious woman who had saved Angel last night in the club.

Then, Solis turned her head, and she looked at Prince, Sol and William by saying that the mysterious woman who had saved Angel last night in the club was not a zombie, but instead an invisible phantom. And Sol told Solis that she was not understanding. Solis said that the zombies fought with their long canine teeth and their venoms, and that the zombies did not have the phantoms, and that the zombies were not invisible through the eyes of the natural human beings. And Solis went on by saying that the mysterious woman who had saved Angel last night in the club was an invisible phantom, because Angel was not seeing that woman, and Angel thought that that mysterious woman was Hero and that it was the reason why Angel was calling that invisible ghost Hero. And that invisible phantom was not fighting like a zombie because that invisible ghost was not using her teeth, but that invisible phantom was fighting instead like a supernatural being.

Prince looked at Solis by saying that even himself he had noticed when he was watching the fight that that mysterious woman was fighting like a supernatural being, and mostly like a supernatural being of the tiger world, and that he had even thought that she was a supernatural being of the tiger world when she was fighting. But he noticed that she did not have any mark of the tiger world, and he did not feel the smell of the supernatural beings of the tiger world when that mysterious woman appeared, or when she was fighting. And Sol said that it meant that the first impression they had had by seeing that woman who had saved Angel last night in the club was true, because when they had all seen that woman in the parking of the club, the first idea that had come in their minds was that that woman was a ghost. And William said that they were not sure that that mysterious phantom who had saved Angel last night was a supernatural being, because she did not look like a supernatural being, and she had no mark of supernatural beings. Prince said that that phantom was not a zombie and she was not a supernatural being too. And Solis agreed with Prince's idea, by saying that she had mistaken when she said that that phantom was a supernatural being. William asked who was that phantom if that phantom was not a zombie and was not a supernatural being? Sol said that probably that mysterious phantom had the same story as Angel, and suddenly Prince, Solis and William turned their heads through Sol by looking at Sol with the surprised faces.

Then, William said that if that mysterious ghost had the same story as Angel, that meant that that phantom had two different genes. Solis said that it was impossible that that phantom had the same story as Angel, because that phantom had not the genes of the supernatural beings. Sol told Solis to not forget that the zombies were in the world of supernatural beings during the fight that had happened two centuries ago, and that during that period of fight a supernatural being had broken one of the rules of the tradition. And Sol went on by saying that they were not sure that that phantom did not have the genes of the supernatural beings. Solis said that if that phantom had the genes of the supernatural beings, they should know because that meant that that phantom was a supernatural being, and that that

# SUPERNATURAL BEINGS

phantom should have the marks of the supernatural beings. William agreed with the idea of Solis by saying that that phantom could not be a supernatural being, because if that phantom was a supernatural being, that meant that the one who had that phantom had two different genes or the body who had that ghost had two different genes.

And that if it was a zombie who had that phantom, that meant that that phantom was coming from the body of a zombie, and if that phantom was coming from the body of a zombie, that meant that that zombie had two genes that were the genes of the supernatural beings and the genes of zombies, and that meant that that zombie had a phantom that was a supernatural being. And that if that zombie had the ghost that was a supernatural being, that meant that there would be the genes of the supernatural beings on that ghost, but that that phantom who had saved Angel last night in the club and that they were seeing on the wall had nothing of familiar with the race of supernatural beings, because that phantom had not the genes of the supernatural beings, and that phantom had not the marks of the supernatural beings, so that it was impossible that that phantom be a supernatural being.

Then, all they all agreed that that phantom was not a supernatural being, and they were also sure that that phantom was not a zombie, but they did not know where that phantom was coming from. And there was a question that was going on in their minds, and that question was why that phantom saved Angel last night in the club? But unfortunately, none of them could answer that question. And Prince was using his magic to try to find out where that phantom who had saved Angel was coming from, but he failed to find out the origins of that phantom. After the hours of thinking, Prince, Solis, William and Sol were already tired, and they did not know what to do, and they had no idea about who that phantom was, and they knew that if they wanted to kill Angel, they should kill that ghost first. And there was the silence in the room, and suddenly they turned their heads through Prince as they heard Prince's phone ringing, and Prince removed his phone from his pocket.

And Prince looked at the screen of his phone, then he stared at Sol by saying that it was Angel who was calling him, and Sol demanded to Prince to pick up the phone. And Prince told Sol that he could not pick up the phone, because Angel was calling him through the number of Hero that he had installed in his phone through his magic. And that if he picked up the phone, Angel would know that she was not texting with Hero yesterday, and she would start to have doubts about him, when she would hear his voice, because she would start wondering how he had the phone number of Hero. And Sol told Prince to communicate with Angel by message, by using the number of Hero that he had in his phone, and to try to get the information from Angel that could help them to find out the identity of that phantom who had saved Angel last night in the club. Then, Prince started to communicate with Angel by message, while Sol, William and Solis were looking at the pictures that were on the wall. After an hour, Solis, William and Sol turned their heads through Prince, as they had heard Prince say that Angel would be in church in less than eleven minutes, and that he had convinced Angel to remove her rosaries.

Sol, William and Solis turned their heads by looking at each other with the amazed faces, as they had heard Prince say that he had convinced Angel to remove her rosaries, then Sol looked at Prince by asking if it meant that Angel did not wear her rosaries now? Prince answered that yes, that Angel was on the way to the church and she had let her rosaries at home. Solis asked Prince how he had succeeded to convince Angel to remove her rosaries? Prince answered that Angel thought that it was Hero who was asking her to remove her rosaries. William asked Prince if Angel did not find it weird that Hero asked her to remove her rosaries. Prince answered that Angel was very surprised when he asked her to remove her rosaries, but he told her that he wanted to kill people who wanted to kill her, that he wanted her enemies to approach her, then he would appear to kill them. Because, it was a good way to end with this war, and it was a good way for her to be safe forever, and that he promised her that she would be safe, that nothing would happen to her, and that he wanted her to live a normal life, and that they lived their love. Sol asked Prince if Angel knew something about the phantom who had saved Angel in the club. And Prince answered that Angel had no idea about that phantom who had saved her in the club, because Angel thought that that phantom was Hero.

And Sol said that they had to organize a plan about how to kill Angel, and that they would make sure to not fail this time, that Angel would not have the rosaries on her wrist and on her ankle, so that it was their chance to kill Angel. Solis told Prince to use his magic and to find out where Angel was, that by knowing the position of Angel, it would help them to make their plan. Then, Prince started to walk through the wall, and the light got out from Prince's eyes and went through the wall, and the pictures appeared on the wall, and they were all looking at the pictures that were on the wall, and they were seeing Angel and her parents who were walking inside the church, and they were noticing that Angel did not wear her rosaries. Then, Solis broke the silence by saying that there was no doubt that Angel would die in a couple of minutes. And Sol turned her head through Solis by looking in Solis's eyes, and by saying that they would think how to prevent that mysterious phantom to protect Angel again. And Solis replied to Sol that that phantom would not prevent them from killing Angel again, because that phantom was not really strong, and that she would fight that phantom alone when that phantom would appear.

William said that he was sure that they would succeed to kill Angel today, because the rosaries on the wrist and ankle of Angel were the obstacles that were preventing them from killing Angel, but that this time Angel was not wearing her rosaries. Sol looked at William and Prince by telling them that they should have their phantoms inside them for this mission, because they did not know what would happen, that they should be ready to fight if they found an obstacle in the church. Because, they could be surprised to see more than one phantom who came to protect Angel, that everyone must have his ghost inside him, and they would make sure that Angel would not leave the church alive. And Sol went on by asking Prince and William to remove their phantoms to the hospital, even if their phantoms were not completely healed.

Then, they all started to talk about their plan, by looking at the pictures of Angel that were on the wall. Angel was sitting in a chair in the church, and she had refused to sit in the same place with her parents, because she was waiting for Hero, and there was an empty chair close to Angel, and Angel had put her purse in that empty chair, and she was reserving that empty chair to Hero. And Angel was not paying attention to what the priest was saying, because she was turning her head by looking for Hero, and she had started to wonder where Hero was. Then, Angel removed her phone from her purse, and she started to send the message to Prince by thinking that it was Hero, and she started to be worried when she noticed that no one was answering to her messages, and she was looking at the screen of her phone with a worried face.

Suddenly, Angel turned her head as she was hearing people who were screaming in the room, and the terror appeared on her face, as she had seen the eagles that were flying in the church. Then, an eagle landed face to Angel, and that eagle turned into a supernatural being who was Sol, then Angel screamed as she had seen Sol face her, and Angel wanted to run away but unfortunately, she was grabbed by William who had appeared behind her. And Angel tried to fight but she was too weak, and William had grabbed Angel from behind, and William looked in Sol's eyes by saying in Latin, "Est tempus." That meant in English, "It's time." Then, Sol handed her both hands, and she grabbed Angel's head and Sol moved her head towards Angel's neck and Sol opened her mouth and there were the long canine teeth in the mouth of Sol, then Sol tried to bite Angel's neck, and suddenly William pushed a loud scream by yelling in Latin, "Et exspiravit." That meant in English, "The ghost." And unknowingly, Sol bit the hand who was between her mouth and Angel's neck.

Then, Sol realized that when she wanted to bite the neck of Angel, the mysterious ghost appeared behind her and that ghost put her hand between her mouth and Angel's neck, and that it was the hand of that ghost that she had bitten. Then, Sol turned, and she started to fight with the phantom, and that phantom was bleeding at her hand, as Sol had bitten that ghost's hand, and there was also the blood on the mouth of Sol, and that blood on Sol's mouth was coming from the wound of the phantom as she had bitten that phantom. And William was running after Angel, because Angel had succeeded to run away from William's arms, because William had lost the concentration on Angel and he had lost the balance too, when he had seen Sol bite the hand of that phantom, and Angel took the opportunity at that moment to run away as William had lost concentration on her. The church was empty, everyone had run away when they had seen the eagles fly inside the church and turned into supernatural beings, and there were only Angel, William, Sol and the phantom in the church. And Angel was running through the door, then she saw a tiger that was running face to her, and Angel stopped running, and she bent face to that tiger by looking in tiger's eyes with the smile on her face by thinking that that tiger was Hero, then the smile that was on her face was disappeared, and the disappointment took place of that smile as she had realized that that tiger was not Hero.

Then, Angel got up and she tried to run away, and suddenly that tiger jumped on her and threw her on the floor, and the tiger was staring at Angel who was unconscious on the floor, then the tiger saw William who had bent close to Angel. William looked at Angel and he opened his mouth and there were long canine teeth in his mouth, then William moved his mouth through Angel's neck, and he touched Angel's neck with his teeth by trying to bite her neck. And suddenly William stopped as he was feeling a wind that was blowing in the church, and he was breathing deeply with the difficulties as if someone was choking him to stop him from breathing, and he was trying to concentrate to bite Angel's neck, but he was not succeeding although the fact that his teeth were still on Angel's neck.

Suddenly, William found himself on the floor, and it was that mysterious phantom who had jumped on him, and threw him on the floor, and both William and the phantom were fighting on the floor. And that wind had stopped blowing, then an eagle flew inside the church and that eagle landed near to Angel, and that eagle turned into a supernatural being who was Solis, and Solis knelt near to Angel, and Solis lifted the head of Angel with one of her hands. Then, Solis started to move her head towards the neck of Angel, and Solis moved her mouth close to Angel's neck, then Solis opened her mouth to bite Angel's neck with her long canine teeth, but suddenly Solis stopped, and Solis turned her head by looking around as she was feeling the wind that was blowing in the church.

Then, Solis let Angel's head that she had lifted with one of her hands, then Solis got up and started to run through Sol, and as Solis had seen Sol who was lying unconscious on the floor. William and that phantom were still fighting, and that phantom was lying on William, and William had held the neck of that phantom with his both hands, and that phantom had held the both hands of William, and that phantom was fighting to remove William's hands from her neck. William was pressing the neck of that phantom with all his strengths, and that phantom was breathing with difficulties by trying to remove the hands of William from her neck, then the eyes of William met with the eyes of that phantom, and they were looking each other in the eyes, and William started to lose the concentration.

Then, William gave up the fight by removing his hands from the neck of that phantom, and that phantom had let the hands of William too, then they were still staring at each other in the eyes. Then, the phantom got up on William, and the phantom walked two steps towards Angel, and the phantom bent close to Angel and the phantom carried Angel in her arms, and the phantom started to walk through the door with Angel who was still unconscious in her arms. Then, William had got up from the floor, then William and the tiger were watching at the phantom who was getting outside of the church with Angel in her arms, then the tiger turned his head through William, and the tiger was looking at William how William was staring at that phantom.

Then, William turned his head through the tiger, and he looked in the tiger's eyes by saying in Latin, "Defecit hoc iterum." That meant in English, "We failed again." William turned his head and he saw Solis who was shaking Sol who was still lying on the floor, then William started to run through Sol and Solis, and the tiger started to follow William by running. Then, both William and the tiger reached where were Sol and Solis, then William bent close to Sol, while the tiger turned into the body of supernatural being who was Prince, and Prince bent near to Sol too and they were all shaking Sol who was unconscious on the floor by calling her name.

## SUPERNATURAL BEINGS

After a few minutes, Sol opened her eyes, and they helped Sol to get up, then Solis looked at Sol by asking what happened for that she be unconscious on the floor? And Sol answered that the phantom with who she was fighting had hit her at her head from behind with a chair when she was trying to run after Angel, that's why she had fainted. Then, Sol asked if Angel was dead, and there was silence and they were all looking at each other without saying a word, then Sol understood that they had failed to kill Angel. Then, Sol opened her mouth by asking in Latin, "Sancti Angeli praetor maledicta suscepit quod amplius?" That meant in English, "How that cursed phantom succeeded to save Angel again?" Prince looked into Sol's eyes by answering in Latin, "Sancti Angeli salus non est." That meant in English, "It's not the phantom who saved Angel." Sol asked in Latin, "Quare Angelus non est mortuorum, si non nisi tenuem illam?" That meant in English, "Why Angel is not dead, if the phantom did not save her?" Prince answered in Latin, "Eodem tempore Willelmi arcani quidpiam Solis utramque Angelus temptabant interficere." That meant in English, "Something mysterious happened at each time when William and Solis tried to kill Angel, and it's that mysterious thing that saved Angel."

Suddenly, the expression on Sol's face changed, and she was looking with an amazed face, then she asked what was that mysterious thing that had happened and that had prevented Solis and William from killing Angel? And Prince told Sol that they would talk about that mysterious thing at home, and together they would try to find out where that mysterious came from, and why that mysterious thing had saved Angel. Then, they all started to walk through the door, and Solis told Prince that she did not know that he spoke Latin, and Prince replied to Solis by smiling that he was a supernatural being, and that the Latin was the traditional language of the supernatural beings. And that since the existence of the race of the supernatural beings, the Latin was the language that the supernatural beings used to speak. Then, they reached outside, and they got inside their car and they drove away.

The phantom was driving through the yard of Angel's house, and the phantom saw Angel's parents in the car who were driving through downtown, and the phantom understood that Angel's parents were going to look for Angel. Then, the phantom parked the car in the yard, and she got out of the car, then she went, and she opened the rear door of the car, and she handed her both hands in the car, then she carried Angel who was lying on the back seat and who was still unconscious, and she put Angel through shoulder. Then, the phantom walked till the front door with Angel, and the phantom grabbed the handle of the door, and she turned the door's handle, then the door opened, and she walked inside, then she closed the door behind her. And the phantom walked until in Angel's bedroom, and she lied Angel in the bed, then the phantom walked till the study's table of Angel, and she took the rosaries that were on that table, and she took a pen that was on the table and she started to write on a sheet of paper that was on the table.

Then, the phantom took that sheet of paper that she had written on it, and she walked till close to the bed with that sheet of paper and with the rosaries, then she wore the rosaries on the wrist and on the ankle of Angel, and she put that sheet of paper on the teddy bear of Angel that was on the bed. Then, the phantom walked till the door, and she opened the door and she got out, then she closed the door behind her, and she left.

Prince, Solis, William and Sol were standing up in the living room of Prince's house, and they were all face to the wall, and they were looking at the pictures that Prince had used his magic to make appear on the wall. And the pictures that were on the wall were the pictures of the fight that had happened in the church a couple hours ago, and they were all seeing all the scenes of the fight, how Sol, William and Solis had failed to kill Angel, and how the phantom had left the church with Angel. And they were all noticing that the phantom who had appeared in the church to save Angel was the same as the phantom, who had saved Angel in the club last night, but they were not worried about that phantom. Because, they were concentrating their ideas and their energies on the wind that had blown in the church, when William and Solis had tried to bite Angel's neck, and they were wondering where that wind was coming from, and why that wind had saved Angel.

## SUPERNATURAL BEINGS

But unfortunately, they had no idea of where that wind was coming from, and they were very nervous, because they were understanding that when they would not find out where that wind that had blown in the church was coming from, they would never kill Angel and if they did not kill Angel, that meant that they would never eradicate the race of natural human beings. After the hours of thinking, Sol started to walk face to the wall, by looking at the pictures that were on the wall with attention, and Sol's eyes were focused on the pictures of William and Solis at the moment that William and Solis were trying to bite Angel's neck. Then, Sol turned her head, and she looked in William's eyes by asking him how he had felt at the moment when he wanted to bite Angel's neck, and that wind started to blow? William answered that he had felt that he was blocked by something, and that he had difficulties breathing, and he was not feeling his teeth, and that the reason why he was not succeeding to bite Angel's neck was because he was not feeling his teeth. Then, Sol turned her head through Solis without saying a word to William, and Sol looked in Solis's eyes and Solis looked in the eyes of Sol by saying that even herself she had felt the same thing as William when she had tried to kill Angel, that she had not succeeded to bite Angel's neck, because she was not feeling her teeth.

Then, Sol opened her mouth and she said, "Joseph." Solis cried out, "What?" by looking at Sol with an amazed face, and William looked at Sol by saying that Joseph was dead. Sol turned her head through William by looking in his eyes and by saying that she had no doubt that the wind that had blown in the church was coming from the magic of Joseph. Solis walked two steps through Sol, and she looked in Sol's eyes by saying that it had been almost a year that they had killed Joseph, and that they were all there the day of Joseph's death. And Sol said that she knew well about Joseph's death, and that she was even the one who had killed Joseph, but that there was something mysterious that was happening, and that she had no doubt that the wind that blew in the church to prevent them from killing Angel was related to Joseph. William said that it was impossible that the wind that had blown in the church was related to Joseph, because

Joseph was dead, and even the powers and the magic of Joseph were dead too.

Sol looked at William by saying that Joseph was so mysterious, that no one knew his real identity, where he was coming from, and that the only thing they knew about Joseph, it was that Joseph had the genes of supernatural beings in his body, but that they did not have an idea about the rest of the genes that were in the blood of Joseph. William replied to Sol that although the fact that Joseph was so mysterious, and that Joseph was not one hundred percent a supernatural being, it did not mean that Joseph was still alive because Joseph was not an immortal. Sol said that the only one who knew well the history of the race of supernatural beings was Joseph, and Joseph knew well the reasons why the world of eagle wanted to kill Angel, and that it was the reason why Joseph had appeared to the hospital the day that Rebecca was giving birth to Angel, and Joseph started to protect Angel since the first second that Angel was born. Solis said that it would be a waste of time to focus their energy on Joseph, because Joseph was dead.

Sol looked at Solis by saying that Joseph had the ability to trigger the wind through his magic, and that Joseph knew well that the wind that was coming from his magic was a poison that was preventing the supernatural beings of the eagle world to breath. And that Joseph knew well that that wind coming from his magic was making the long canine teeth of the supernatural beings weak and unusable, as if that wind was killing the teeth of supernatural beings of the eagle world, and that Joseph used to fight to protect Angel by using that wind coming from his magic. William said that the wind that had blown in the church could not come from Joseph, because that wind was very weak compared to the wind that was coming from the magic of Joseph. Solis looked at Sol by telling Sol to remember that the wind that was coming from the magic of Joseph was very strong, and that that wind used to carry them and throw them in space, and that when that wind was blowing everything was shaking even the houses as if there was an earthquake.

Then, they turned their heads through Prince as they had noticed that Prince was walking through the wall, and they were looking at the wall with surprised faces, as they were seeing the light that was getting out from Prince's eyes and going through the wall, and that light was turning into the pictures. Then, they all walked till face to the wall, and they were looking at the pictures that were on the wall, as they were seeing that fight that had happened between the supernatural beings of the eagle world and Joseph in the forest, and it was in that fight that Sol had killed Joseph by using the nails of her fingers. But, the eyes of Prince were focused on Joseph, and Prince was noticing that Joseph was an old man with long dark beard, with purple eyes, and with a beauty mark near to the left side of his ear, then Prince started to understand who Joseph was and the origins of Joseph.

Then, Prince turned his head through the pictures were Sol was killing Joseph, and Prince was seeing on those pictures that Sol and Joseph were fighting on the top of a mountain, and Sol had used her magic to make her nails become long, and she had stabbed at the belly of Joseph by using her long nails, then she had pushed Joseph, and Joseph fell in the ocean that was under the mountain. Then, Prince turned his head by looking at other pictures on the wall, and he was seeing that William, Collin and Solis were there during the fight, and he was also seeing the dead body of a supernatural being of the eagle world that Joseph had killed during the fight, before Sol killed him too. Then, Prince turned his head and he looked at Sol by asking what was the phantom of Joseph? Sol answered that she had no idea about the phantom of Joseph, because she had never seen the phantom of Joseph, and Joseph had never turned into his phantom even when Joseph was in danger, because Joseph was still fighting with his body. Prince asked why they had said that Joseph was a supernatural being? Sol answered that because Joseph had the marks of a supernatural being, like his eyes color and his beauty mark, and Sol added that she had read in the holy book that the supernatural beings had the purple eyes, that was the eyes colors of Joseph. And Solis looked at Prince by asking if he had the doubt about the identity of Joseph? Prince looked in Solis's eyes by answering that the origins of Joseph were full of mysteries, and that they would talk about who Joseph was another time, but that Joseph had the good reasons to protect the race of natural human beings, and that it was the reason why Joseph was fighting to protect Angel. Because, Joseph knew that the race of natural human beings would be eradicated by the race of supernatural beings, if the supernatural beings had succeeded to kill Angel.

Then, Prince looked at Sol by telling Sol that he wanted her to make her nails become long, as she had done to kill Joseph. And Sol answered Prince that she could not make her nails become long in the world of natural human beings, because the part of her magic that she used to make her nails become long was blocked by their enemy. Then, Prince asked Sol why she stabbed Joseph with her nails? Sol answered that her nails were one of her weapons to kill an enemy, that she could even kill an animal by using her nails, and that her nails contained the poison, and that it was the reason why an enemy could not survive if that enemy had been stabbed by her nails.

Prince demanded Sol why she did not kill Joseph since the first day that Joseph had started to protect Angel, if she knew that she could kill Joseph by using her nails? Sol answered Prince that Joseph had appeared unexpectedly at the hospital where Rebecca was giving birth to Angel, and that they had arrived at that hospital a second after the birth of Angel to kill Angel, but unfortunately for them Joseph was already at that hospital to protect Angel. And they were surprised to see Joseph who was protecting Angel, because they did not expect that Angel should be protected by a supernatural being, and they were more surprised to see that Joseph who was a supernatural being was fighting against his family to protect an enemy as Angel.

Prince looked at Sol by saying that she did not answer his question. Sol replied that she did not kill Joseph since the first second, that she had seen him fighting to protect Angel, because Joseph was in the world of natural human beings, and most of part of her magic already was blocked in the world of natural human beings by their enemy. And that during almost sixteen years Joseph was always in the world of natural beings, and it was impossible to kill him in the world of natural human beings like most part of her magic was not working to kill him in the world of natural human beings, till

# SUPERNATURAL BEINGS

the day that Joseph made a mistake and he got out of the world of natural human beings. And she found out that Joseph was in a forest close to the ocean, then she went in that forest with other supernatural beings and they fought Joseph, and she killed him, then she pushed his dead body in the water. Prince asked Sol that why after the death of Joseph, they did not go to kill Angel? Sol answered that they could not kill Angel the same day that they had killed Joseph, because during the fight with Joseph, they had lost a member of their family who was killed by Joseph. And that according to one of the rules of the tradition of the eagle world, when a member of the family of the eagle world died, the eagle world would spend three of mourning and during all those three days of mourning all activities were stopped, even the fight against an enemy. And as they had lost a member of their family in that fight against Joseph, they could only kill Angel after three days, but unfortunately for them when they came after those three days to kill Angel, they found out that Angel had another savior who was Hero.

Prince asked if it was Joseph who had given those rosaries to Angel? Sol answered that yes, that it was Joseph who had given those rosaries to Angel, and that it was even three rosaries, but Angel had lost one, the one that was on her neck. Prince asked if Angel and Joseph were very close? Sol answered that yes, that both Angel and Joseph were very close and that Joseph was the godfather of Angel. Then, Prince took a deep breath and he said that they would need the help of Angel to kill Joseph. And Solis looked at Prince by asking if Joseph was still alive? Prince answered Solis that one part of Joseph was dead, and another part of Joseph was still alive, but that the part of Joseph who was still alive was very sick, and that the wind that had blown in the church was coming from the magic of Joseph that was very sick.

And suddenly the expression of the faces of William and Solis changed, and they were looking with surprised faces, and by looking at them, we could see that they were not believing that Joseph was still alive. Then, William looked at Prince by saying that he was not understanding how one part of Joseph was dead, and another part was alive. Prince told William that there was no time to talk about the origins of Joseph, but that Sol had done a big mistake by pushing Joseph in the water after that she had stabbed him, because Joseph was not completely dead, and that when Joseph fell in the water, one part of the magic of Joseph had succeeded to survive in the water.

Sol looked at Prince by saying that she was not understanding. Prince told Sol that Joseph had the genes in his body that had the links with the water, and that those genes could not die in the water, and that the genes of Joseph who had succeeded to survive in the water were the genes who contained the magic that had prevented Solis and William to bite Angel's neck, and that Joseph had inherited those genes from one part of his ancestors. Solis asked Prince if the magic of Joseph was located in his genes? Prince answered Solis that Joseph had different genes in his body, and those genes were coming from his different ancestors, and that almost all the ancestors of Joseph had the magic, and some parts of the magic of Joseph were located in his genes. And Prince went on by saying that Joseph had inherited all the magic of his ancestors, but that Sol had killed all the genes of Joseph who contained the magic, except the genes who had survived in the water, but that those genes who had survived in the water were very sick, and that was the reason why the magic that was coming from those genes could not fight. William asked Prince why those genes who had survived in the water were sick? Prince answered William that even if those genes had survived in the water, those genes had got hurt by the nails of Sol, and that those genes should die too if Sol had not pushed Joseph in the water after that she had stabbed him, that those genes were very lucky to survive in the water. Because those genes would die if those genes were outside of the water, but those genes were very sick because those genes had not been cured since those genes had been injured by the nails of Sol.

Then Sol asked Prince why during all those times that magic coming from those genes of Joseph who had survived in the water did not protect Angel when Angel was in danger? Prince answered Sol that the magic coming from those genes of Joseph who had survived in the water did not protect Angel during almost a year, because those genes were very sick, and as those genes were very sick, that meant that the magic coming from those genes was very weak. And

## SUPERNATURAL BEINGS

that that magic could not really protect Angel, because that magic was not strong enough to protect Angel, and that it was the reason why the wind that had blown in the church in the morning was very weak, that that wind could not blow as it used to blow by shaking the houses, and by throwing people in the space. And that it was the reason why that wind had blown only for a few seconds, because that wind could not blow for a long time, and that that wind had blown in the church to save Angel, because the magic coming from that wind had found out that Angel was really in danger, but that that magic could not protect Angel for a long time.

Sol asked Prince how it could be possible that one part of the genes of Joseph had survived, while the rest of his genes were dead. Prince answered Sol that one part of the ancestors of Joseph were coming from the race of supernatural beings who were a little bit different from their race, and that it was very hard to kill the supernatural beings of the race where one part of the ancestors of Joseph were coming from. Because, those supernatural beings had the links with the water, and that the only way to kill those supernatural beings was to kill their genes, and Joseph had inherited those genes from his ancestors, and that was the reason why one part of the genes of Joseph had succeeded to survive in the water. Sol asked Prince if that meant that Joseph was still alive? Prince answered that he could not really answer that question, because he tried to find the body of Joseph, but he did not succeed because he could not use all the abilities of his magic like most part of his magic was blocked by their enemy. And Prince added that Joseph would be very sick and weak, if Joseph was still alive. Sol asked where was the magic of Joseph that had prevented William and Solis to bite Angel's neck? Prince answered that it was almost impossible to find that magic, because that magic was like the wind, and that the only way to kill that magic, it was to know the weaknesses of Joseph, and the only way to kill Angel, it was to kill that magic first. Because, if they did not kill that wind, every time when they would try to kill Angel that wind would blow to prevent them to kill Angel, except if Angel was killed by a supernatural being who was not a supernatural being from the eagle world, like that wind that blew to protect Angel was an obstacle for the supernatural beings of the eagle world.

Sol told Prince that to forget that idea that Angel could be killed by a supernatural being who was not from the eagle world, because Angel had important treasure that the eagle world was looking for, so that only a supernatural being of the eagle world would kill Angel. Solis asked Prince if there were two different races of the supernatural beings? Prince answered Solis that there was another race of supernatural beings, who was a little bit different from their race. Solis asked Prince where was that other race of supernatural beings? Prince answered Solis that the history of the races of the supernatural beings was more than a thousand years old, and that they would talk about it another time.

Then, Prince, Solis, William and Sol spent their rest of the day thinking how they could kill that magic of Joseph who had blown in the church. Angel opened her eyes, and she saw that letter that the phantom had put on her teddy bear, and she took that letter, and the first thing that she had noticed on that letter, it was that that letter was not coming from Hero, as she had remarked that the writing that was on that letter was not the handwriting of Hero. Then, Angel read that letter with the fear on her face, and that letter was telling her to stop sending and answering those messages that were sent to her through the number of Hero, because it was not Hero, but instead one of those who wanted to kill her. And that to never remove her rosaries again, because she was very lucky that her enemies did not succeed to kill her in the church. And Angel was very afraid, and she spent her whole night trying to answer the questions that were going on in her mind like, where was Hero? Who had put that letter in her bedroom? Who had saved her in the club, and in the church if it was not Hero? And who was sending her the messages through the number of Hero? And the letter did not tell her that it was Prince who was sending her those messages. But unfortunately for Angel, she could not answer any of those questions, and she was very worried for Hero by wondering where he was, and why he had disappeared, and she had started to be afraid as she was feeling inside her that Hero was not doing well, and that he was in danger.

## SUPERNATURAL BEINGS

The days were passing, and Hero was hiding under the bed of his hotel bedroom, because he did not want the employees of the hotel to see him in the state he was in, because the employees would call the emergencies if the employees had seen him in the health condition that he was. And there was a young woman who was living in Hero's bedroom, and the employees of the hotel had rented Hero's bedroom to that young woman by thinking that Hero had left the hotel like his stay had been already expired, and Hero had not renewed his stay, and if Hero had not renewed his stay, it was because he could not walk to go to the hotel reception to renew his stay, and he was even unable to talk because all his whole body was freezing. Hero was living a torture under that bed, and he was not anymore feeling his body, all the genes of his body till his brain were freezing by the ices, that he could not even think, and Hero was not even remembering what had happened, because he was unable to think, and the worst was that Hero could not even use any part of his magic. And Hero was in those conditions because his invisible ghost was still prisoner in that cold box in the world of eagles. Angel was having a hard time, she was going to school every day with the intention to see Hero in the classroom, and she had no doubt that Hero was in danger, but she did not know where she could find him, or how she could help him. And Angel was spending some of her time with Prince who had returned to school, and Prince had returned to school because he wanted to be close to Angel, and if Prince wanted to be close to Angel, it was because he wanted to get the information from her about Joseph. And Prince could not anymore use the number of Hero to try to communicate with Angel, because he had found out through his magic that the mysterious ghost that had saved Angel in the church, had left a letter to Angel to tell Angel that the one who she was communicating with, was not Hero.

It was been the weeks now, that the world of natural human beings was terrified by what was happening in their world, except Angel and few people, the rest of inhabitants were afraid by what they were reading in the newspapers, as they were reading about the mysterious eagles that were turning into the bodies of human beings. And almost all newspapers had the pictures of eagles in front of their newspapers with the headlines like, "Who are those eagles?" "Where those eagles come from?" And "What those eagles want?" And people were wondering who those people who had the shape of the eagles were, because there was no picture of a supernatural being in the newspapers. And most people were living with the fear, and they were wondering where those eagles were coming from, but there were few people who were not believing in what they were reading in the newspapers, because for them, it was impossible that the eagles turned into the bodies of human beings. But there were some people who were believing one hundred per cent what they were reading in the newspapers, because they had seen those eagles turned into the bodies of human beings in front of them in the church, in the drugstore and in the club. After the months the invisible phantom of Hero was still prisoner in the eagle world, and Prince had not yet succeeded to get the information from Angel about Joseph.

It was early morning, a young girl of nine years old opened the box that the invisible phantom of Hero was locked inside, and it was the first time that that box was opened, since that phantom was locked in that box, then that young girl knelt close to the box. And she stared inside that box as she was seeing the ice that had frozen in that box, and Hero's ghost was covered by that frozen ice, then that young girl put her both hands through that ice inside the box, and the light started to shine on the palm's hands of that young girl, and that light was going through the ice, and the ice was dissolving like the light that was coming from the palm's hands of that young girl was shining on the ice.

After a minute, all that ice had disappeared, but that young girl had not removed her hands, and the light was still shining on her palm's hands and that light was going through the phantom that was in the box. And that young girl was looking at the phantom that was in the box, then that phantom opened his eyes, and that young girl looked in the eyes of that phantom by saying, "My name is Kerry, and I am a supernatural being of the eagle world." And Kerry added, "I am not here to release you, but I am here to help you, I know how it's hard to be prisoner in this box, and that's why I broke one of the rules of the tradition of the eagle world by coming here to warm you through my magic." The phantom that was in the box was trying to turn into the light, and to run away without succeeding, and that phantom could not turn into the light to disappear, because the light that was coming from the palm's hands of Kerry, and that was shining on the phantom was preventing that phantom to turn into the light and to disappear. And Kerry was feeling that that phantom was trying to run away, and she looked in the eyes of that phantom by telling that phantom to stop trying to run away, because he could not run away, and that she would not let him run away. And the phantom understood that it was impossible for him to run away, because the light that was shining on him was preventing him from running away.

Hero was still under the bed of his hotel, and he was not anymore feeling cold, and he was feeling warm as Kerry was warming his invisible phantom, and Hero started to feel his body, and all the genes of his body, and he started to remember what had happened, and where he was. Then, Hero started to remember about Angel, and suddenly he used his magic to try to find Angel, but he failed, and his heart started to beat with fear as he was unable to find Angel through his magic, then he used his magic to find Prince, and he saw Prince who was walking in the classroom through his magic. Then, Hero started to think that maybe Angel was dead, and he suddenly started turning under the bed to get out from under the bed, then Hero got up from the floor and the door opened face to him, and he saw a young woman who was trying to walk inside the room. And Hero and that young woman were looking at each other in the eyes without saying a word, and that young woman opened her mouth, but no word was coming out, and Hero was understanding that the young woman who was facing him was the one who was living in that bedroom.

Then, Hero started to walk through the door, and that young woman moved from the door, then Hero got out and he started running on the veranda of the hotel by going towards the parking. After a few seconds, Hero jumped from the balcony of the veranda where he was, and he landed in the parking, then he ran till a car that was close to him, and he opened the door of that car, and he got in that car, then he drove away.

Angel was sitting in the class, and she was listening to the instructor who was explaining the course, then the phone that was on the table close to her started to vibrate, and Angel turned her head towards her phone, and she noticed that she had got a message. Then, Angel took her phone, and she remarked that that message was coming from Bella, and suddenly she got up, and she started to run through the door as she had read in the message of Bella that Hero was at the home of Bella. Bella and Hero were in the basement of Bella's house, and Hero was lying in the bed, and Bella had covered Hero with the blanket, and Bella was standing up in the room, and she was staring at Hero who was shaking of cold in the bed, without understanding what was going on. Then, Bella turned, and she started to run towards upstairs as she had heard ringing at the door, and she reached the front door, then she opened the door, and Angel rushed inside the house by asking where Hero was? And Bella told Angel that Hero was in the basement. Then, both Angel and Bella ran till the basement, and Angel got in the room, and she started to breath deeply as she was looking at Hero who was shaking in the bed, and Hero did not know that Angel was in the room, because he had turned, and he was face to the wall, and Angel was face to the back of Hero.

Then, Hero turned in the bed as he had heard Angel called his name, and he was staring at Angel with a smile on his face, while Angel was staring at him with the sadness on her face by breathing deeply, then Angel ran through the bed, and she got on the bed and she hugged Hero. Then, Angel noticed that Hero was freezing, and she looked at Hero by telling him that he was freezing, and Hero looked at her without saying a word, then Angel looked at Bella asking Bella if Bella could turn on the heating. But Hero refused by saying that the heating would not help him, and Bella asked Hero if he wanted more blankets, and Hero refused, then Bella told Angel that they should take Hero to the hospital. Angel looked at Bella by saying that Hero hated the hospital, then Angel told Bella that Bella could go to school, that she would stay with Hero. And after a few minutes, Bella left. And Angel turned her head through Hero by looking at him with a sad face how he was suffering by wondering how she could help him, and Hero was freezing because Kerry had locked the box where the invisible phantom of Hero was kept prisoner, and that invisible phantom of Hero had started to freeze again, and that was the reason why Hero was that condition. But, this time it was not all the parts of Hero body who were freezing, there was one part of his body who was not freezing, and that's part was the part where his identity phantom was located, and that part was not freezing because Hero had removed his identity phantom from his body when his body was warmed by Kerry couple hours ago. Angel was still staring at Hero with a worried face, and Hero was staring at her too, and by looking at Hero, we could see the joy on his face, that he was very happy to see that Angel was still alive.

Then, Angel took off her clothes and she lifted one side of the blanket that was on Hero, and she got inside the blanket, and she tried to take Hero in her arms, and he refused by saying that he was freezing, and she told him that she did not care that she wanted to warm him, and Angel finally took Hero in her arms although the fact that he tried to refuse. Then, both Hero and Angel started to talk, and Hero had the difficulties to talk because he could not pronounce the words well, as it was hard for him to make the gestures with his mouth, and it was also hard for him to make the gestures with his hands, or even to turn in the bed. And Angel was very surprised as she was hearing Hero who was talking about who he was, about the supernatural beings, the world of the tiger and his mission in the world of the natural human beings. Angel and Hero spent their whole day talking, and Angel even spent the night at Bella's house with Hero, despite the fact that Hero had tried to convince Angel to return to her house. The weeks were passing, and Angel had stopped going to school, and she was spending her whole day at Bella's house with Hero, and they were talking about the race of the supernatural beings, and the tradition and cultures of supernatural beings.

And Angel was very surprised when she had heard Hero say that in the culture of the supernatural beings, the supernatural beings believed in their ancestors as their gods, and that their king had the powers to communicate with their ancestors. Hero had told Angel about his invisible phantom who was prisoner in the eagle world, and also about the strengths of his identity phantom that had been destroyed by the king of the tiger world on the demand of the ancestors. But Hero did not tell Angel that he was sentenced to death by his ancestors, because he wanted to protect her, because he knew that she would be worried if he had told her that he was sentenced to death. And Hero wanted to talk to Angel that Prince was a supernatural being, but he remembered that his magic had warned him to not talk to Angel about who Prince was, and Hero had decided to keep the silence about Prince. And Angel had told Hero about her godfather named Joseph, and she had also told Hero about what had happened in the church, and in the club, and about the letter she had found in her bedroom.

And Angel was spending the hard moments near to Hero, it was very hard for her to see Hero who was suffering, and she was wondering how she could help him, but she had promised him that she would release his invisible phantom from jail. And Hero had laughed at Angel when she had told him that she would release his phantom from prison, and Hero had not told Angel about what he had heard from the supernatural beings of the eagle world about her, because he did not want to stress her. But both Angel and Hero did not know why the supernatural beings of the eagle world wanted to kill Angel.

It was an evening. Prince, Solis, William and Sol were sitting in the living room of Prince's house, and they were all already tired and they were wondering if they would succeed to kill Angel and to eradicate the race of natural human beings. And the worst was that Prince had completely lost control on Angel, and although the fact that Angel had not broken up with him, it had been the months now that both Prince and Angel had not seen each other, because since that Angel was spending her time with Hero, Prince had not put his eyes on her again, and Angel had turned off her phone because she did not want people to disturb her. Prince was very angry, and he had found out through his magic that Angel was spending her time with Hero, and it had been the months now that Prince wanted to join Angel through her phone, but he could not because Angel's phone was off. And Prince did not know how he could get the information about the weaknesses of Joseph, as Angel was always spending her time with Hero, and Prince had told Sol, William and Solis that they would never kill Angel, if they did not find the weaknesses of Joseph to get rid of the magic of Joseph. And there was the silence between all of them, then Prince got up from his chair, and he walked till face at the wall, and he stared at the wall and the light started to get out from his eyes and going through the wall, and those lights were turning into the pictures on the wall, and those pictures on the wall were the pictures of Hero and Angel.

Then, Sol, William and Solis got up from their chairs and they walked till face to the wall, and they were all staring at those pictures on the wall, and they were all seeing Hero who was suffering in the bed with the blanket on him, and Angel who sat in the bed staring at Hero with a sad face, and with tears that were flowing down her cheeks. And they were also noticing that almost the whole body of Hero was frozen, that Hero could not even make a gesture with his hands, or his feet, and that he could not even turn in the bed, and they were seeing too that both Hero and Angel were talking. And that Hero had the difficulties to talk, because it was hard for Hero to make the gestures with his mouth for the words to come out of his mouth. And Prince was staring at the pictures that were on the wall, by reading the conversation between Angel and Hero through his magic, and Sol turned her head through Prince by asking Prince what were Angel and Hero talking about? Prince answered Sol that Hero was begging Angel to return to school, that Angel should return to school to prepare for her final exams. Sol said that they had forgotten something very important. Solis asked Sol what they had forgotten? And Sol answered that they had forgotten to kill Hero, that they should kill Hero since that had kept the invisible ghost of Hero prisoner. And Sol added that it was time to kill Hero, that they must burn the corpse of Hero tonight.

Solis said that they had focused their energy to kill Angel, that they had forgotten to kill Hero. William said that it would be easy to kill Hero at Bella's house, as Hero could not fight in the condition where he was. And William added that they would burn Hero with

Hero's ghost inside him as they could not remove his ghost from his body. Prince took a deep breath by saying that they could not kill Hero, because Hero did not have his identity ghost inside his body. And that they had forgotten to kill Hero when Hero was under the bed of his hotel bedroom, because their energies were focused on Angel, on the mysterious ghost, and on Joseph. And Prince went on by saying that Hero had his identity ghost inside him when Hero was under the bed of his hotel, but that Hero had removed his ghost from his body, and that the identity ghost of Hero was wandering in the space in the shape of light. And that it was impossible for them to catch the identity ghost of Hero that was wandering in the shape of light, and that meant too that it was impossible for them to kill Hero, because the only way to kill Hero, it was to kill his identity ghost. Suddenly, the disappointment appeared on the faces of Sol, William and Solis as they had understood that they could not kill Hero.

And Solis asked Prince how he knew that Hero did not have his identity ghost inside his body? And Prince answered that when he saw Angel and Hero together through those pictures on the wall, he got the idea to go kill Hero to have the control on Angel, because he lost the control on Angel because she was spending her time with Hero, but when he checked through his magic, he found out that Hero did not have his identity ghost inside his body. Then, there was the silence in the room, and Prince was staring at the pictures that were on the wall, then William and Solis turned their heads through Prince, as they had noticed the light was getting out from Prince's eyes, and going through the wall, then they all turned their heads through the wall, and they remarked that the light that was getting out from Prince's eyes and shining on the wall were turning into the pictures of Hero. And they were all looking at the pictures of Hero on the wall, and they were noticing through those pictures that Hero was lying with his back in the bed on all those pictures, and they were understanding that it had been months now that Hero had not changed the position in the bed. Then, Prince turned his head through Sol, and he looked in her eyes by saying in Latin, "Habemus novum inimicum." That meant in English, "We have a new enemy." Sol cried out, "What?" And she asked in Latin, "Quis est inimicus?"

## SUPERNATURAL BEINGS

That meant in English, "Who is that enemy?" Prince answered in Latin, "Quod hostes in mundo aquilae." That meant in English, "That enemy is in the eagle world." Sol cried out in the Latin, "Aquila in mundo?" That meant in English, "In the eagle world?"

Then, Sol turned her head through William and Solis, and they were all looking at each other with the surprised faces, and Solis turned her head through Prince by asking Prince who was that traitor? And Prince answered Solis that he did not know yet who that traitor was. And William asked Prince why he was saying that there was a traitor in the eagle world? Prince answered William that if Hero had left his hotel room, and drove till Bella's house, it was because an enemy had warmed the invisible phantom of Hero, because Hero could not walk, could not drive and he could not even get out of under the bed of the hotel where he was. Because, Hero could not move with a member of his body, as his foot, his hand or even his mouth, because the invisible phantom of Hero who had been frozen had had an impact on body's Hero. Solis told Prince that she did not think that the invisible ghost of Hero had been warmed by a supernatural being of the eagle world.

Prince told Solis that if it was not a supernatural being of the eagle world who had warmed Hero's phantom, that meant that they had another mysterious enemy, the Prince turned his head through the wall and the light got out from his eyes and went through the wall. And they were all looking at the pictures that were on the wall with the surprised faces, as they were seeing Kerry who was warming the invisible phantom of Hero, and suddenly the eyes of Sol became dark green, and she turned into the eagle and she flew through the window that was opened. And Prince, Solis and William looked at each other with silence, as they had understood that Sol went to the eagle world to talk about the betrayal of Kerry. And Prince asked Solis who Kerry was? Then, Prince, Solis and William spent the whole night talking about Kerry.

The next day, it was 9:00 a.m., in the eagle world. And the weather was beautiful and there was a little sun outside. And all supernatural beings of the eagle world were in the sacred yard of the eagle world, except Sol, William and Solis who were not there because they were in the world of the natural human beings. And all supernatural beings had all worn the black clothes, as their tradition required them, because in the tradition of the eagle world when a supernatural being had broken a rule of the tradition, the inhabitants should wear the black clothes at the time of the torture that occurred before the judgement of the one who had broken the rule of the tradition. Kerry was in the middle of the sacred yard, and she was surrounded by the supernatural beings, and Collin started walking through Kerry, then Kerry started shouting by crying the pains that she was feeling inside her body. And Kerry was screaming in pain because she was tortured by the magic of Collin, and the eyes of Collin were dark green as he was staring at Kerry. And most supernatural beings were looking at Kerry who was tortured by Collin with the sadness on their faces, as Kerry was turning on the ground still by screaming the pains, then the eyes of Collin started to turn as he was looking at Kerry, and Kerry started to fly through the space. And suddenly, a loud scream was pushed by some supernatural beings as they were seeing Kerry who was hitting her body against the trees that were around the sacred yard.

Then, Kerry was tortured during eleven hours by Collin and by a young woman named Mel, then Kerry was kept prisoner in a jail, and Kerry was waiting the decision of the ancestors in three weeks, and Kerry was tortured and kept prisoner because she had warmed the invisible phantom of Hero. And most supernatural beings were afraid that Kerry was going to be killed in three weeks on the demand of the ancestors.

The days were passing, and Angel had started to go to school, and all her classmates had noticed that Angel was sad, that she had lost her smile since she had returned to school, and only Bella knew the reasons why Angel had lost her joy of living. And when people were asking Angel if everything was all right, she was answering them that everything was fine, but Angel was lying to them, and Angel was sad because Hero was suffering. Angel was coming to class not because she wanted to, but to please Hero because she had promised to Hero, and most of time she was just spending some hours in class, she was not staying in class until the end of the courses, because she was spending the rest of her time with Hero. Prince and Angel were spending some time together when Angel was on the campus, but that time had never exceeded an hour, and all the time that both Angel and Prince were talking, Angel was not focused on the conversation and Prince had tried to make Angel talk about Joseph during their conversation without succeeding.

Prince, Solis, William and Sol were spending their time together by trying to find out the weaknesses of Joseph, and the walls of the living room of Prince were full of the pictures of Joseph and Angel, because Prince was spending his time to make the pictures of Angel and Joseph appear on the wall through his magic. And the photos that were on the wall were the photos of the moments that both Angel and Joseph were spending time together, and Prince was staring at the photos that were on the wall by reading the conversation that Angel and Joseph had had through his magic. And Prince had tried to find the weaknesses of Joseph through those pictures on the wall without succeeding, and even by following most of the conversation that had happened between Joseph and Angel, Prince did not succeed to find out what the weaknesses of Joseph were.

Hero was still in the basement of Bella's house, and Bella's parents did not know that Hero was in their house, although the fact that Bella's parents had noticed that Bella and Angel were spending most of their time to the basement, and when Bella's parents had asked Bella and Angel what they always doing in the basement? Angel and Bella had lied to Bella's parents by answering that they were studying in the basement. Angel had moved to Bella's house, because she wanted to be close to Hero, but Angel had lied to her parents that she was moving to Bella's house, because she wanted to study with Bella, to be ready for the final exams. Bella and Angel were spending the sad moments, because it was hard for them to see Hero who was lying in the bed like a corpse, and almost the whole body of Hero had frozen. And although the fact that Angel had told Bella that Hero was a supernatural being, Bella was not really afraid, but Bella was completely lost, and Bella was not understanding how the body of Hero had frozen as if Hero was in the freezer. And what was weird for Bella was that there was not the ice on the body of

Hero, but when she was touching the body of Hero, it was as if there was the ice on his body, and Bella was a little bit scared by what was happening to Hero, and she was seeing it as a mystery. Angel was sleeping with Hero, and most of the nights she was just sitting in the bed staring at Hero by talking to him, and she knew that he was listening to her, even as he could not reply to her, because Hero's mouth had already completely frozen that Hero could not anymore open his mouth.

All the parts of Hero's body had frozen, except the parts of his body where the magic that was linked to his identity ghost was located, and that part had not frozen because the identity phantom of Hero was out of his body, so that part of his body could not feel the torture of his invisible phantom. Although the fact that Hero was lying in the bed like a dead supernatural being, he was trying to know what was going on outside through his magic, and he was spending his time to follow Prince, Solis, William and Sol through the part of his magic that was linked to his identity phantom, like that part of magic had not frozen. And Hero was aware of the plan of Prince, William, Sol and Solis. And Hero knew that Sol, William, Solis and Prince were trying to find out the weaknesses of Joseph to get rid of the magic of Joseph. But there was a mystery that Hero was not understanding, and Hero was finding it very weird that his magic that was linked to his identity ghost was able to see supernatural beings and natural human beings that he wanted to see except Angel.

And every time that Angel was in school or was not near to Hero, and when Hero was using his magic to see if she was doing well, he was not succeeding, because his magic could not find Angel. But, when Hero was using his magic to find Bella, his magic was succeeding to find Bella, and his magic was succeeding to find other natural human beings as Bella's parents and Angel's parents, also the supernatural beings of eagle world like the tiger world, and Hero was aware of what was going on in the tiger world through his magic. And Hero could not explain why his magic was able to find both the supernatural beings and natural human beings except Angel, and Hero had even told Angel about it when he was talking to Angel about who he was.

## SUPERNATURAL BEINGS

And Hero had noticed that his magic was unable to find Angel since the day that Kerry had warmed his invisible phantom, and he had started to look for Angel without succeeding since under the bed of the hotel where he was living. And Hero had come to Bella's house, because he thought that Angel was dead as his magic was unable to find her. And another mystery that Hero was not understanding was about his body, Hero was not understanding why the fact that his invisible phantom was prisoner in a cold large box was affecting his whole body when his identity phantom was in his body. And Hero had let his identity phantom inside his body when his invisible phantom was kept prisoner, because he did not know that the fact that his invisible phantom was going to be kept prisoner would affect his whole body. Because he thought that the fact that his invisible phantom was kept prisoner would only affect the part of his body which was linked only to his invisible phantom, he did not know that even the part of his identity phantom should be affected by the fact his invisible phantom was kept prisoner. And since that Hero had removed his identity ghost from his body as his invisible ghost had been warmed by Kerry's magic, only the part of his body who was linked to his invisible ghost was affected by the fact that his invisible ghost was still prisoner in that cold box. And Hero was wondering if his identity phantom and invisible phantom were linked? But he could not answer that question and he was very confused, and he had two ideas in his mind.

The first idea was that Hero thought that his both phantoms were linked because the fact that his invisible phantom was in jail was affecting his whole body till his identity phantom, when that identity phantom was inside his body. And the second idea was that Hero thought that his both phantoms were not linked, because the fact that most of the strengths of his identity phantom had been destroyed did not affect his invisible phantom. And Hero was also wondering why the supernatural beings of the eagle world had not yet killed his invisible phantom? But unfortunately, Hero could not answer that question, he was understanding that he did not know his own powers and magic, also his own body. It was an evening, Prince, Solis, William and Sol were in the living room of the Prince's house by thinking how they would get rid of the magic of Joseph that was still alive, then Sol got an idea and she started to talk about her idea to the rest of supernatural beings, and they spent the whole night to make a plan on the idea of Sol.

The next day, it was 11:00 a.m., and Angel was in class sitting in her place with her face full of sadness as usual, then Angel felt that Bella was touching her hand, and she turned her head through Bella who sat near to her, and Angel noticed that Bella had the eyes focused on the door, and Angel turned her head through the door. Then, Angel saw Prince who was walking in her classroom with a flower in his hand, and she understood that Prince was coming to give her the flower, and she said in her head that it was the time to break up with him, that she had to talk to Prince that she was in love with someone else. Suddenly, Angel screamed the name of Prince with her face full of fear, as she had seen an eagle fly inside the classroom through one of the windows of the classroom that was opened, and all students started to scream by running through the door by trying to get out of the classroom, as they had seen that eagle landed face to Prince and turned into a supernatural being who was William, then William knocked Prince in his face, and William turned into the eagle and flew away. Angel rushed through Prince, and she knelt close to Prince who was unconscious on the floor, and she was shaking Prince by calling his name with the fear on her face, then Angel noticed that the blood was coming out from Prince's mouth, and she started to scream by calling for help.

Then, Angel noticed that no one was coming, then she turned her head to her right, and she remarked that the classroom was empty, and she understood that everyone had run away, then she turned her head through Prince and the smile appeared on her face as she had observed that Prince had opened his eyes. Then, Angel helped Prince to get up, and she wanted to take Prince to the hospital, but Prince refused by saying that he was fine, that he wanted to sit, then Angel held Prince's hand, and she helped him to walk till the chairs that were close to them, and they sat. Then, Angel took a handkerchief and she cleaned the blood that was on Prince's mouth, and Prince gave her the flower that he had kept her, then they started to talk about what had happened, and Prince noticed that Angel was very worried about him, then Prince removed an envelope from his school's bag, and he handed that envelope to Angel. Angel took that envelope in Prince's hand by looking at him without asking a question, then Angel turned the envelope and she saw her name that was written on the envelope, and she noticed too that there was not the name of the sender on the envelope, then she looked at Prince by asking him where he got that envelope. And Prince answered her that he saw the envelope in front of his door this morning when he was opening the door, and Angel demanded him what an envelope with her name on it was doing in front of his door, and Prince answered her that he had no idea, that himself he was very surprised when he saw that envelope.

And Angel was looking at him, and by looking at the envelope at the same time without knowing what to say and what to do, the Prince looked at Angel by asking her to open the envelope, and Angel replied to him that she was afraid to open because she had no idea about where that envelope was coming from. And Prince told Angel that he could open the envelope, if she was afraid, but Angel refused then she opened the envelope, then she removed a sheet of paper that was folded in the envelope, and she opened that sheet of paper, then suddenly her eyes opened widely, and her heart was beating faster than the normal as she was staring at that sheet of paper in her hand. And Prince was staring at Angel by asking her if everything was all right, but Angel was not paying attention to Prince, and she was just focused on that sheet of paper that was in her hand.

Then, Angel took a deep breath and she started to read what was written on that sheet of paper, and after a minute she had finished reading, and she looked at Prince with a worried face, then she told Prince that the letter was coming from her godfather named Joseph. Prince looked at Angel by asking, "Where is Joseph?" Angel answered, "I have no idea." And added, "It's been almost a year that I have not seen him." Prince asked, "Why did he send you that letter?" Angel looked in Prince's eyes by answering, "Because, you are in danger, and Joseph wants me to talk to you about him, because by knowing about him, you would find a way to protect yourself."

Then, Prince asked Angel if she was sure that that letter was coming from Joseph, and Angel replied to Prince that she had no doubt that that letter was coming from Joseph, that she had recognized the handwriting of Joseph on that letter, also the drawings that were on that letter were the drawings of Joseph. But that letter was not coming from Joseph, and it was Prince who had written that letter through his magic by using the handwriting of Joseph, and even the drawings that were in that letter were made by Prince through his magic. And everything was planned by Sol, William, Solis and Prince even the fact that William had knocked Prince in Angel's classroom was a part of the plan to attract the attention of Angel that Prince was really in danger. Then, both Prince and Angel started to talk about Joseph, and Prince was asking the questions to Angel about Joseph, and they spent the whole day in the classroom to talk about Joseph.

It was evening. Prince, Solis, William and Sol were in the living room of Prince's house, and they were all standing up face to the wall, and they were all staring at the pictures that were on the wall, that Prince had made appear on the wall through his magic. And the pictures that were on the wall were based on the conversation that Prince and Angel had had during the day in Angel's classroom, and they were all looking at the pictures that were on the wall by trying to find the weaknesses of Joseph on those pictures. Suddenly, Prince started to remember that during his conversation with Angel, she told him that when she was playing with Joseph, she liked to tease Joseph by using a small stick that she had put the fire on it. Then, the light got out from Prince's eyes and went through the wall, and the photos of Joseph and Angel appeared on the wall, and on those pictures on the wall, Prince was noticing that Angel was five years old on those pictures, and he was seeing Angel and Joseph who were playing on those pictures. And Prince was seeing Angel who was running after Joseph with a small stick in her hand, and there was the fire on that stick that was in Angel's hand.

Then, the light got out from Prince's eyes, and went through the wall, and the photos of Angel and Joseph appeared on the wall, and on those photos, Prince was noticing that every time that Angel was using a stick with a fire on it, Joseph was running away, and

Joseph was afraid. Prince's eyes were focused on those pictures where Angel had a small stick in her hand with the fire on it, and Prince was staring at those pictures by using his magic to understand what had happened. While, Solis, William and Sol had still the eyes focused on the photos that were on the wall, and they had not seen the pictures that Prince was staring at the wall. Suddenly, Sol, William and Solis turned their heads through Prince, by looking at him with amazed faces as they had heard Prince say that he had found the weakness of Joseph. And, Sol asked Prince what was the weakness of Joseph? Prince answered Sol that the weakness of Joseph was the fire, that the magic of Joseph could not stand anything that was burning, then Prince showed the pictures that were on the wall to them, by explaining to them what had happened in those pictures. And they all spent the entire night talking about how they would get rid of the magic of Joseph and kill Angel, then started their mission that was the destruction of the race of natural human beings.

The days were passing, and Prince, Solis, William and Sol were spending their time to plan to kill Angel. While Angel and Hero were spending their time together, although the fact that the situation of Hero had not changed.

It was 10:00 p.m., both Angel and Bella were in a shop, and they were looking for the stuff to buy for breakfast the next day, because they had noticed less than an hour ago when they were at home that there was nothing for breakfast. Angel was walking in the shelf of bread with a basket in her hand, then she saw two big men who were walking face to her, and she noticed that those two men were staring at her, then Angel tried to turn but she felt the hands on her body, and she noticed that she was grabbed by other men. And Angel opened her mouth to scream, but one of men who had grabbed her, closed the mouth of Angel with his palm's hand, and two men who were walking face to Angel rushed through her and they cut the rosaries that were on the ankle and on the wrist of Angel, while Angel was trying to fight against people who had held her.

Suddenly, there was a huge scream in the shop, and people were trying to run through the door, as they were seeing the eagles that were flying inside the shop. Then, an eagle landed face to Angel and that eagle turned into a supernatural being who was Sol, and men who had grabbed Angel ran away once they had seen that eagle turned into Sol. Angel wanted to run away, but she was grabbed from behind by William, and Sol walked two steps face to Angel, and Sol grabbed Angel's head, and Sol bent her head to bite Angel's neck.

Suddenly, Sol turned her head and she looked around, as she had felt the wind that was blowing in the shop, then she noticed that the wind started blowing with low pressure and there was Prince on the other shelf. And there was the light that was getting out from Prince's eyes and shining in the shop, and that light that was getting out from Prince's eyes was burning like the fire, and the wind that was blowing in the room was becoming more and more weak like the light that was getting outside from Prince's eyes was burning that wind. And Angel was still held by William and Sol, and Angel was trying to fight to escape from the hands of William and Sol, but she was too weak, then Sol smiled at William as she had noticed that the wind had stopped blowing, and Sol started to bend her head to bite Angel's neck. And suddenly, William screamed the name of Sol as he had seen a light appear behind Sol, then Sol felt the hands around her neck, and that light that had shone behind Sol had turned into the mysterious phantom, and it was that mysterious phantom who had grabbed Sol's neck.

And Sol had let Angel's head, and Sol was fighting to remove the hands of that phantom from her neck, then Sol screamed at William who had still held Angel to bite Angel's neck, and William moved his head to bite Angel's neck, and suddenly William pushed a yell and he let Angel, and William was holding his right shoulder that was bleeding. And William was bitten on his shoulder by the tiger, and that tiger was the phantom of Hero, then William turned and he saw a tiger that was staring at him angrily, then that tiger jumped on him, and before William throws that tiger away, that tiger had bitten him at his hand, then the tiger picked up the rosaries of Angel that were on the floor with his mouth, and the tiger ran away. Angel was running through the door, then an eagle flew through her, then that eagle turned into Solis, and Solis jumped on Angel, then Solis threw

Angel on the floor and Solis was on Angel, and Solis was trying to bite Angel's neck.

And suddenly, Solis screamed, and she lost the concentration and the balance on Angel, then Angel got up from the floor, and Angel noticed that Solis was bleeding on her back, and she turned her head, then she saw the tiger that was looking at her. And Angel started to smile at the tiger, as she had understood that it was that tiger that had bitten Solis's back, and that that tiger was Hero, then Angel started to walk through that tiger, and she suddenly screamed the name of Hero, as she had seen another tiger that was coming from behind Hero's phantom, and Hero's phantom turned and he saw that tiger.

Then, the two tigers were looking at each other angrily, then the two tigers started to run through each other, and they started to fight, and Angel was looking at both tigers that were fighting with her heart who was beating faster than the normal. Then, Angel felt a hand on her hand, and she felt that she was grabbed by someone, and she turned her head through her hand that was grabbed by someone but she was not seeing that person who had grabbed her, and she was trying to remove the hand who had held her hand, then she heard a voice told her to not feel afraid that she was there to help her, and that they should run away. And Angel replied that she could not let Hero alone. And that voice told Angel, that the only way to save Hero, it was that they get out of that shop. And that voice who was talking to Angel was the voice of that mysterious phantom who had grabbed Angel's hand, then that mysterious phantom saw Sol and William who were running through Angel, and that phantom pulled Angel's hand, and both Angel and that phantom started to run through the door.

William and Sol were running after Angel and that phantom, then William screamed the name of Solis with fear on his face, as he had seen Solis who was lying on the floor bleeding on the back, then both William and Sol rushed through Solis and they bent near to Solis, and they started to shake Solis by screaming Solis's name. While the two tigers were still fighting, and the tiger that was Hero's phantom was losing the fight against the tiger that was Prince, suddenly the two ghosts stopped fighting and they were looking at each other, as they were hearing the sirens of the police's cars. Then, the tiger that was Hero's phantom turned and he started to walk through the door, and the other tiger walked till where Sol, William and Solis were, and that tiger turned into Prince. Then, Prince noticed that Solis was unconscious and that she was bleeding too, and Prince asked Sol if the phantom of Solis was injured, and Sol answered that she had no idea.

Then, they all turned their heads through the door as they had heard the footsteps coming from the door, and they saw policemen who were walking through them, and one of the policemen started to ask them the questions. And Sol looked in the eyes of those policemen and her green eyes became blue, then that policeman stopped asking them questions, and those policemen were just looking at them with the silence how they were shaking Solis who was still unconscious on the floor. After eleven minutes, Solis opened her eyes, and Sol and William helped Solis to get up, and those policemen had turned their heads looking at Prince, Solis, William and Sol who were getting out of the shop. And the police were called by people who had run away from the shop when the eagles were flying inside the shop. Angel was lying in her bedroom with her night dress on her, and Angel was worried about Hero although the fact that she had called Bella to ask how Hero was doing, and Bella had answered her that nothing had changed about the situation of Hero. And Angel wanted to go to Bella's house to sleep with Hero, but she remembered that the phantom that had taken her at home had asked her to not get out of the house.

Hero was in bed and he was thinking about Angel, and he was worried about her, he did not know where Angel was as he could not find her through his magic. And Hero was remembering of the fight that happened in the shop, and Hero had sent his ghost to the shop because he had found out through his magic that the supernatural beings who wanted to kill Angel were inside that shop, and Hero had also found out through his magic that Bella was in that same shop where those supernatural beings were.

Then, Hero had imagined that Angel should be in that shop too, as Bella and those supernatural beings were inside that shop, and although the fact that Hero could not find Angel through his magic, Hero had the feeling that Angel was in danger. And those supernatural beings were inside that shop to kill Angel, and that was how Hero had sent his ghost inside that shop to protect Angel. Prince, Solis, William and Sol were in the living room of Prince's house sitting in the chairs, and William and Solis had the wounds on their bodies, but William was not feeling any pain, because his phantom was not hurt, while Solis was feeling a little bit pain on her back, because her phantom was a little bit hurt as Hero's ghost had bitten and scratched her back. And they were all talking about what had happened in the shop, and they were not understanding how they had not succeeded to kill Angel, mostly that Prince had got rid of their big obstacle that was the wind.

Then, Sol told Prince that they had to go and kill Angel, that they could not sleep without killing Angel, then Prince got up from his chair, and he started to walk through the wall, and there was the light that was getting out from his eyes and going through the wall. And Sol, William and Solis got up from their chairs, and they started walking through the wall, by looking at the wall with the amazed faces as they were seeing Angel who was asleep in her bed, and Solis asked them if they were noticing the same thing as her. And Prince replied to Solis that he was seeing that Angel had not her rosaries, then Sol told them that Angel had lost her rosaries in the shop, that men that they had hired had succeeded to cut the rosaries of Angel. And Solis said that it was time to kill Angel, and that they had to go now and kill Angel in her bedroom, and they all agreed with Solis's idea, and they turned through the door and they started to walk through the door.

Suddenly, they all stopped walking and they turned their heads through Prince, as they had heard the phone of Prince that was ringing, and Prince removed his phone from his pocket and Prince looked at the screen of his phone, then they all noticed that the expression of the face of Prince had changed, that Prince was looking at his phone with an astonished face. Then, Sol broke the silence by asking Prince if everything was all right, and Prince turned the screen phone through them, and they all noticed that it was King Philip who was calling Prince, and they were wondering why Philip was calling Prince at that time. Then, Solis turned her head though the clock that was on the wall, and she said that it was midnight, and Sol looked at Prince by telling him to pick up the phone, and Prince replied to Sol that he was afraid that he had the feeling that something bad had happened.

Then, they turned their heads looking at each other without saying a word, as they had remarked that Prince's phone had stopped ringing, then they heard a noise coming from Prince's phone, and Prince noticed that he had got a message, then he read that message, and he handed the phone to Sol without saying a word, and Sol took the phone in Prince's hand and she read that message that was in the phone. And Sol handed the phone to Solis, and Solis read the message, and she handed the phone to William and William read that message which was sent by King Philip and that message was ordering Prince to stop all activities for seventy-two hours, because the tiger world had just lost two of his kids. And they were all looking at each other with the silence, then Prince started to walk through the wall and the light were getting out from his eyes and going through the wall, and Sol, William and Solis were walking through the wall with their eyes focused on the wall, as they were seeing two young supernatural beings of the tiger world a man and a woman kissing in the forest at the night, and suddenly Solis cried out in Latin, "Immortui?" That meant in English, "Zombies?" as Solis had seen on the pictures that were on the wall, the zombies who were fighting against the young couple of supernatural beings who were kissing in the forest.

Then, the expression of the face of everyone changed, as they were seeing the zombies who were killing that couple of supernatural beings, then Sol walked two steps through the wall, and she was staring at the pictures on the wall as she was staring at the two dead bodies who were on the ground, and Sol was noticing that there were the wounds on the necks of the two dead bodies who were on the ground.

## SUPERNATURAL BEINGS

Then, Sol turned her head through Prince, and she looked in his eyes by asking him if he could make the images appear on the wall of how those zombies had killed those supernatural beings by biting the necks of those supernatural beings? Then, the light got out from the eyes of Prince and went through the wall, and they were all seeing how those zombies were biting the necks of those supernatural beings, but what was attracting their attention it was the small and thin venom that they were seeing on the tongues of the zombies who had bitten the necks of those supernatural beings. And except Prince and Solis, the rest of supernatural beings were very surprised to see that the zombies had the venoms, because they had not noticed those venoms last time when Prince had used his magic to make the pictures of the zombies appear on the wall.

Then, they turned their heads by looking at each other with surprised eyes, and Sol asked Prince if the zombies killed the venom. And Prince answered Sol that the zombies had two ways to kill, they could kill by using their long canine teeth, or they could kill by using their venoms, and that their venom was the poison, that no one could survive a wound coming from the venoms of the zombies. And that most of the time the zombies were using their venom to kill the race of natural human beings, because it was harder for the zombies to kill the race of supernatural beings by using their venoms, because it was hard for the zombies to bite the phantoms of the supernatural beings by using their venoms. And Sol asked Prince if those zombies had bitten the necks of that couple of supernatural beings by using their venoms, because that couple had their ghosts inside them? Prince answered Sol that the zombies could bite the neck of the supernatural beings by using their venoms, but that the supernatural beings would not die if the supernatural beings were bitten by the venoms of the zombies when their phantoms were outside from their bodies. But if the supernatural beings were bitten by the venoms of the zombies when the supernatural beings had their phantoms inside them, the supernatural beings would die, like that couple of supernatural beings dead in the forest, because they were bitten by the zombies when their phantoms were inside them.

Then, Prince turned his head through the wall, and the light got out from his eyes and went through the wall, and the pictures of the fight that had happened in the past between the zombies and the race of supernatural beings appeared on the wall. And they were all seeing the fight that had happened between their ancestors and the zombies, and they were all noticing that the zombies were trying to use their venoms to kill the supernatural beings. But that the supernatural beings were not dying, although the fact that the supernatural beings were bitten by the venoms of the zombies, and they understood that if the supernatural beings were not dying, although the fact that they were bitten by the venoms of the zombies, it was because the supernatural beings had not their phantoms inside them. Then, Solis opened her mouth, and she asked Prince if he was close to the supernatural beings who were killed in the forest by the zombies? Prince answered that he was not really close to that young couple of supernatural beings, but that he loved that couple.

Sol said that she supposed that the zombies killed that couple of supernatural beings to get their revenge for what had happened in the past, between the race of the supernatural beings and the zombies. Prince said that the goal of the zombies was to eradicate the race of the supernatural beings, as the goal of the supernatural beings was to eradicate the race of natural human beings. And Prince added that the zombies found out that that young couple of supernatural beings were alone in the forest at 11:00 p.m., and they appeared, and they killed that young couple. And Sol asked Prince if he was going to the world of tigers? And Prince answered that he was going to the tiger world, and that he would be back in three days. And Sol said that they were all going together in the tiger world. And Solis told Sol that they had to kill Angel first, before going to the tiger world even if Prince could not go kill Angel with them, that Angel had lost her rosaries and they could go kill Angel without a problem. Sol told Solis that they could not kill Angel without the help of Prince, because that wind that was coming from the magic of Joseph would prevent them from biting Angel's neck.

Solis told Sol that Prince had killed that magic that was like the wind a couple hours ago in the shop. Then, they turned their heads through Prince, and the light got out of Prince's eyes and went through the wall, and they turned heads through the wall, and they read what was written on the wall. Then, they understood that that magic that was like the wind was still alive, and they understood that they could not kill Angel without the help of Prince. And they all decided to go to the tiger world and come back in three days to kill Angel, then they all left for the tiger world.

Angel was deeply asleep in her bed, and she felt a hand at her shoulder who was shaking her, and it was that mysterious phantom who was shaking Angel, then Angel jumped, and she opened her eyes. And that phantom asked Angel to wake up and to come with her, and Angel refused but that phantom succeeded to convince Angel, then Angel wore her shoes, and phantom grabbed Angel's hand and they walked till the yard of the house, and that phantom opened the car's door and Angel got inside the car, and that phantom got in the car too. Then, that Phantom drove during the whole night with Angel, and Angel was asleep in the car, and she had no idea where that phantom was taking her.

## CHAPTER XI

# THE INITIATION OF ANGEL AS A SUPERNATURAL BEING

It was 6:00 a.m., and that phantom parked the car in a forest, and that phantom woke up Angel who was still asleep and Angel opened her eyes and she looked around by asking where she was? And that phantom answered Angel to not worry that she was safe. And suddenly the fear appeared on Angel's face, as she had turned her head through the car's window, and she saw the trees around, and she understood that she was in the forest, then Angel heard the car's door open and she felt that her hand was grabbed by another hand. And Angel got out of the car, then Angel screamed with her face full of fear as she had noticed that she had not her rosaries on her wrist and on her ankle, and she asked where her rosaries were. And that phantom told Angel that Angel had lost her rosaries last night in the shop during the fight, but that to not worry because she was safe. And that phantom grabbed Angel's hand and they started to walk in a huge forest, and after a few minutes walking, Angel saw a small shack, and she noticed that they were walking through that shack. Then, they reached the door of that shack, and Angel saw that door opens, then the expression of Angel's change, and Angel was looking with an astonished face an old woman who was smoking the pipe face to her, and Angel was staring at that old woman as Angel was noticing that

that old woman had the gray eyes, with the long gray hair and with a scar on her forehead.

Then, that old woman turned her head and that old woman looked in the eyes of that phantom, and that phantom let Angel's hand, and that phantom turned and left, and Angel turned her head by looking around with her face full of fear, and by asking if that phantom was still there with her, as Angel had felt that that phantom had let her hand. And that old woman handed her hand through Angel by saying that her name was Marie, but Angel just looked at Marie without shaking Marie's hand, and without saying a word to Marie. Then, Marie moved from the door, asking Angel to walk inside, and Angel refused to walk inside, and Angel told Marie that she wanted to return to her home, but Marie succeeded to convince Angel by saying that Angel was safe, then Angel walked inside the shack, and Marie closed the door. Angel was walking inside the shack with her head turned through the walls, and she was staring at the pictures that were on the walls with an amazed face, as she was seeing her pictures on the walls, the pictures of Hero, Sol, William Solis, Matt, Joseph and there were also other pictures on the wall, but Angel did not know who were on those pictures, and there were no the pictures of Prince on the walls. Then, Angel turned her head, and she noticed that Marie was looking at her, and they were staring at each other in the eyes with a silence, then Angel broke the silence and asked, "Who are you?"

Marie answered, "I am a seer, and I am going to help you."

Angel asked, "What do you mean by a seer?"

Marie answered, "I was born with the gifts to initiate humans, and I was born with a lot of powers and magic."

Angel cried out, "To initiate?" By looking at Marie with an astonished face. And she added, "To initiate who?"

Marie answered, "To initiate the supernatural beings."

Angel cried out, "To initiate supernatural beings?" By looking at Marie with her mouth opened.

Marie answered, "Yes, to initiate the supernatural beings who do not know their identities like you."

Angel asked, "What do you mean by like me?"

Marie answered, "Like you, because you are a supernatural being."

Angel cried out, "What?" By looking at Marie with a face full of fear, and she asked, "A supernatural being?"

Marie answered, "Yes, you are a supernatural being."

Angel smiled and said, "You are kidding."

Marie replied, "I am not joking."

Angel looked into Marie's eyes and said, "Please, take me back to my home."

Marie said, "You can not run away from your identity."

Angel asked, "Which identity?"

Marie said, "You are a supernatural being"

Angel looked at Marie angrily and said, "I am a natural human being."

Marie said, "It's true that you are a natural human being, but you also have the genes of the supernatural beings in your body."

Angel said, "It's impossible, because I can not have the genes of supernatural beings."

Marie said, "You have the genes of the supernatural beings of the eagle world, and it's the reason why the supernatural beings of the eagle world want to kill you."

Angel said, "I do not understand."

Marie looked into Angel's eyes and said, "You were born with a lot of magic and powers, and the eagle world wants to take that magic and those powers from you, because the eagle world claims that those magic and powers are the legacy of the eagle world."

Angel said, "Still, I do not understand."

Marie said, "You have inherited those magic and powers from your ancestors on the side of supernatural beings, because your great grandfather was the king of the eagle world, and in the race of the supernatural beings the magic and the powers are sometime located in the genes, and those genes are transmitted to the descendants from generation to generation. That means if you are a supernatural being and that you have the magic and powers that are located in your genes, your kids would inherit those powers and magic, and your grandkids would inherit those powers and magic from your kids.

## SUPERNATURAL BEINGS

And how those magic and powers would be transmitted to the future generation, because the genes are transmitted from generation to generation."

Angel asked, "Why my parents never told me that I was a supernatural being?"

Marie answered, "Because, your parents do not know that you have the genes of the supernatural beings in your body."

Angel asked, "How do my parents not know that I have the genes of supernatural beings? If my parents themselves have the genes of the supernatural beings."

Marie said, "Your parents do not have the genes of the supernatural beings, because your both parents are one hundred per cent the natural human beings."

Angel asked, "How I got the genes of the supernatural beings if my both parents are one hundred per cent the natural human beings?" And Angel added, "You just say that the genes are transmitted from generation to generation, so if my parents are one hundred per cent the natural human beings, that means that I do not have the genes of the supernatural beings in my body, and that I am one hundred percent a natural human being."

Marie said, "Your story is a long story, that began over a century ago."

Angel said, "I am sixteen years old, so it's impossible that I am related to a story that had happened more than a century ago."

Marie said, "I know well that you born sixteen years ago, and the fact that you are sixteen years old do not prevent you to be linked to a story that had happened more a century years ago, because as I told you the genes are transmitted from generation to generation, and all the supernatural beings are linked to their ancestors through the genes. Even the supernatural beings who were born today are linked to their ancestors who existed a thousand years ago through the genes, and if those ancestors had the powers and magic that were located in the genes, their generation who was born today would inherit those magic and powers."

Angel said, "That means that the videos of my birth I had watched, when my mom was giving birth to me were fake, even the photos of my mom when she was pregnant with me were fake, because I am not the kid of my parents."

Marie said, "Those videos of your birth, and the photos of your mom pregnant with you are not fake, those videos and photos are true and authentic, and you are the kid of your parents, and there is no doubt about that."

Angel asked, "How it's possible that I am the daughter of the parents who are one hundred percent the natural human beings, if I have the genes of the supernatural beings in my body."

Marie replied, "It's a long story, and we do not have the time to talk about it now."

Angel said, "I have the time, and I am even ready to sleep here to know exactly who I am."

Marie said, "We do not have the time, because we must start your initiation."

Angel cried out, "Initiation?" By looking at Marie with an astonished face. And she added, "I did not tell you that I wanted to be initiated, because I do not want to be an eagle that flies in the sky and turns into the body of a human to scare and to kill people."

Marie said, "It's your destiny, and you can not run away from your destiny."

Angel looked into Marie's eyes and said, "I prefer to die than to be a supernatural being."

Marie said, "If you choose to die, know that it would be a tragedy that you caused, because by killing yourself, you are also killing the race of the natural human beings."

Angel asked, "What do you mean?"

Marie replied, "You are the one who is protecting the race of natural human beings, because the goal of the supernatural beings is to eradicate the race of natural human beings."

Angel cried out, "Me?" By looking at Marie with a face full of fear, she asked, "How am I the one protecting the race of natural human beings?"

Marie said, "I know that Hero told you about the mysterious enemy who is protecting the race of natural human beings."

## SUPERNATURAL BEINGS

Angel said, "Yes, Hero told me about that mysterious enemy, who was preventing the supernatural beings from destroying the race of natural human beings."

Marie said, "You are that mysterious enemy."

Angel said, "That's impossible, because Hero told me that that mysterious enemy was invisible."

Marie said, "Yes, Hero could not see that enemy through his magic, because that enemy is inside your genes, but the supernatural beings of the eagle world know that you are that enemy."

Angel said, "I do not understand."

Marie looked into Angel's eyes and said, "You have two identities, one of your identity is your natural human being side, and your other identity is your supernatural being side. And it's your supernatural being who has magic and powers, and it's one part of your magic who is protecting the race of natural human beings."

Angel said, "I am completely lost."

Marie said, "You are the one who has blocked one part of the magic of all the magician supernatural beings who came in the world of natural human beings to eradicate the race of natural human beings."

Angel asked, "How I blocked one part of the magic of the supernatural beings?"

Marie answered, "You blocked one part of the magic of the supernatural beings through your powers."

Angel said, "I have no idea about the magic and powers you are talking about."

Marie said, "You did everything mystically, without even knowing who you were and what you were doing, but now after your initiation you are going to control those powers and magic by yourself.

Angel said, "Hero told me about his invisible ghost, and he told me that all the natural human beings who have the magic could see his invisible ghost, and why I did not see the invisible ghost of Hero if I have the magic."

Marie answered, "You could not see the invisible ghost of Hero because the genes of the supernatural beings that are inside your body are not yet initiated, and it's also the reason why your body did not reject the body of Hero when you were making love with Hero. But, After your initiation your life would completely change, you would be able to recognize all the supernatural beings, and you would be able to see all the invisible ghosts, and you would remove your supernatural being side from your body any time when you would like to kiss or to make love with Hero, or any natural human being."

Angel said, "I do not know how you do the initiation, but I do not want to be initiated."

Marie said, "You do not have the choice."

Angel said, "Of course that I have the choice."

Marie said, "If you refuse the initiation, the supernatural beings of the eagle world would take all the magic and powers that you have inside you, and they would kill you, then they would start destroying the race of natural human beings."

Angel asked, "How the supernatural beings of the eagle world would take the magic and powers that are located in my genes?"

Marie answered, "The supernatural beings would take the powers and magic that are located in your genes by biting your neck, and they would remove those powers and magic mystically from your genes."

Angel asked, "If I am a supernatural being of the eagle world like them, why do they want to kill me and steal my powers and magic?"

Marie answered, "The supernatural beings of the eagle world hate you, you are their worst enemy, and they would never accept you as a member of their family, not only because you have the genes of natural human beings inside you, but because you are a curse for them. And they consider you as a natural human being and not as a supernatural being, and they always call you a natural human being, and they talk about you as a natural human being. And for them, you are cursed, and it's important for them to get rid of you as soon as possible. And they think that the magic and powers you have inside you belongs to them."

Angel asked, "Why do they hate me?"

Marie answered, "They hate you because you are protecting the race of natural human beings, but mostly because when they see you,

you remind them of the sad story that had happened more than a century ago between the race of natural human beings and the race of supernatural beings."

Angel said, "I do not understand."

Marie looked into Angel's eyes and said, "It's a long story we do not have the time to talk about now, but your origins of the supernatural being come from the story that had happened more than a century ago between the race of natural human beings, and the race of supernatural beings."

Angel said, "Hero told about that story that had happened more than a century ago, but Hero did not know how the race of natural human beings was responsible for the destruction of the race of supernatural beings. Mostly that the natural human beings could not win a war against the supernatural beings."

Marie said, "The race of natural human beings did not make the war against the race of supernatural human beings, but the race natural human beings was responsible of the war that had happened between the race of supernatural beings, and it's the reason why this generation of supernatural beings want to get their revenge on the race of natural human beings for what had happened to their ancestors."

Angel asked, "How was the race of natural human beings responsible for the war that had happened between the races of the supernatural beings?"

Marie answered, "It's a long story, and we do not have the time to talk about it today."

Angel asked, "How is it possible that the supernatural beings of the eagle world steal my powers and magic, if you say that those powers and magic are only transmitted from generation to generation, and that we could only inherit those powers and magic?"

Marie said, "The supernatural beings of the eagle world could steal those powers and magic inside you because you are not initiated as a supernatural being, but when you would be initiated, they could not anymore steal those powers and magic. And it's one of the reasons why I need to initiate you."

Angel asked, "What are the other reasons why you need to initiate me?"

Marie replied, "There are a lot of reasons why I need to initiate you now, and we can not talk about those reasons today because we do not have the time, but one of those reasons is that you are in danger and there is nobody to protect you again. And as you know by yourself that Hero could not anymore protect you, and Joseph also could not anymore protect you, and you have lost your rosaries, and if the supernatural beings kill you, they would eradicate the race of natural human beings."

Angel asked, "Where is Joseph?"

Marie answered, "We would talk about Joseph another day, because we do not have the time."

Angel asked, "Who took me here?"

Marie answered, "It's Light."

Angel asked, "Who is Light?"

Marie answered, "Light is the twin of Hero who had left the tiger world when she was just a kid, and now she is living in a world called Mont Coupe', and she used her invisible phantom to save you and to take you here, and nobody knew who she was because she was disguised as a zombie."

Angel said, "Hero told me about her twin who had left, but why did Light help me?"

Marie said, "Light helped you for a lot of reasons, but we will talk about it another day, because we do not have the time now."

Angel said, "Hero told me about his ancestors, and how he had broken some rules of the tradition of the tiger world, and his ancestors found it out, but his ancestors did not mention the fact that he had broken those rules to protect me. And I want to know why the ancestors of Hero did not mention the fact that Hero had saved me."

Marie said, "If the ancestors of the tiger world did not mention the fact that Hero had saved you, it's because those ancestors were not aware that Hero had saved you."

Angel said, "Hero told me that their ancestors are their gods, and that their ancestors are aware of everything that they do."

## SUPERNATURAL BEINGS

Marie replied, "The supernatural beings born with ten senses, but Hero born with eleven senses, and the ancestors could only control ten senses. And even Hero did not know himself that he has eleven senses."

Angel said, "I do not understand."

Marie said, "One part of the magic of Hero is located in his eleventh sense."

Angel said, "Still I do not understand."

Marie said, "We will talk about Hero another day, and I would also explain you the reasons why Hero could not find you through his magic since that his invisible ghost is prisoner to the eagle world, and why the strengths of the invisible ghost of Hero had not been destroyed when most parts of the strengths of his identity ghost had been destroyed."

Angel said, "There are a lot of questions that you did not answer, and I am wondering when you would answer those questions."

Marie said, "We would meet again, but I do not know when, but we would meet to end your initiation that we would start now. And the next time when we would meet, I would answer those questions that I did not answer."

Angel asked, "Why can you not finish my initiation today?"

Marie said, "Your initiation would happen in eleven days, but we would only spend three days together, because I do not want the supernatural beings to find out that you are doing your initiation, because if they find out that you are here, they would come here and kill both of us."

Angel said, "We can not run away from the supernatural beings, because I have no doubt that they would find us here, when they would try to find me."

Marie said, "The supernatural beings who have the mission to kill you, would not try to kill you during those three days, because they are in the tiger world, and the tiger world lost two of their kids, and the tradition of tiger world forbids all kids of the tiger world to make a mission, or an activity during the period of mourning."

Angel said, "Hero told me about that tradition. But even the supernatural beings of the eagle world want to kill me, and the supernatural beings of the eagle world could find me here, mostly that they are not concerned by the tradition of the tiger world."

Marie said, "It's true that the supernatural beings of the eagle world are not concerned about those three days of the mourning in the tiger world, but the supernatural beings of the eagle world can not kill you without the help of the supernatural beings of the tiger world. Because there is a supernatural being in the tiger world who uses his magic to help the supernatural beings of the eagle world to kill you, and as that supernatural being of the tiger world can not do any activity for three days, the supernatural beings of the eagle world are obliged to wait."

Angel asked, "What would happen during those three days of initiation?"

Marie said, "You would be initiated, and you would be able to use some of your powers and magic, and some of your abilities. And when we would finish your initiation, you would be able to use all your abilities, your magic and powers."

Angel asked, "What would happen after those three days?"

Marie looked into Angel's eyes and said, "You would start your mission."

Angel cried out, "My mission?" by looking at Marie with an astonished face, then she asked, "Which mission?"

Marie answered, "You were born with a destiny, and with a mission. And that mission is to protect the race of natural human beings, because even after your initiation the supernatural beings would try to kill you, and to eradicate the race of natural human beings."

Angel asked, "How am I going to protect the world of natural human beings?"

Marie answered, "By fighting against all the enemies of the race of the natural human beings."

Angel asked, "Why is it me who would protect the world of the natural human beings?"

Marie answered, "No one can answer that question."

Angel said, "Light should never take me here."

Marie said, "Light did not have another choice, because you were very lucky that the death that happened in the tiger world happened in a good time, because after that the supernatural beings had failed to kill you in the shop, they were on their way to your house to kill you when they received the message coming from the tiger world that was announcing them the death of those two kids. And if the supernatural beings had reached your house, you would be dead now, because they had already got rid of all those who were protecting you, and they would be destroying the race of the natural human beings now."

Angel asked, "I would make that war for how long?"

Marie said, "That war may be would never end, and your future generation would keep defending the world of natural human beings, that's why it's important for you to give birth after the end of your initiation, because if you die during the war, your kid would keep protecting the race of the natural human beings."

Angel said, "That means that I would spend the rest of my life fighting."

Marie answered, "You do not have a choice, it's your destiny."

Angel asked, "What would happen if I kill all the supernatural beings?"

Marie answered, "The supernatural beings already trained the future fighters who would come in the world of the natural beings in less than a week, to help those who are already in the world of natural human beings to eradicate the race of natural human beings. And the world of supernatural human beings is already training the next fighters to be ready for the war against the race of natural human beings, in case that generation who is in the world of natural human beings fail their mission."

Angel said, "That means that even my kids would spend their life fighting."

Marie said, "Your kids would inherit your destiny."

Angel said, "Hero told me about the marks of the supernatural beings, but I do not understand why I do not have those marks, if I have their genes, and why I was not born once as a supernatural human being."

Marie said, "You were not born as a supernatural human being because the dominant genes in your body are the genes of the natural human beings, because you only have twenty-five percent of the genes of the supernatural beings in your body."

Angel asked, "Where those twenty- five percent of genes are coming from if my both parents are natural human beings?"

Marie said, "It's true that your both parents are one hundred percent natural human beings, but I would explain to you another day how you had inherited those twenty-five percent genes of supernatural human beings from your ancestors who were the supernatural beings." And Marie added, "You have some marks of the supernatural beings of the eagle world on your body, and when the supernatural beings of the eagle world see you, they recognize those marks on you, and they know that one part of your body belongs to their family who is the family of eagles."

Angel asked, "What are those marks on my body, that are the marks of the eagle world?"

Marie said, "Follow me."

Then, Marie turned, and she started to walk through the mirror that was on the wall, while Angel was following her, then Marie stopped face to the mirror, and Angel stopped close to Marie. And both were looking at the mirror, and Marie told Angel that the beauty mark above the left side of her lips was a mark of the supernatural beings of the eagle world, then Angel started staring at the beauty mark that was on her face through the mirror.

Then, Marie asked Angel to close her eyes, and Angel closed her eyes, and Marie demanded Angel to rub her eyes, and Angel put both hands on her eyes and she started rubbing her eyes. And after a couple of minutes, Marie asked Angel to open her eyes, and Angel opened her eyes, then the expression of Angel's eyes changed, and Angel was looking with a surprised face without understanding what was going on, as she was noticing that her blue eyes had become green, and she was wondering how her eyes color had changed. And Marie told Angel that her green eyes were the eyes color of the supernatural beings of the eagle world, and Angel asked Marie how it was possible that she had two colors of eyes. Marie answered Angel that Angel had the genes of supernatural beings inside her, and that meant

## SUPERNATURAL BEINGS

that Angel had all the marks of the supernatural beings of the eagle world inside her, because Angel had two identities.

Then, Angel was very surprised when Marie showed her again other marks of the supernatural beings of the eagle world on her body, and Marie told Angel that if Angel did not eat meat, it was not because Angel was allergic to meat, but it was because the supernatural beings of the eagle world did not eat meat. And Angel understood why she always hated the smell of the meat, and why she had never tasted the meat since she was born, then Angel understood too that the reason why she hated some foods. And Angel understood that some of her behaviors were coming from her nature of supernatural being, and Angel also understood that she loved the carrots because the carrots were the favorite dish of the supernatural beings of the eagle world as Marie told her, and that she loved the volleyball because the volleyball was the traditional sport of the supernatural beings.

And Marie also told Angel that if Angel was very smart and stronger, and if Angel could spend the days without eating or drinking water, it was because Angel had the genes of supernatural beings, because the intelligence quotient of the supernatural beings was quite high. And Angel understood that she had the brain and the strengths of the supernatural beings, and she also understood why Hero was smart enough.

Then, Marie took Angel in a room, and Marie gave a black pant, a black t-shirt, the black socks and the black shoes to Angel to wear, and Angel took those black clothes in Marie's hands. And Angel noticed that the clothes had a weird smell, and that there were the drawings of the eagle on those clothes, that even on the shoes there were the drawings of the eagle, and she asked Marie the meaning of the smell and the drawings that there were on the clothes. And Marie answered Angel that black clothes was the traditional clothes of the eagle world, and that the smell that Angel was feeling on the clothes would help her to communicate with the ancestors of the eagle world, because the ancestors of the eagle world would understand that one of their kids was calling for them through those smell coming from those clothes.

Then, Angel changed her clothes, and she wore her black clothes, and Marie demanded Angel to sit in the chair that was in the middle of the room. And Angel walked till the middle of the room, and she sat in that chair, then Marie stood face of Angel by asking Angel if Angel had put something in her mouth before Light brought Angel for the initiation. And Angel replied that she did not remember the last time she had put something in her mouth, that she had lost her appetite since Hero was living the torture as if he was in the freezer. Marie told Angel that it was good news that Angel had not put something in her mouth since midnight, because if Angel had put something in her mouth after 11:00 p.m., of yesterday, they should interrupt the initiation because the initiation occurred in fasting.

Then, Marie lifted her both hands through Angel's head, and a star shone in the room, then a blanket appeared, and that blanket had covered Angel, and there were the drawings of the eagles on the blanket that had covered Angel. Then, Marie started to pronounce the words in Latin still with her both hands lifted through Angel's head, and the words that were getting out from Marie's mouth were going to the ancestors of the race of supernatural beings, and those words were specially for the ancestors of the eagle world. And Marie was demanding the ancestors in Latin to accept Angel as their daughter, to protect Angel and to help Angel to achieve her goal, also to be with Angel in those hard moments of her life and to help Angel in her initiation for that her initiation goes well.

After three hours, Marie was still talking to the ancestors in Latin, and Marie noticed a star that was shining in the room, and Marie understood the reasons why that star was shining, and Marie turned her head to her left side and she looked at the window that was opened, and she saw the eagles that were flying in the sky, and those eagles were flying through the window. And Marie understood that those eagles in the sky were coming to welcome the phantom of Angel, then Marie turned her head and she looked at the blanket that had covered Angel, and Marie was still talking to the ancestors. Suddenly, the blanket that was on Angel's head disappeared, and there was an eagle on Angel's head, and that eagle that was on

Angel's head flew outside through the window, and met other eagles that were outside, then Marie turned her head through the window, and she saw the eagles that were flying away by singing.

Then, Marie handed her hand to Angel by asking Angel to get up, and Angel grabbed Marie's hand and Angel got up from the chair where she was sitting, and Angel asked Marie what happened? Marie answered Angel that she was introducing Angel to the ancestors, then Marie grabbed a small handbag that was on the floor, and she put that handbag on her shoulder, and she demanded Angel to follow her so that they were going into the forest.

After a couple of minutes, Angel and Marie were walking in the forest, and Angel was staring at the forest with a surprised face, as she was seeing the tall trees and the big stones, and Angel was understanding those stones and trees that she was seeing meaning something. Because some of those stones and trees had the shape of animals, and humans, and for Angel it was like a miracle to see the stones and the trees that had the shape of the animals and humans, and she was wondering how it was possible. Angel and Marie walked till close a small river that was in the forest, and Angel noticed that that river was surrounded by the trees, and that there were the big stones in that river, and that the stones that were in that river had the shape of the animals like the lion, the eagle, the snake, the tiger and other species of animals, and that the water was flowing among those stones in that river. Then, Angel turned her head and she looked at Marie by asking Marie how it was possible that the stones that were in the water had the shape of the animals? And Marie answered Angel that they were in a sacred forest, and everything that was in that forest like the river, the stones, the trees and other things were related to the history of the race of the supernatural beings, and that that sacred forest and everything inside was created by the gods of nature of the world of supernatural beings.

Then, the expression of Angel's face changed, and there was the dread on her face as she had lifted her head through the sky, by watching at the eagles that were singing at top of the trees, and Angel had also noticed that the sun that was shining had disappeared, and that there was darkness. And Angel turned her head looking around, and she was seeing the sun that was shining in the whole forest, except where she and Marie were, and the eagles had stopped singing, and there was an eagle that was flying around where they were.

Then, Marie demanded Angel to take off her dress and get inside the water, and Angel turned her head, and she looked at Marie with her face full of fear, and Marie told Angel to not feel fear, that she was safe. Then, Angel took off her clothes, and Marie told Angel that Angel would get inside the water naked, as Angel had not removed her bra and her panty, then Angel took off her bra and panty. Then, Angel and Marie walked close to the water, and Marie got inside the water, and Marie turned face to Angel, then Marie handed her hand to Angel, and Angel grabbed Marie's hand, and Marie asked Angel to come in the water, and Angel got inside the water, and Marie showed a stone that had the shape of eagle to Angel to sit on it, and Angel sat on that stone, then an eagle flew and that eagle landed on Angel's head. And Marie put her hand on that eagle that was on Angel's head, and Marie started to talk in Latin to the gods of the race of the supernatural beings. And Angel had the eyes closed, and the body of Angel was shaking, and she was feeling that something was happening inside her body, that it was as if her body was transforming, and Angel was feeling a connection with the eagle that was on her head. Then, the eagle that was on Angel's head, started walking on Angel's head and on Angel's shoulder, and Angel was not feeling the eagle that was walking on her head and on her shoulder, but she was instead feeling something that was walking inside her whole body. Then, the eagle stopped walking, and the eagle was on Angel's head, and the eagle had lifted her head through the sky, and Marie was still talking to the gods of the world of supernatural beings.

Then, a light started shining between that eagle on Angel's head and the whole body of Angel, and Angel was feeling that something strange was happening that she was not herself, that it was as if she was someone else. And After a few minutes, that light stopped shining, and the blond long hair of Angel had become long black hair, and there was the drawing of the wings of the eagle that looked like the tattoo on the back of Angel. Then, the wind started blowing and the eagles that were at the top of trees started flying around, and the eagle that was on Angel's head flew in the water, and that eagle got under the water, then Angel started to feel fear as she was feeling that her whole body was wet, and that it was as if she was under the water. Then, Angel started to feel as if she was swimming in the water, as that eagle that was in the water was swimming, then Marie removed the small boxes in the handbag that she had on her shoulder, and Marie opened those boxes and she threw the content of those boxes in the water. And After a few minutes, the sun started shining, and that eagle got out of the water, and that eagle started flying around Angel by touching Angel with her wings, and Angel was feeling that, it was as if she was the one who was flying.

Then, that eagle flew through the sky, and joined the other eagles that were flying in the space, and all the eagles flew away, and Angel opened her eyes and she looked at Marie who was staring at her, and the blue eyes of Angel had become green. And Marie handed her hand to Angel, and Angel grabbed Marie's hand and Angel got up from the stone where she was sitting, and both Angel and Marie got out of the water, and Angel wore her clothes, and they started to walk in the forest.

Then, Angel noticed that the color of her hair had changed, and she asked Marie why she had the black hair, and Marie answered Angel that the black was the color of the hair of the supernatural beings of the eagle world, and Angel told Marie that she was feeling that she was someone else. And Marie replied to Angel that it was normal what she was feeling, because Angel was someone else for the moment, and Angel asked Marie who she was if she was not Angel? Marie answered Angel that the gods who were the ancestors had not yet given the name of her new identity, then the expression of the face of Angel changed, as she was seeing a huge place with the big stones, and there were the skulls and the skeletons of the animals on those stones, and there were also the trees in that place, and they walked in that place.

And Angel asked Marie why there were the skulls and the skeletons of the animals on the stones. And Marie answered Angel that the skulls and the skeletons of the animals that Angel was seeing on the stones were the skeletons and the skulls of the ghosts of the race of the supernatural beings who had died more a thousand years ago. Angel asked Marie if where they were it was another world of supernatural beings? Marie answered Angel that it was a long story, and that they would talk about it another time, and that there were a lot of secrets in the history of the race of the supernatural beings. And Angel noticed that Marie was turning her head by looking around, as if Marie was looking for something, and she demanded Marie what Marie was looking for? And Marie answered that she was waiting for Angel's ghost to show them the way, and the place where they should stay, then Marie noticed an eagle that was flying, and Marie grabbed Angel's hand and they started to walk by following that eagle.

Then, the eagle landed on a stone, and there were the skulls and the skeletons of the eagles on that stone, then Marie and Angel stopped in front of the stone that there was the eagle on it, and Angel was staring at the eagle that was on the stone, then Marie noticed that the eagle was making the gestures with her head. And Marie demanded to Angel to kneel face to that stone, and to lean her forehead on that stone, as Marie had understood the meaning of the gestures of that eagle, then Angle knelt, and Angel leaned her forehead on that stone, and the eagle that was on that stone flew and landed on Angel's head. Then, Marie handed her both hands through Angel and the eagle, and Marie started to talk to the ancestors of the race of the supernatural beings, and there were the eagles that were flying in the sky by singing.

After a few minutes, the wind started blowing, and the shadows of humans and the shadows of the eagles appeared in the spaces around Angel, then the eagle that was on Angel's head flew through those shadows who had surrounded Angel. And those shadows were the shadows of the ancestors of supernatural beings, and the shadows of the eagles were the shadows of the phantoms of the ancestors, then that eagle that was flying in front of those shadows started flying slowly. And those shadows were lifting their hands and putting their hands on that eagle that was flying in front of them, and the shadows of eagles were touching that eagle that was flying in front of them with their heads and their wings. And Angel was feeling as if there were people who were putting their hands on her head, and

## SUPERNATURAL BEINGS

who were touching her, and if Angel was feeling those reactions, it was because the ancestors were blessing the supernatural being who had become Angel through the hands of their shadows, as the ancestors were putting their hands on the phantom of Angel, that was that eagle that was flying around the shadows of the ancestors.

And after a few minutes, all those shadows disappeared, and that eagle started to fly around, and Marie demanded Angel to get up, and Marie held Angel's hand by helping Angel to get up. And Angel looked in Marie's eyes by asking Marie who was putting the hands on her head? And Marie answered Angel that the ancestors were blessing her through her ghost, and Angel turned her head and she looked at that eagle that was flying around her, and Marie demanded Angel to hand her hand to that eagle by showing her palm's hand. Angel looked at the eagle that was flying around her with the fear on her face, and Marie looked at Angel by telling Angel to not be scared, that that eagle was herself, and Angel handed her hand through that eagle by showing her palm's hand to that eagle, and that eagle flew through Angel's hand, then that eagle landed on the palm's hand of Angel. And Angel was shaking like that eagle was walking on her palm's hand.

And after less than a second, the eagle flew through the sky, and joined the other eagles that were in the sky, and Angel noticed that something was written on her palm's hand, and Angel looked at her palm's hand and she read, "Terra." And Angel showed her palm's hand to Marie by asking Marie what was the meaning of that word on her palm's hand? And Marie answered Angel that Terra was her name of supernatural being in Latin who was giving by the ancestors, and Angel told Marie that she already had a name, and Marie replied to Angel that she had two identities one identity who was a natural human being named Angel, and another identity who was a supernatural being named Terra. And Angel looked at Marie without saying a word, and Marie demanded Angel to follow her, and they started to walk in the forest and there was silence between them, and after a few minutes, Angel broke the silence by asking Marie if all the supernatural beings who were born were initiated in the same way as she? And Marie answered Angel that the supernatural beings did not need to be initiated because they were born already as the supernatural beings, just that they received some training.

Then, Marie and Angel stopped in front of a small hut that was built with the glass, and Marie turned head and she looked at Angel by telling Angel to take off her dress and to get inside that hut, and Angel asked Marie if she should get inside that hut alone, and Marie answered that yes, that Angel should get in that hut alone, because Angel was going in touch with her magic and powers. And Angel looked at the hut and she noticed that the hut did not have the door, and she asked Marie how she should get inside that hut because she was not seeing the door on that hut, and Marie replied to Angel to not worry to just take off her dress and walk till close to the hut.

Then, Angel took off her clothes, and she walked naked without the shoes in front of that hut, she stared at it and realized that it was built with glass, then Angel remarked that there was an eagle that was flying around her, then that eagle started to hit her wings on that hut, and that eagle landed on Angel's shoulder, and both the eagle and Angel were staring at that hut. Then, that eagle started to make the noises with her mouth, and the one part of the glass of that hut opened as if it was a door, and Angel walked inside with the eagle on her shoulder, then that part of the glass that had opened closed again. Angel was standing up inside that hut, then a white smoke started appearing in that hut, and Angel started to breath deeply as she was feeling something that was happening in her body, and the smoke had invaded that hut that Marie who was outside was not anymore seeing Angel. And after twenty-one minutes, the smoke in the hut disappeared but there was no Angel and the eagle in the hut, and Marie was still staring at the hut.

After three hours, the light started to shine in the hut, then Angel appeared in the middle of the hut without the eagle and that light was shining on her, and after eleven minutes that light stopped shining, and Angel walked till close of the glass, then Angel looked at left palm's hand and the light got out from her eyes and shone on that left palm's hand, and Angel put that left palm's hand on the glass, and the light shone between her palm's hand and the glass, and the glass

## SUPERNATURAL BEINGS

opened as if it was a door, and Angel got outside, and she walked till close to Marie.

Then, Angel wore her clothes and her shoes, and she looked in the eyes of Marie with a tired face by asking, "Can we return to home now?" Marie answered, "Angel, we would spend three days in this forest working the day like the night." Angel said, "I am Terra for the moment and not Angel, because Angel is not a supernatural being." Marie said, "I know well that you are Terra." Terra said, "I am Terra since the first second I put my feet in this forest." Marie asked, "How did you want me to call you?" Terra answered, "Call me Terra when I am a supernatural being and call me Angel when I am a natural human being." Marie asked, "Why you suddenly changed you mind, and you want me to call you Terra?" Terra answered, "The sorcerer doctor told me that my ancestors who were the gods were not happy that I am still using the name of Angel as a supernatural being, and that I should use the name of Terra that the ancestors gave me as a supernatural being." Marie asked, "Who is the sorcerer doctor?" Terra answered, "The sorcerer doctor is the magician who trained me to use my powers and magic." Marie asked, "How it happened that training?" Terra answered, "I spent three hours with the sorcerer doctor, and he showed the basics of how to use my magic and my powers, and he told me that we would meet again when I would finish my eleventh day of initiation, and he would train me how to use all my magic and powers." Marie said, "We can not spend eleven days together, because your enemies would start to look for you in less than seventy-two hours, so you would return to the world of natural human beings in less than seventy-two, because we could not take the risk that your enemies find you here."

Then, Marie turned by asking Terra to follow her, and they were walking in the forest with the silence, suddenly, Terra started walking slowly with her heart that was beating with fear as she had seen a big lion that was walking face to her, by looking at her angrily. And Marie told Terra to not feel afraid, then Terra noticed that the lion was running through her, and suddenly the green eyes of Terra became dark green and the light got out from Terra's eyes and that light turned into the eagle, and that eagle flew though the lion, and both the eagle and the lion started to fight. And Terra and Marie had stopped, and they were watching the fight between the eagle and the lion, but Terra was not focused, and she was losing the balance as she was feeling the reaction of the fight of that eagle inside her body.

Suddenly, Terra pushed a loud scream as she had felt pains in her right hand, and she looked at that right hand and noticed that she was bleeding, and she also noticed the marks of the claws coming from the claws of the lion on her hand, and she understood that the lion had injured her phantom. Then, the light got inside Terra's eyes, and the lion turned and ran away, and Terra looked at Marie by asking Marie why she was attacked by that lion? And Marie answered Terra that It was a part of the initiation, then they continued walking.

After a few minutes of walking, the expression on Terra's face changed, and she turned her head through Marie by looking at Marie with a surprised face, and she asked Marie where they were? And Marie answered that they were still in the forest. Terra told Marie that she knew well that they were still in the forest, but that she wanted to know why the trees that were in front of her were tight, and why there was darkness in those trees. Marie looked in Terra's eyes by saying, "You are going to run among those trees." Terra cried out, "What?" And she added, "It's impossible to run among those trees." Marie said, "It's a part of the training." And Marie added, "An animal would appear, and you would follow that animal, by running like that animal." And Terra was staring at Marie with an amazed face without knowing what to say. Suddenly, Terra started to breath deeply with her face full of fear as she was seeing a Cheetah that was walking face to her, and Terra turned her head by looking in Marie's eyes by saying, "I can not run with the Cheetah." Marie asked, "Why can you not run with a Cheetah?" Terra answered, "Because, I am a human, and the Cheetah is the fastest animal on this planet." Marie said, "You are a supernatural being, and the supernatural beings are not different from animals."

And Terra just looked at Marie without saying a word, and Terra turned her head, and she noticed that the Cheetah was close to her, and a violent wind started blowing and Marie told Terra to be ready because when the weather would change, she would start to follow the Cheetah. And after three seconds, the wind stopped blowing and the sun appeared, and suddenly the Cheetah started running faster through the trees, and Terra started running faster like the Cheetah through the trees too. Marie was watching the Cheetah and Terra who were running among the trees with an astonished face, and Marie was amazed to see how Terra was faster, how Terra was following the rhythm of the Cheetah.

After three hours, the Cheetah and Terra were still running among the trees, and the night was falling, then the moon appeared in the cloud, and that moon was shining in the forest, and Terra was still running among the trees although the fact that she was very tired. After more than six hours, it was midnight and the Cheetah stopped running, and Terra stopped running too, and both the Cheetah and Terra were looking at each other, and the Cheetah made the gesture with his head, and Terra smiled at the Cheetah as she had understood the message of the Cheetah that was telling her that she was very good, then the Cheetah turned and ran away. Then, Terra walked till close to Marie, and Marie told her that she was very good.

Then, Terra lifted her head through the sky as she had heard the noise coming from the sky, and Terra saw a big eagle that was flying in the sky, and Marie told Terra to get ready, that when the weather would change, she would fly in the sky and she would follow the eagle that was in the sky. And Terra asked Marie how she would follow the eagle in the space? And Marie answered Terra that Terra would use her magic, and she would fly in space by following the eagle. Suddenly, the rain started falling, and the light started shining in Terra's eyes, and after three seconds, Terra's eyes started spinning, then Terra flew in the space. And Marie lifted her head through the sky, and she was staring at Terra in the space as Terra was flying in space by following the eagle.

In the world of natural human beings, it had been more than twenty-four hours now that no one had seen Angel, and Angel's parents were very worried till they had already called the police to talk about the missing of Angel. And Bella was looking for Angel by calling all their friends that they had in common, and Hero was still lying in the bed, and he was aware of Angel's missing, and he was trying to find Angel through his magic without succeeding. But Hero knew that it was not Prince, Solis, William and Sol who had Angel, because he was seeing through his magic that Prince, Solis, William and Sol were in the tiger world for the mourning.

And Hero was following the conversation of Prince, Solis, William and Sol through his magic and Hero knew that they did not kill Angel, because in their conversation they were talking to kill Angel when they would be back in the world of natural human beings. And Hero was wondering where Angel was, and Hero was very worried about her, and he was afraid that something bad had happened to Angel, and the worst for Hero, it was that his magic could not find Angel.

The next day, Terra and Marie were still in the forest, and Terra was still practicing her initiation, and Terra was working days like the nights. And in the world of tiger, Prince, Solis, William and Sol were having a good moment, and Sol was very happy as she was spending her time with Brad. It was midnight, Terra had done with her initiation, and she was in the shack with Marie, and they were looking at the pictures that were on the wall, and Terra put her hand on the picture of Kerry that was on the wall, and she turned her head through Marie and asked, "Who is this girl?"

Marie answered, "Her name is Kerry, and she is the one who has warmed the invisible phantom of Hero, through her magic."

Terra asked, "Where is Kerry?"

Marie answered, "Kerry is in jail, because she had broken one of the rules of the tradition of the eagle world by warming the invisible phantom of Hero. And she would be killed tomorrow on the demand of the ancestors."

Terra cried out, "Kill?"

Marie replied, "The king of the eagle world is in the secret room talking with the ancestors about the betraying of Kerry, and the ancestors would sentence Kerry to death, but the eagle world would not succeed to kill Kerry because Kerry is protected by her magic, but Kerry would spend the rest of her life in jail."

Terra asked, "Where Kerry got her magic?"

# SUPERNATURAL BEINGS

Marie answered, "Kerry has inherited her magic from her ancestors."

Terra asked, "Kerry is undying?"

Marie answered, "We would talk about the story of Kerry the next time when you would come for the next step of your initiation."

Terra said, "I would release Kerry from the jail, when I would go to the eagle world to release the invisible phantom of Hero."

Marie looked at Terra with a surprised face and asked, "Are you going to the eagle world?"

Terra answered, "I have to release the invisible ghost of Hero."

Marie said, "You can get killed in the eagle world."

Terra said, "I do not have a choice, I must release the invisible ghost of Hero."

Marie said, "If you want to go to the eagle world, you must be there before 5 am, and before Hector gets out of the secret room, because you would not succeed to release the invisible phantom of Hero if Hector is out of the secret room."

Terra said, "I imagine that Hector is the king of the eagle world."

Marie replied, "Yes, Hector is the king of the eagle world, and he has a lot of powers and magic, and he is also very strong, so he would not hesitate to kill you if he sees you in his world."

Terra said, "If my ancestors were the kings of the eagle world, that means that I am related to Hector, as Hector is the king of the eagle world."

Marie said, "It's a long story, and a lot of things have changed after the war that had happened more than a century years ago between the race of supernatural beings."

Terra asked, "What do you mean?"

Marie said, "It's a long story, we would talk about it the next time when you would come."

Terra asked, "Why did the gods of the supernatural beings accept me as their kid, if I am a curse for the supernatural beings?"

Marie answered, "That's a good question, but I would answer you that question the next time when we would meet." And Marie added, "You must know that the history of the race of supernatural beings is full of the mysteries and secrets."

Terra asked, "Why did the ancestors of the supernatural beings give me those powers and magic, if they knew that I am going to use those powers and magic to fight the supernatural beings by protecting the race of the natural human beings who are the race of the enemies of the supernatural beings?"

Marie looked into Terra's eyes and asked, "There is a good reason why the ancestors of the supernatural beings accepted you and gave you those powers and magic."

Terra asked, "What is that reason?"

Marie answered, "You would understand that reason in the future when the time would come."

Terra said, "I want to know a little bit about myself."

Marie said, "You are Terra and you are a supernatural being of the eagle world, and you are the one who is protecting the race of natural human beings by fighting against the supernatural beings." And Marie added, "Before, you were existing mystically because you were not yet initiated as a supernatural being, and the reason why Hero could not find you through his magic when he was looking for the mysterious enemy who you are, it was because you did not exist physically as you were existing mystically in the genes of Angel."

Terra said, "I understand now why Hero could not find me through his magic when he was looking for the mysterious enemy who was preventing them from destroying the race of natural human beings." And Terra added, "Hero told Angel during their conversation that he had the powers to know all the humans who had the magic, and why Hero did not find out through his powers that Angel had the magic."

Marie answered, "Angel does not have magic, so Hero could not find magic in Angel."

Terra said, "I know well that Angel is a natural human being who has no powers and magic, but Angel has the genes of supernatural beings, and my magic and powers are located in the genes of the supernatural beings who are inside the body of Angel, because the body of Angel is made up of supernatural being's genes and the natural human being's genes. So, I want to know why Hero was unable to find out through his magic that Angel had the genes of supernatural beings in her body and that those genes had the powers and magic."

Marie said, "If Hero did not find out through his magic the genes of the supernatural beings that have the powers and magic in the body of Angel, it's because the magic of Hero was unable to find the genes of the supernatural beings that were in the body of Angel. So, Hero did not know that Angel had the genes of the supernatural beings."

Terra asked, "Why could n't Hero find out through his magic that Angel had the genes of the supernatural beings in her body?"

Marie answered, "I would answer that question the next time that we would meet."

Terra said, "When I met with the sorcerer doctor last night during my training, that sorcerer doctor demanded me to find the secret book."

Marie said, "Yes, it's very important that you find that secret book."

Terra asked, "Where is that book? Because, the sorcerer doctor did not tell me where I could find it."

Marie said, "I have no idea about where that book is."

Terra said, "The sorcerer doctor told me that I would learn a lot from that secret book, that that book would save me, and that I would not succeed to save the race of natural human beings without reading that book."

Marie said, "That secret book had been lost during the war between the race of supernatural beings, and all the supernatural beings are looking for that book, because that book is a treasure."

Terra said, "My mission is not going to be easy."

Marie said, "I am very worried about you."

Terra said, "Do not worry, I would be fine, and I would succeed to manage my two identities."

Marie said, "I am afraid, because your worst enemy is in love with you."

Terra said, "Hero is my lover, not my worst enemy."

Marie said, "Hero is in love with Angel, and your enemy is in love with Terra."

Terra asked, "Who is that enemy?"

Marie answered, "It's a supernatural being that you know well."

Terra asked, "What is his name?"

Marie said, "I can not tell you his name, because you would find out who that supernatural being is by yourself."

Terra asked, "Why can you not tell me his name?"

Marie said, "That supernatural being is very dangerous, even Hero and Light wanted to tell Angel who was that supernatural being, but the magic of Hero and Light forbade them to tell Angel who that supernatural being was. Because, if that supernatural being find out that Angel know his real identity the worse is going to happen in the world of natural human beings, because that supernatural being is very powerful, and he has some powers and magic that no one can stop, and that's the reason why the magic of Hero and Light forbade them to tell Angel who that supernatural being was." Then, Marie looked in Terra's eyes by saying, "When you would find out who that supernatural being is, you would do everything to have control on that supernatural being, and that supernatural being would not know that Angel and you are in the same body."

Terra looked into Marie's eyes and said, "Do not worry, I would succeed to have the control on that supernatural being, and it would be easy if he is really in love with me." Then, Terra asked, "Why did Light not release the invisible ghost of Hero from jail?"

Marie answered, "Light can not release the invisible ghost of Hero from jail, and she could not even help Hero when Hero was fighting, because Light is not allowed to help the supernatural beings of the tiger world."

Terra asked, "Why is Light not allowed to help the supernatural beings of the tiger world?"

Marie answered, "Light is an inhabitant of the world of Mont Coupe' and one of the rules of the Mont Coupe' ban Light to help an inhabitant of the tiger world."

Terra said, "Why does that rule ban Light to help the inhabitants of the tiger world, if Light herself was born as a supernatural being of the tiger world, even if she lives in the world of Mont Coupe' now?"

Marie answered, "We would talk about the reasons why Light could not help or save a supernatural being of the tiger world the next time when you would come."

Suddenly, Marie stayed silent, and Terra was looking at Marie with a surprised face by asking Marie if everything was fine. After less than a minute, Marie opened her mouth, and she told Terra that her enemies were on their way for the world of natural human beings, and that Hector would be out of the secret room at 5 am. And Terra told Marie that it was time to go, then Marie removed a small box from her purse that she had on her shoulder, and she opened that box and she walked two steps face to Terra, and she threw the oil that was in that box in her palm's hand, and she started rubbing that oil on the body of Terra. And Marie told Terra that the oil that she was rubbing on Terra's body would protect Terra when Terra would be in the world of eagle, because that oil would prevent the supernatural beings of the eagle world from feeling by the sense of smell that Terra was a member of their family.

After a minute, Marie walked a step away from Terra and she looked at Terra by asking Terra if Terra could make a little bit of training. Then, the green eyes of Terra became Blue, and Terra turned into the body of a natural human being who was Angel, then the eyes of Angel became green and she turned into the body of a supernatural being who was Terra, and her eyes became dark green and she turned into an eagle. Then, the eyes of the eagle became blue, and the eagle turned into the natural human being who was Angel, and the light got out from Angel's eyes, and that light turned into a supernatural being who was Terra, and both Terra and Angel were looking at each other.

Suddenly, Terra saw a lion that was running through Angel, and Terra rushed, and she pushed Angel away, and the lion tried to jump on Terra, but Terra grabbed the lion and she threw the lion away against the wall, and Marie went and hit her back against the wall. And Terra turned into the light and she got inside Angel's eyes, and Angel turned her head, and she saw Marie on the floor and she rushed through Marie as she had understood that the lion that Terra had thrown against the wall was the phantom of Marie, then Angel helped Marie to get up, and she apologized to Marie. And after a few minutes of conversation between both Marie and Angel, Marie gave a mask to Angel to wear it when she would be in the world of eagle, and Angel took Marie in her arms by thanking Marie, then Angel left. Angel was running in the forest, and there was the moon that was shining in the sky.

After a few minutes, Angel was still running in the forest, and her blue eyes became green, and Angel turned into a supernatural being who was Terra, and Terra looked at her left palm's hand, and the light got out from her eyes and shone on her left palm's hand. And a map appeared on her left palm's hand, and Terra lifted her left palm's hand through her face, and she was staring at the map that was on that palm's hand, and that map was showing her the direction of the eagle world. Then, the green eyes of Terra became dark green and Terra turned into her phantom that was the eagle, and the eagle flew through the sky in the direction of the eagle world.

It was almost 5:00 a.m., in the eagle world and most of the inhabitants were still asleep, even in the palace most of the supernatural beings were still asleep, then an eagle landed in the yard of the palace, and that eagle turned into a supernatural being who was Terra. Then, Terra started looking around by wondering where the phantom of Hero could be kept prisoner, then she got the idea to use her magic to find where the ghost of Hero was kept prisoner, and she lifted her left palm's hand through her face, and the light got out from her eyes and shone on her palm's hand, and a map appeared on her palm's hand. Terra looked at the map that was on her palm's hand, and she removed the mask from the pocket of her jacket, and she wore that mask to cover her face and her hair.

Then, Terra looked at the map that was on her palm's hand, and she started running through the entry door of the palace. After less than a minute, she reached the entry door, and the light got out from her eyes and shone on the door, then she put her both palm's hands on the door and she pushed the door, and the door opened. Then, she ran inside the palace, and she suddenly stopped running like the clock that was on the wall face to her had attracted her attention, and she had her eyes focused on that clock and she was noticing that in a minute it would be 5:00 a.m., and Hector would be out of the secret room, and she was understanding that she had less than a minute to release the phantom of Hero.

Suddenly, Terra turned her head to the right side as she had heard the voice coming from that side, and she saw three supernatural beings who were looking at her with the amazed faces, and she looked at the map that was on her left palm's hand, and she started running to the left side of the corridor, and those three supernatural beings started running after her. Then, Terra saw other two supernatural beings who were coming face to face, and her eyes started spinning, then she flew above them, and those two men lifted their heads through the ceiling, and they were looking at Terra who was flying with the surprised faces, and one of them started screaming. And the supernatural beings who were still asleep were getting up from their beds, as they were hearing the noises, and they were wondering what was going on.

Terra was on the third floor running to the right side of the hallway, and two big supernatural beings came face to face and she started fighting against those two big supernatural beings, and she was stronger than them, then she beat them, and she carried them and threw them outside through the window. And Terra kept running by looking at the map that was on her palm's hand, then she reached a door and she opened that door, and she got inside a room, and she saw another door, and she looked at the map on her palm's hand, then she rushed till that door, and she opened that door. And suddenly the expression of her face changed, and she was looking with a surprised face as she was seeing the steam in the room, and it was very cold in the room, then she saw a big box that was like a coffin and she ran through that box as she had understood that that box was where the invisible phantom of Hero was kept prisoner, and she knelt near to that box and she was trembling of cold, then she opened that box, and she saw the invisible phantom of Hero who was lying in that box, but the ice had covered that phantom.

Then, Terra started thinking how she could remove the ice that was on that phantom for that that phantom run away and she was not seeing a solution of how to remove that ice, then she turned her head by looking around by trying to find a solution with her heart that was beating with fear as she was hearing the noises of supernatural beings in the palace who were looking for her. And Terra saw a window and she got up and ran till the window and she opened that window, then Terra looked at her left palm's hand, and the light got out from her eyes and shone on her left palm's hand, and the clock appeared on that left palm's hand, and she looked at the time and she understood that she had nine seconds to save Hero's phantom. Because, it would be 5:00 a.m., in nine seconds, and Hector would be out of the secret room, then she rushed till close to the box, and her green eyes became blue and she turned into the body of natural human being who was Angel, then the light got out from Angel's eyes and that light turned into Terra.

Then, Terra and Angel carried that box and they walked until the window with that box, and they threw that box outside through the window, and that box fell on the stone, and that box broke and even the ice that was inside that box broke too, then Terra looked through the window how the invisible phantom of Hero turned into the light and disappeared. Then, Terra turned into the light and got inside Angel's eyes, and the blue eyes of Angel became green, and she turned into the body of supernatural being who was Terra.

Then, Terra walked till the door and she opened the door and she looked through the door, and she noticed that the palace was full of supernatural beings who were looking for her. And Terra understood that it was a risk to get out, then she looked at her left palm's hand and the light got out from her eyes and shone on that left palm's hand, and a map appeared on that palm's hand, and she looked at that map and she saw the prison where Kerry was kept prisoner. And Terra turned, and she ran till the window where she and Angel had thrown the box where Hero's phantom was kept prisoner, and she looked in the sky, and she saw the eagles that were flying in the sky, and she understood that those eagles in the sky were looking for her.

Then, Terra got an idea, and her green eyes became dark green and she turned into an eagle, and she flew through the sky, and she was flying among the eagles that were in the space, but she was flying through the jail where Kerry was kept prisoner. The palace was full

## SUPERNATURAL BEINGS

of supernatural beings and everyone was looking for Terra without even knowing who she was, because none of them had seen the face of Terra or the colors of her eyes because she had worn the mask. Kerry was asleep in a small bed in her jail, and she suddenly jumped from the bed as she had heard the noises coming from the window of her jail, and she sat on the bed then she turned her head through the window and she noticed that the window glass was broken, and she saw an eagle that was flying in the room, then that eagle landed close to her and that eagle turned into Terra.

And both Terra and Kerry were looking at each other in the eyes, and Terra handed her hand to Kerry without saying a word, and Kerry was just looking at Terra's hand who was handing to her. After a couple of seconds, Kerry handed her hand and she grabbed Terra's hand, and Kerry got off from the bed, and they ran till close to the window, and Terra looked at the sky through the window and she noticed that the sky was empty that there was no eagle flying in the sky. Then, Terra bent close to Kerry, and she demanded Kerry to climb on her back, and Kerry climbed on Terra's back and Terra got up, then Terra's eyes started spinning and she flew outside through the window that she had broken the glass. Terra was flying in the sky with Kerry on her back, then Terra looked at her left palm's hand and the light got out from her eyes and shone on that left palm's hand, and a map appeared on that palm's hand, and she kept flying by following the map that was on her palm's hand.

After nineteen minutes, Terra was flying in the sky of a forest, then she saw a big lion that was running on the ground, and she looked at the map that was on her palm's hand and she started flying through that lion, then she landed face to that lion, and that lion stopped face to her. And both Terra and that lion were looking each other in the eyes, then Terra walked till close to the lion and she put Kerry on the lion's back, and Terra kissed Kerry's forehead, and the lion turned, and the lion looked at Terra, and Terra smiled at the lion, then the lion ran away with Kerry. And the green eyes of Terra became dark green, and she turned into an eagle and she flew through the sky.

After six hours of flying, the eagle landed close to a car that was parked close to the sidewalk and that eagle turned her head by looking around, and the eagle noticed that there was nobody around, then the eagle turned into a supernatural being who was Terra. And Terra walked till close to the car's door, and she opened the car's door and she got inside the car, and the light got out of her eyes and shone in the car, and the engine of the car started, and she drove away. After an hour driving, Terra saw a car on the other side of the road and that had lost the direction of the road, and that car was going through a shop, and people who were in front of that shop were running away.

Suddenly, the green eyes of Terra became blue and she turned into the natural human being who was Angel, and the light got out from Angel's eyes, and that light went out through the car's window, and Angel parked the car on the sidewalk, then she got out of the car. And that light that had got out from Angel's eyes was going through the car that had lost the direction of the road, then that light turned into the supernatural being who was Terra, and Terra appeared face to the hood of the car, and Terra stopped the car by putting her both hands on the hood of the car. And everyone who was running away turned and they were all looking with surprised faces as they were seeing that car that had stopped, but they were not seeing Terra who was still face to the car's hood, and even the driver who was in the car was not seeing Terra. And they were not seeing Terra, because they were all the natural human beings, and Terra was like the invisible phantom of Angel and only the magicians, the wizards, the sorcerers, the zombies, the vampires, the natural human beings who have the magic and the supernatural beings could see Terra when Terra was out of the body of Angel. But, when Terra was inside the body of Angel and that she had turned into her side of supernatural being, everyone could see her, even the natural human beings who did not have the magic.

Then, Terra removed her hands from the car's hood, and she turned, and she started walking away, then Terra turned her head and she noticed that there was a young man who was staring at her and she kept walking by staring at that young man too. And Terra was noticing that the eyes of that young man were still focused on her,

# SUPERNATURAL BEINGS

and she was wondering who was that young man, and she was noticing that that young man was not a supernatural being but instead a natural human being, and she was seeing that that young man had the blue eyes, short blond hair, with a long nose and with no beauty mark on his face. And Terra was wondering if that young man was really staring at her? And If he was looking at her, it meant that that young man may be a vampire, a magician, wizard, a zombie or a natural human being who had the magic but not a supernatural being, because she could recognize any supernatural being. Then, Terra turned into the light and she disappeared. Angel was standing up near to her car, and the light got inside Angel's eyes and the blue eyes of Angel became green, and she turned into a supernatural being who was Terra and she got inside the car, then she drove away.

Prince, Solis, William and Sol were in the living room of Prince's house, and they had just arrived in the world of natural human beings coming from the tiger world, and they were talking about the plan to kill Angel in the evening. And suddenly, Sol's phone started ringing and they all turned their heads through Sol, and Sol picked up her phone, and everyone was looking at Sol who was talking on the phone. After a few seconds, Sol hung up the phone, and she looked at everyone by telling them that a mysterious enemy got inside the palace of the eagle world and released the invisible phantom of Hero and Kerry. And the eyes of everyone opened widely, and they were all looking at Sol with surprised faces, and William and Solis had their mouths open as they were looking at Sol. Then, Sol got up from her chair by telling her that she was going to the eagle world to see what had happened, and she turned into the eagle and she flew through the window that was opened.

Then, William and Solis got up from their chairs, and they turned into the eagles and they flew through the window too, and Prince got up and he went to his bedroom. Hero and Bella were in Angel's house with Angel and Angel's parents, and they were all happy to see that Angel was doing well. And when Hero and Bella asked Angel where she was? Angel lied to them by saying that she had been kidnapped by unknown people, and that she did not know the reasons why those people had kidnapped her. And Angel asked Hero what had happened? And Hero answered her that he did not know what happened in the eagle world, but that some supernatural beings had released his invisible phantom. And Angel asked Hero if he knew the supernatural beings who had released his invisible phantom. Hero answered that no, that he had no idea about the supernatural beings who had released his phantom. Angel told Hero that she was happy that he was doing well by pretending to not know what had happened, but although the fact that the invisible phantom of Hero was released from the jail of the eagle world, Hero was very sick and tired. Hero, Angel and Bella spent the afternoon talking, and they decided to go to the nightclub in the evening to celebrate the return of Angel and the releasing of the invisible phantom of Hero from jail.

# CHAPTER XII

## THE HANGING OF HERO

It was evening, Prince was sitting in a chair in the nightclub alone and he had his eyes on the front door and he had decided to go to the nightclub because he was bored at home alone as Sol, William and Solis had not come back from the eagle world, and suddenly the expression of Prince's face changed and he was looking at the door with an amazed face, and he was seeing Terra who was walking inside the club.

And Prince was wondering who Terra was and he was like troubled as he was staring at Terra who was walking inside the club, and Prince was feeling as if he knew Terra, and he was wondering where and how he knew Terra. And the heart of Prince was beating faster than normal and he was feeling something strange, as if he already had felt it before, and suddenly he started to remember Angel. And Prince remembered that he was feeling the same feelings that he felt when he was always near to Angel, and that his heart was beating in the same way that when he was close to Angel, and the reaction that he was feeling, it was the same reaction that he was feeling when he was near to Angel.

And Prince was wondering why he was feeling those reactions by seeing Terra, then Prince got up from his chair and he walked till face to Terra and he handed his hand to her by saying, "My name is Prince." And Terra shook the hand of Prince by making a fake smile at him and by saying, "My name is Terra." Prince said, "I have the feeling that we already met." Terra said, "I do not think so, because it's my time to be here, and I am here for holidays." Prince said, "Let's go have a sit, and I would find you something to drink." Terra said, "Sorry, I am waiting for someone." And she added, "We can use this time to dance, like my friend is not yet here." And Prince agreed to dance with Terra, and both were dancing by looking at each other in the eyes, and Terra was noticing the marks of the supernatural beings of the tiger world on Prince's face, that Angel had never paid attention to those marks, and Terra was understanding that Prince was a supernatural being from the tiger world.

Then, Terra started remembering about the words of Marie as Marie had told her that one of her enemy was in love with her, and she understood that that enemy was Prince, and she started remembering everything that had happened, and she understood that Prince was pretending to be in love with Angel to help the supernatural beings of the eagle world to kill Angel. And although the fact that Prince was dancing with Terra by staring at her, he had not noticed that Terra was a supernatural being, and there were a lot of questions that were going in the mind of Prince like who was Terra? Why was he feeling those feelings that he felt when he was near to Angel? And why was his body reacting as if he was close to Angel? But Prince could not answer those questions, although the fact that he was saying in his mind that he was feeling those feelings as if Terra was the mysterious supernatural being who was inside Angel's body as he knew well that Angel had the genes of the supernatural beings.

Then, Terra saw Hero who was walking in the club, and she noticed that Hero was looking for Angel, because both Angel and Hero should meet in that club, then Terra stopped dancing and she told Prince that she was going to the washroom, that she would be back. Then, Terra started walking through the washroom, and she saw the same young man that she had seen the morning who was looking at her when she had stopped the car that had lost control on the road. And Terra noticed that that young man was still staring at her, but she knew too that everyone was seeing her, that even the natural human beings who did not have the magic could see her, because she was in the same body as Angel. Because, the natural human beings who did not have the magic could not see Terra only when Terra was out of the body of Angel.

Then, Terra stopped walking as she had noticed that that young man was walking towards her, and he walked till face to her, then that young man handed his hand through her by saying, "My name is Martin." And Terra shook his hand by saying, "My name is Terra." Then, they talked for six seconds, and Terra walked till the toilet, and her green eyes became blue and she turned into the body of a natural human being who was Angel, and the light got out from Angel's eyes, and that light turned into a supernatural being who was Terra.

Then, both Terra and Angel looked at each other, and Angel turned and walked until to the dance floor, and she saw Prince and Hero who were looking at each other angrily, as if they would be ready to fight, then Angel looked at Hero by asking if everything was all right? And Hero grabbed Angel's hand and he tried to walk away with her, and Prince grabbed Angel's other hand by telling Hero that Hero could not go with Angel because Angel was his lover. And Hero replied to Prince that Angel was his beloved, and Angel was in the middle of Prince and Hero who were arguing, and suddenly Hero punched Prince by telling Prince to let Angel's hand, and Prince fell on the floor.

Then, Angel bent, and she helped Prince to get up with other people who were dancing around, and Prince was bleeding from his nose, and Angel was preventing both Hero and Prince from fighting, so Terra joined them. And Terra looked at Prince by asking him why he was bleeding? Then, Prince, Angel, Hero and Terra were looking at each other without saying a word, and Hero was very surprised as he was looking at Terra, then Terra turned, and she started walking through the door and Prince started following Terra. Then, Angel and Hero spent the night dancing, and they returned to Angel's house where they spent the rest of the night to make love.

It was early morning, Angel was still in the bed asleep, then she opened her eyes and she did not see Hero in the bed, and she turned and she saw a sheet of paper on the teddy bear, then she handed her hand and she took that sheet of paper and she noticed the handwriting of Hero on that sheet of paper, and she read what was written on that sheet of paper, and her heart started beating with fear as she was reading that letter of Hero in which he was wishing her his farewell by telling her that she was his first and his last lover, and that no matter where he would be, he would always love her, and that she would be always in his heart. And that through her, he found out that the only thing that we could not control was the heart, and that their hearts beat for each other despite the fact that they were coming from different races, as he was a supernatural being and she was a natural human being.

Then, Angel threw the letter away without even finishing to read, and there were the tears that were flowing down her cheeks, and she jumped from the bed and she rushed till the window and she opened the window and the light got in her eyes. And that light was Terra, and Terra had spent the night outside as Angel had spent the night with Hero, because Terra could not be in Angel's body as Angel had spent the whole night to make love with Hero. Then, the blue eyes of Angel turned into green and Angel turned into a supernatural being who was Terra, and Terra looked at her left palm's hand and the light got out from her eyes and shone on that left palm's hand and a map appeared, and she looked at that map on her palm's hand and she saw Hero in a car who was driving through the tiger world.

Then, Terra suddenly lifted her head through the window as she had heard a noise coming from the window, and she cried out, "Light?" With an astonished face as she had seen an invisible phantom face to her. And that invisible phantom answered, "Yes, I am Light." Terra said, "I am glad that I can see you now." Light said, "You are seeing me now because you are a supernatural being." Terra said, "I am glad that you came." Light said, "I am here for Hero." Terra said, "Hero left this early morning." Light said, "Hero would die in a couple of hours." Terra cried out, "What?" by looking at Light with her face full of fear. Light said, "Hero was sentenced to death by the ancestors for betraying his family, and for breaking some rules of the tradition, and since Hero was sentenced to death, he never put his feet in the tiger' s land because he did not want to abandon you. But today, Hero decided to go to the tiger world, and he would be killed on the base of the rules of the tradition when he would put his feet in the tiger land." Terra asked, "Why did the Hero decide to go to the tiger world knowing that he would be killed?" Light answered, "Hero could not keep living in the world of natural human beings, because his two phantoms were very sick, mostly his invisible phantom as his invisible phantom had spent the months in a cold jail that was freezing. And the cold had destroyed his invisible phantom, and even his identity phantom was very sick as his identity phantom had got hurt a lot during the fight, and Hero could not anymore cure his both phantoms in the tiger world because he was not anymore a kid of the tiger world since he was sentenced to death."

Terra said, "Hero could keep staying here, and I should take care of him." Light said, "Hero went to the tiger world because he did not want to die here, even if he had decided to stay here, he should die because his phantoms could not survive without treatment, and without food. Because, there is no doctor in the world of natural human beings who could treat a supernatural being, or a food in the world of natural human beings that the phantom of a supernatural being could eat." Terra asked, "How am I going to survive without treatment and without food?" Light answered, "Your case is different, because you are two different beings in the same body, so you can only feed your natural human being side, and you must only avoid your supernatural being side to get hurt, but your supernatural being side could stay without food." Terra said, "I have to go because I must prevent Hero from putting his feet in the tiger world." Light said, "The only way to save Hero it's to go to the tiger world and change the weather by using your magic to trigger the rain at the moment when they would try to hang Hero." Terra asked, "Why should I trigger the rain?" Light answered, "Because, by triggering the rain, they would cancel the hanging of the Hero." Suddenly, the green eyes of Terra became dark green and she turned into the eagle and she flew through the window, and Light turned her head through the window, and she saw the eagle that was flying through the sky, then Light turned into the light and she disappeared.

It was 12:00 p.mHero put his feet in the tiger world, and he was suddenly surrounded by the supernatural beings who were keeping the border of the tiger world, and Hero was arrested, and he was taken to jail. After an hour the whole inhabitants of the tiger world were aware of the arrest of Hero, and they were all called to the death place for the hanging of Hero as the tradition required, and most of the supernatural beings were sad about the arrest of Hero.

It was 3:00 p.m., and the sun was shining outside, and the whole inhabitants of the tiger world were standing up to the death place and they had all worn the blue clothes as the tradition required them. Because, the blue was the color that was meaning the death or the sad events in the tradition of the tiger world, and they had all their eyes focused on the rope that was tied on a tall tree called the tree of the death, and they were all waiting for Hero who was going to be hanged on that tree. And Hero would be hanged with his two ghosts inside his body, because his dead body would be burned after with his ghosts in his dead body, so the ghosts of Hero would not be buried in the tiger's land, because Hero was a traitor, and the tradition banned to bury the ghosts of the traitors, also to bury the ghosts of all the supernatural beings who were sentenced to death by the gods in the tiger's land. And most supernatural beings were staring at that rope with the sadness on their faces, and they were trying to not cry, because it was banned by the tradition to shed the tears to the death place, then they saw the king and his advisors who were walking through the tree of the death. And suddenly, the expression on the faces of most of them changed as they were looking at Hero who was walking behind King Philip with his both hands tied, and Hero was holding the guards. Then, King Philip reached under the tree of death, and he started to make a speech to the ancestors in Latin, and he was telling the ancestors that Hero was going to leave the tiger world forever in a couple of minutes.

After fifteen minutes, Philip was done with his speech, and the guards walked with Hero till under the tree near to the rope, and the eyes of all supernatural beings were focused on the rope. And some supernatural beings were breathing deeply with their hearts who were beating faster than the normal as if they were going to have a heart attack, as they were seeing the neck of Hero in the rope. Philip was face to Hero and Philip was looking at Hero who had the neck in the rope and with his both hands tied, then Philip started lifting his

## SUPERNATURAL BEINGS

left hand through the sky and a green light was shining on Philip's hand, and the rope started lifting Hero. All supernatural beings had the heads lifted through the rope that was lifting Hero, and as Philip was lifting his hand, the rope was lifting Hero because the green light that was shining on Philip's hand had the impact on the rope, and it was that green light that was lifting the rope mystically. Also, that green light that was shining on Philip's hand was controlling the two phantoms that were in Hero's body, and Hero could not remove his phantoms from his body, because that green light was preventing Hero to do that.

Suddenly, the fear appeared on the faces of most supernatural beings as they had noticed that Hero had started having difficulties breathing, and they looked at the hands of Philip and they noticed that the green light that was shining on Philip's hand had become red. And although the fact that they were banned to cry to the death place, some of them had the tears in their eyes as they had understood that Hero was dying, because they knew that the red light that's shining on Philip's hand was killing the phantoms of Hero, and while others had the smile on their faces as they were seeing Hero who was dying on the rope.

Suddenly, they all lifted their heads through the sky as they had heard the thunder that was rumbling in the sky, and they were all noticing that the weather had changed that the sun that was shining was gone, and the darkness had taken place of that sun, and there were all seeing an eagle that was flying in the sky and they thought that that eagle was just an ordinary bird, but that eagle was Terra. Then, a violent wind started blowing and the smile appeared on the faces of all those who had the sadness on their faces, with the tears of happiness in their eyes, as they had seen the rain that was coming to the left side of the forest, and Brad screamed in Latin, "Nisi Hero." That meant in English, "Save Hero."

Suddenly, the rain started falling where they were, and Philip turned his head through Hero and the light got out from Philip's eyes and went through the rope that had tight Hero's neck, and immediately there were the shouts of joy as they had noticed that the light that got out from Philip's eyes had cut the rope that was hanging

Hero. All Hero's friends who had faces full of sadness a couple minutes ago were jumping in the rain by singing, with their faces full of smiles, and they were singing by thanking the ancestors for having save Hero. While, Prince's friends who had smiles on their faces a couple minutes ago were sad, and they were hating the ancestors for having saved Hero's life by changing their decision to kill Hero.

Some supernatural beings as King Philip and his advisors were just staring what was going on with the surprised faces by wondering why the ancestors had changed their decision about Hero, and for them it was like a miracle because it was the first time in the history of the tiger world that the ancestors changed their decision about a supernatural being who was sentenced to death. Hero was lying on the ground still with the rope in his hands, and another half of the rope on his neck, and his friends as Brad and others rushed till him and they lifted Hero, and they removed the rope that was in the neck of Hero, and they also untied the rope that was in Hero's hands. Then, Brad looked in Hero's eyes and there were the tears flowing down the cheeks of Hero and Brad. And Brad opened his mouth to talk but a word was not coming out from his mouth, then he took Hero in his arms, then Sarah ran among the crowd and she took Hero in her arms with the tears of joy that were flowing down her cheeks.

They all thought that it was the ancestors who had sent the rain to cancel the hanging of Hero, but it was instead Terra who had triggered the rain through her magic to cancel the hanging of Hero, because the tradition of the tiger world banned killing or hanging a kid of the tiger world in the rain. So, even if a supernatural being was sentenced to death by the gods, and that the rain fell at the moment to hang that one who was sentenced to death, the king must cancel that hanging. Because, according to the tradition a kid of the tiger world could not be hanged in the rain, and if the rain fell at the moment to hang a supernatural being, that meant that the ancestors had changed their decision by cancelling that hanging, and the change of the decision of the gods was known by the rain that was sent by those gods. But it did not mean that the doomed rain had cancelled his hanging was free, because this doomed was going to spend the rest of his life in prison as the tradition dictated, so Hero was going to spend the rest of his life to jail as the tradition dictated. Hero's friends were still celebrating their joy, and Philip ordered the guards to take Hero to the jail, then Hero was held by the guards, and the eyes were focused on Hero as Hero was walking through the prison with the guards around him.

Then, Hero stopped walking and he lifted his head through the sky, as he had heard the noises coming from the sky, and he saw an eagle that was flying in the sky in the rain by making noises, and Hero stared at that eagle and he noticed that that eagle was staring at him too. Then, Hero and the eagle were looking at each other in the eyes, and Hero was feeling something strange inside him, and Hero was feeling that he had already seen the eyes of that eagle somewhere, but he did not remember where he had seen those eyes. And Hero was noticing that that eagle was sad, and that it was as if that eagle was crying, and after a few minutes that eagle flew away, and Hero was taken to his jail, and all the supernatural beings returned to their houses.

Sol, William and Solis had returned to the world of natural human beings, and they were in Prince's house with Prince, and they were all standing up in the living room face to the wall with their faces full of sadness. And they were completely lost, they were not understanding what was going on, they were looking for Angel without succeeding, even Prince was unable to find Angel through his magic. The lights were getting out from Prince's eyes and going through the wall and the pictures were appearing on the wall, but those pictures on the wall were empty, Angel was not appearing on those pictures on the walls. They were all not understanding what was happening, and they were feeling that they were losing control of their war, mostly that they did not know who had released the invisible phantom of Hero from the jail, and who had taken Kerry, and they were also aware that the gods of the tiger world had cancelled the hanging of Hero. And they were concentrating to find Angel, who had not used his magic to find out who had released the invisible phantom of Hero and Kerry from the jail.

Then, after the hours without succeeding to find Angel, they understood that there was a mystery that was going on, and Sol looked at Prince by saying, "We have another mysterious enemy who is not Angel." Prince replied, "I have no doubt that there is an enemy who is protecting Angel, by preventing me from finding Angel through my magic." Sol asked, "What is the solution?" Prince said, "We would need more magicians, and together we would use our magic, and we would try to find Angel." Sol said, "It means that we would need more supernatural beings." Prince said, "We have to make a new plan, with the magician supernatural beings." Sol said, "I would call King Hector, and I would ask him to send me some magicians." Prince said, "I would call King Philip, and I would ask him to send me more supernatural beings." Then, they started talking about their new plan to find Angel, and to destroy the race of the natural human beings, and they decided to find a new house, and to settle in the world of natural human beings to focus on their goals.

Terra was lying in her bedroom with her face wet of tears, and she was thinking about Hero who was in jail, and she was thinking how she could save him. And Terra knew that Prince was looking for Angel through his magic, and that was the reason why she staying in her supernatural being side, because she knew that Prince could not find Angel through his magic when she had not turned into the natural human being who was Angel, and Terra was only turning into the body of natural human being who was Angel when she was with her parents and her friends. So, the reason why Prince could not find Angel through his magic, was because Angel was inside Terra's body, and Angel was unseen when she was inside Terra's body, so Angel did not exist when she was in Terra's body, and no one could see her.

After three days, Prince, Solis, William and Sol had welcomed the magician supernatural beings coming from the tiger world and the eagle world who were sent by King Philip and King Hector to help them in their mission. Prince, Solis, William, Sol and other supernatural beings were in the living room of their new house called the house of the supernatural beings, that they had bought in the world of natural human beings. And they were talking about their new plan to find Angel and kill her and then to eradicate the race of

## SUPERNATURAL BEINGS

natural human beings, while Terra was still in her bedroom crying for Hero who was in prison.

To be continued in Supernatural Beings 2